AGE OF INFLATION

Age of Inflation

by

Hans F. Sennholz

Published by
Western Islands
395 Concord Avenue
Belmont, Massachusetts 02178

Printed in the United States of America
ISBN: 0-88279-234-2

CONTENTS

Preface

Man sometimes learns more from the sight of evil than from an example of good. Especially when evil is very common and its harmful effects are clearly visible, it affords an excellent opportunity for learning. When it finally becomes insufferable it may touch its point of cure.

Inflation is one of the great evils of our time. Because it is spreading at accelerating rates, its dire consequences are visible nearly everywhere, bringing forth ever greater evils. Therefore, there may be no greater task for a contemporary economist than to encounter it, unmask it, and help to overcome it. He must expose the popular errors causing the inflation, establish the truth, and thereby correct the popular misconceptions. It is a difficult task, for popular errors are always presumptuous, the putative guardians of the common good pointing in the wrong direction. At times, it may even be a dangerous task that requires true courage and a just sense of duty.

This volume deals with several errors and mistakes that compound the inflation and cause much evil. It brings together some of the essays on money and credit written by this economist in the past decade. May it shed some light on a subject that is enveloped in deep darkness.

Grove City, Pennsylvania   *Hans F. Sennholz*
June 1978

Introduction

All free societies are governed by public opinion, and the quality of this public opinion shapes the character of government and its policies. If public opinion favors individual freedom and self-reliance and is suspicious of political authority, it brings forth a system that governs least. If, on the other hand, public opinion favors political governance and chooses to allocate income and wealth by force, it gives birth to a system of authority and conflict; it creates authority, *i.e.*, government force, that is commensurate to the political objectives desired, and generates economic and social conflict, not only between the beneficiaries and victims of the political process, but also among the beneficiaries themselves. After all, there is no government wealth and income other than that taken from individuals. What government distributes to its beneficiaries it must first seize from its victims. The transfer or welfare society, with its millions of beneficiaries, is also a victim society that is torn by internal conflict.

The role of money differs fundamentally in the two social orders. The system that governs least leaves the selection of a medium of exchange as well as all other economic activity to the choice and discretion of its people. Money that springs from voluntary exchanges is left free and unhampered. In a transfer society, money becomes a tool of political force and economic redistribution, a tool that is freely wielded by government, the transfer agency. To cover the chronic deficits which government may suffer in its transfer policies, or to generate economic boom conditions with rising employment and activity, the central bank is called upon to expand the supply of its legal tender money. As the quantity of government money multiplies, its exchange value and purchasing power must shrink and the prices of goods must rise, calling forth many undesirable social and economic consequences. The public commonly calls these consequences "inflation." It decries and condemns them while it clamors for their causes, easy money and credit for federal deficits and economic stimulation.

Ours is an age of inflation. All national currencies have suffered serious depreciations in our lifetime. In terms of 1933 consumers' dollars, we are today making purchases with twenty-cent dollars; and in terms of construction costs, which are so vital for business, we are buying supplies and labor with six-cent or even five-cent dollars. Although the inflation may not have been the stated intention of the monetary authorities, its symptoms and consequences are real and serious. Inflation destroys individual thrift and self-reliance as it gradually erodes personal savings. As it benefits debtors at the expense of creditors, it creates a massive flow of unearned income and loss. It consumes productive capital and destroys the middle class that invests in monetary instruments. It generates the business cycle, the stop-and-go, boom-and-bust movements of business that hurt millions of people. It invites government price and wage controls and other restrictive policies that hamper individual freedom and activity. In short, inflation breeds economic upheaval and social disorder, and generally erodes the moral and social fabric of a free society.

Surely every true American sincerely wishes to halt the inflation and save the dollar. But the difficulty arises from the public addiction to the very policies that either are directly inflationary or necessitate the creation of money. The public condemnation of the consequences of such policies is most inconsistent. It sounds like a public confession of sins in church on Sunday morning. The preacher intones the confession, the congregation accompanies him in loud voices, and then they return home to sin again. The President denounces inflation on Monday, and signs another multi-billion-dollar appropriations bill on Tuesday. Politicians who are the noisiest inflation fighters on Wednesday submit more costly bills for economic stimulation and distribution on Thursday. The news commentators publicly enlist in the war on inflation on Friday, and bravely endorse another costly program for economic improvement on Saturday. The following week the ritual is repeated.

The federal government that again and again declared war on inflation actively commenced the inflation, conducted it, and now continues to press it forward with ever greater force. The same politicians who at times sound like militant inflation fighters are pushing hard for every dollar of deficit spending. In just thirteen years, from fiscal year

Introduction

1965 to 1978, the federal government boosted its annual spending from $118.4 billion to an estimated $440 billion. Expenditures on "human resources," *i.e.*, income redistribution, alone rose from $35.4 billion to an estimated $224.8 billion. (Education and manpower from $2.3 billion to $19.4 billion; health care from $1.7 billion to $43.2 billion; income security, *i.e.*, retirement and disability, unemployment insurance, public assistance, social services, from $25.7 billion to $143.9 billion; veterans' benefits and services from $5.7 billion to $18.3 billion.)[1]

Such a rapid growth of government alone would have strained the American economy as economic resources were withdrawn from business and individual taxpayers. But this process of redistribution was made worse by far as it was accomplished by the most insidious of all possible methods, deficit spending and money creation. The quantity of Federal Reserve credit was inflated from $39.9 billion on January 1, 1965, to $126 billion at the present. The total money stock consisting of demand deposits in commercial banks and currency in circulation subsequently rose from $160 billion to $349 billion at the present (June 21, 1978).

This has been the worst monetarization of federal debt since World War II. In fact, the 1960's and 1970's have been the longest period of deficit spending and currency inflation since the Continental Dollar debacle during the American Revolution. And the end is nowhere in sight. If the federal deficit spending were merely to exact economic resources in the amount of the deficit, let us say $50 billion, the economic loss to money holders would be very small indeed, only $50 billion. But the given deficit and its monetarization causes goods prices to rise and the purchasing power of the monetary unit to fall, which alters the creditor-debtor relationship of over $3 trillion of long-term debt. When the dollar falls at the modest rate of ten percent per year, the creditors are losing $300 billion and debtors are gaining this very amount. Since the United States government is the largest single debtor with an estimated 1978 debt of nearly $800 billion, it is gaining $80 billion annually through debt depreciation in addition to the $50 billion deficit that triggered the inflation in the first place. But many millions of American creditors are losing a total of $300 billion. This is why inflation is not only a federal tax on money holders, but also a terrible instrument for the redistribution of wealth and income. In fact, the magnitude of this redistribution through federal inflation, in addition to that accomplished through social policy

---

[1] Compare Executive Office of the President, Office of Management and Budget, *The Budget of the United States Government* (Washington, D. C.: Government Printing Office, Fiscal Year 1965), p. 52; Fiscal Year 1978, p. 52.

and taxation, probably exceeds one-third of American disposable income, and as such is the most massive transfer of wealth in the history of man.

A free society that deliberately embarks upon such a road is suffering a terminal case of redistribution cancer. It is bound to suffer ever more symptoms of social conflict and strife. A democratic society that has been led blithely and ignorantly to such a policy may yet redeem itself by turning off the inflation road and returning to honest money. To stabilize the dollar it must be taken out of the hands of politicians, *i.e.*, the United States government must be deprived of its monopolistic power over money and banking. Since inflation is a federal policy, the federal government must mend its ways and permit a return to honest money. In particular,

> 1. The federal budget must be balanced now, next year, and every year thereafter.
> 2. The engine of inflation, the Federal Reserve System, must be inactivated, or better yet, abolished.
> 3. The Federal Reserve money now in circulation must stay in circulation and be made fully redeemable in gold.
> 4. With these steps we will have achieved monetary stability. But we will face a recession which past deficit spending and credit expansion have made unavoidable. Without an engine of inflation to accommodate new deficit spending and credit expansion, we will need to cut federal spending even further as federal revenue declines. And to facilitate speedy recovery from the recession, business taxes must be cut. We are confident that in a year or two the American economy will resume full speed again, with stable prices and a sound monetary system.[2]

Balancing the federal budget through reductions in spending does not signal the end of economic and social policy by the federal government. Taxes could still be raised in order to facilitate more transfer. But it would mean open redistribution from taxpayers to beneficiaries. Every new expenditure would have to be met with new tax revenue. Both the Congress and the Administration would have to regain the lost virtues of fiscal discipline and honesty. They would have to cut programs and allocations or raise taxes now in order to avoid large deficits next year.

A balanced budget would greatly reduce the pressures for debt monetarization and currency inflation. But it would not yet be enough for the desired dollar stabilization. The Federal Reserve System as it is now constituted has independent powers of currency inflation and

---

[2] From an open letter to President Gerald R. Ford by the Faculty of the Economics Department of Grove City College, October 1, 1974.

credit expansion. These powers must be revoked *immediately* through either inactivating the System or abolishing it altogether. Only when the engine of inflation has been removed from our financial scene can monetary stability be regained permanently.

Experience alone would dictate an immediate inactivation of this central command post over the economic lives of the American people. In the sixty-four years of its existence, the Federal Reserve System has presided over unprecedented economic instability — over two depressions, of which one was the longest and severest in American history, over numerous booms and recessions, and over an inflation that reduced the American dollar to less than twenty percent of its pre-Federal Reserve value. Few economists, if any, would defend its long record of money mismanagement.

Even if the System had been managed by the greatest financial minds of the century its very premise of central management of money and credit is alien to economic freedom and contrary to economic and social stability. The very existence of a money monopoly that endows its *fiat* issues with legal tender standing is antithetic to individual choice and freedom. By its very nature as a central bank it must seek to place currency in the loan markets, or withdraw it, in order to manage and manipulate those markets. But we are convinced that neither the addition nor the reduction of *fiat* money imparts any social utility, which leads us to conclude that Federal Reserve policies necessarily are disruptive to monetary stability. In particular, its frequent bursts of currency expansion, so popular with government officials, politicians, and their beneficiaries, have given our age the characteristics of unprecedented monetary instability.

To inactivate the engine of inflation does not mean withdrawal of all its money and credit. For lack of other money, Federal Reserve Notes now in the people's cash holdings and member bank reserves now held by the System must not be withdrawn. After all, deflation, *i.e.,* reduction of the money stock, would necessitate painful price and wage reductions, for which neither business nor labor is prepared.

But when the quantity of money is stabilized, the control of money could then be returned to the people by redeeming dollars (Federal Reserve Notes) again in gold. When man is free, he chooses natural money that is free from all strictures of government and politics. Gold is world money that unites all countries in one monetary system and facilitates peaceful exchange and division of labor. For more than two thousand years its natural qualities made it man's universal medium of exchange. In contrast to political money, it is honest money that survived the ages and will live on long after the political *fiats* of today have gone the way of all paper.

Redemption of the dollar in gold would be a simple undertaking that needs no central bank, no federal plan or policy, merely payments in gold. At a given market exchange ratio between the paper and the gold, the federal government merely resumes payment of the gold it forcibly seized from the American people in 1933 for the paper it has issued since then. People thus would be free again to choose between the paper notes, the quantity of which is rigidly limited, and the gold now hoarded in Fort Knox. Every ounce of gold that is withdrawn would reduce a quantity of paper, which would become a mere substitute for gold, the money proper. Thus, once again, the people of the United States would have hard and honest money, the golden symbol of a truly great society.

The gold standard sooner or later will return with the force and inevitability of natural law, for it is the money of freedom and honesty. Society may temporarily deny it in the vain hope of replacing it with political money that is managed and manipulated for political ends. But when the political paper finally disintegrates because its very nature lends itself to appalling abuse as an instrument of public plunder, people must again choose between political money, of which they may try another issue or series, and natural money. In the end, a society that prefers social peace over conflict, individual freedom over government coercion, and wealth over poverty has no alternative but to use honest money, which is gold.

Return to the gold standard, it is true, would precipitate a serious economic readjustment, commonly called a recession. But this is not the fault of gold. The political paper leaves behind a vast array of maladjustments and malinvestments that need to be corrected. In fact, they would be corrected in any case, sooner or later, when the creation of paper comes to an end. The economic recession need not be long and severe provided the federal government does not stand in the way of the necessary readjustment. After so many years of false stimulation through easy money and credit, many mistakes need to be corrected, some projects abandoned, and others begun. The whole economy needs to readjust to the wishes and commands of millions of consumers, who are the only sovereigns of a free economy.

It is important that the federal government should not intentionally or inadvertently obstruct the return to hard money. When the readjustment recession sets in, the federal government must not be allowed to resume deficit spending. Like anyone else, it must reduce its spending when its revenue declines. In particular, it must not be allowed to impose new tax burdens on business at this critical moment of recession and readjustment. It must not repeat the supreme folly of the Hoover Administration which, in 1932, doubled the tax burden. Also, the federal government must not be permitted to suffer deficits that are financed with the people's savings. Were the United

States Treasury to enter the loan markets at that critical moment of readjustment, it would deprive business of urgently needed funds and greatly raise business costs through soaring interest rates. These, in turn, would aggravate the recession and generate more unemployment. Who would be blamed for the dilemma? The *fiat* inflation that caused the maladjustments, the deficit spending that is aggravating it or the gold standard? The deficit spenders would lay the blame on gold.

An administration that welcomes monetary stability and therefore conducts and cooperates with the reform would balance its budget as its revenue declined. It would avoid placing new burdens on business during the readjustment period. In fact, it might want to lighten the tax load in order to hasten the recovery. But such a reduction of tax costs must not be negated by new deficits that burden the capital markets and raise interest costs. To reduce the costs of government and facilitate speedy recovery means to *reduce government consumption* of economic resources, not merely to change the method of financing from taxation to borrowing.

A significant reduction of federal spending not only would save funds and resources but would also enhance productive employment. For currency stability it does not matter which particular expenditures are reduced so long as the budget is balanced. Of course, it would be conducive to productivity and rapid readjustment if federal expenditures and economic controls were substantially reduced and bureaucratic regulations relaxed or abolished. Many industries can be revived through all kinds of de-regulation. It should be clear to anyone willing to see that with distressing monotony federal regulation has produced sick and anemic industries. The Interstate Commerce Commission's strangulation of the American transportation industry, for instance, has done incalculable harm that exceeds by far the budget expenditures for the controllers. The boost to productivity from a liberation of business energy could not come at a better time.

An administration that welcomes monetary stability would want to facilitate a speedy readjustment through significant cuts of business taxes. A rollback of corporate income taxes, for instance, would make corporations more profitable, which would boost capital investments, create new jobs, raise output and wage rates, and otherwise hasten the readjustment process.

The time clearly has come for a public commitment to the preservation of the dollar. The ultimate destination of the present road of political *fiat* is hyperinflation with all its ominous economic, social, and political consequences. On this road, no federal plan, program, incomes policy, control, nationalization, threat, fine, or prison can prevent the continuous erosion and ultimate destruction of the dollar.

Therefore, we must mend our ways and return on the proven path of our forebears to honest money, which is gold.

I
The Value of Money

Carl Menger's theory of the nature and origin of money still provides the cornerstone for our knowledge of money.[1] Tracing all monetary phenomena back to the choices and actions of individuals, Menger rejected the doctrines so popular then and now that would make the State the inventor and guardian of money. The origin of money was "entirely natural" as economizing and enterprising men sought to exchange their goods and services for more marketable goods that facilitated exchange for other goods. "Money is not an invention of the state," wrote Menger. "It is not the product of a legislative act. Even the sanction of political authority is not necessary for its existence."[2]

What then were the marketable goods that were sought by man in early times? Paleolithic man, who lived mainly by hunting, used furs and skins that served as clothing. Neolithic man, who learned to

---

[1] Carl Menger, *Grundsätze der Volkswirtschaftslehre* (Vienna, 1871), p. 250 *et seq.* English edition, *Principles of Economics* (Glencoe, Illinois: The Free Press, 1950), p. 257 *et seq.*
[2] *Ibid.*, pp. 261, 262 (English edition).

9

cultivate the soil and tame animals, used a great variety of commodities, such as grain and oil, dried fish, tortoise and cowry shells, sheep, horses, and especially cattle. The ox was one of the most marketable of all available goods and therefore a popular medium of exchange in the ancient world. It was used by ancient Greeks, Hebrews, Romans, Arabs, and many other peoples even until late in the middle ages.[3]

With the gradual improvement of the division of labor and the development of urban societies, the cattle-money was slowly replaced by other goods, especially the metals then in use. Where handicrafts were practiced, the tools of the craft or the materials used acquired great marketability. Copper, bronze, gold, and silver became goods of most general acceptability, at first in finished forms as tools, weapons, or ornaments of all kinds, and later, when their uses were widely recognized, also as raw materials. They could be easily divided, transported at low cost, and stored in relative safety. With the extension of trade over large areas of the world the precious metals gradually became the most marketable commodities and thus the money of civilized people.

To avoid the inconvenience of constant testing and weighing of the metals, the Lydians of Asia Minor in 650 B.C., and soon thereafter the Greeks, began to use coins, which were small pieces of metal with a visible mark of guarantee of weight and fineness. They were manufactured by private and public mints,[4] made of electrum, the natural mixture of gold and silver, and later of bronze, copper, pure gold, and silver, and carried a great variety of symbols and portraits. Coins made of precious metals gradually became the most popular medium of exchange all over the world and constituted universal money until the beginning of the twentieth century.[5]

Where coins were the accepted media of exchange, money substitutes were also payable in coins. In the ancient world, papyrus notes and clay tablets functioned as promises to pay precious metals on

---

[3] Paul Einzig, *Primitive Money* (London: Eyre & Spottiswoode, 1948), p. 228 *et seq.*; A. Hingston Quiggin, *A Survey of Primitive Money* (London: Methuen and Company, Ltd., 1949), pp. 271, 272; Arthur R. Burns, *Money and Monetary Policy in Early Times* (London: Routledge & Kegan Paul Ltd., 1927), pp. 1-36.

[4] The oldest coins were probably issued privately to meet the requirements of markets or fairs. Cf. Burns, *ibid.*, p. 75 *et seq.*

[5] According to Paul Einzig, *op. cit.*, p. 231, coinage may have been invented during the Late Mycenaean period (1400-1100 B. C.) but subsequently perished because of deterioration of civilization. It had to be invented over again in Lydia many centuries later. Cf. also Philip Grierson, *Coins and Medals: A Select Bibliography* (Historical Association, 1954), pp. 14-20. See also George MacDonald, *Evolution of Coinage* (New York: G.P. Putnam's Sons, 1916), p. 7. MacDonald believes that "coins were in use in China at a date much anterior to that of the archaic electrum of Asia Minor," during the eleventh century B.C. or even earlier.

demand. In modern times, the early goldsmiths began to issue paper receipts — later called bank notes — for gold and silver deposited with them for safekeeping. These notes enjoyed wide acceptance among merchants and manufacturers because they afforded both convenience and safety. After all, the transport of precious metals was often hazardous and expensive. In some cases the depositors even waived their right to paper receipts and maintained open book accounts — later called bank deposits — which they transferred to others by check.

People grew accustomed to paper money as a substitute for gold and silver. Then, in periods of emergency, governments could suspend redemption requirements, which made the paper substitutes the only money in circulation. In order to facilitate deficit financing, governments even resorted to "legal tender" legislation that forced the people to accept paper in settlement of government debts. After many decades of such emergency use of money substitutes, governments and central banks then withdrew all commodity money from individual cash holdings, which left the promissory notes as the only available exchange media. The stage thus was set for irredeemable government paper, called *fiat* money.

Ours is an age of paper money. The gold and silver coins of yesteryear have given way to irredeemable government paper, the quantities of which can be expanded with little effort. This is also a reason why ours is an age of inflation and money depreciation. Huge quantities of *fiat* money are created to meet budgetary deficits or to stimulate the economy. In addition, large volumes of money substitutes in the form of bank deposits are created by the banking system under the direction of the central bank. They are payable and redeemable on demand in this *fiat* money. The certainty that the owner can exchange his deposits against money at every instant makes these bank deposits money substitutes that render all the services of money. Thus demand deposits subject to withdrawal or transfer by check, as well as time deposits — inasmuch as the owner looks on them as cash, and banks stand ready to redeem them on demand — serve as media of exchange and are money in the broader sense. They are the major portion of the money holdings of most individuals today.

Monetary Theories

There is, and always has been, wide disagreement among economists on the basic principles that determine the purchasing power of all this money. But in spite of all the disagreements among economists, there are only two basic schools of thought. One endeavors to explain the purchasing power of money on the basis of individual choice and action and to develop the theory of the value of money from a general theory of value. Its monetary doctrines remain an integrated part of general economics, and as such may be called the *integrated* or *catallactic* monetary doctrines. The other school embodies all doctrines and theories that are alien to any theory of exchange or system of the market society, and thus deny the principles of individual choice and exchange. Such monetary doctrines may be called *segregated* or *acatallactic*, for they do not view money as a market phenomenon.

Most contemporary theories of the value of money must be classified as acatallactic. Presented in mathematical, holistic equations, they either ignore individual choice and valuation, or merely pay lip service to individual action while theorizing about collective wholes. Some writers, especially in government, resemble the medieval schoolmen who ascribed the power to fix the values of coins to their princes.[6] They hold that the value of money is a *valor impositus*, a value authenticated by the President and enforced through price and wage controls. To them, monetary phenomena, like all the phenomena of social life, are merely manifestations of the exercise of political power and government force. Their monetary explanations are not fallacious theories — they are not theories at all.

Some even deny the very existence of the science of economics. The radical inflationists, for instance, question the natural scarcity of economic goods and services, which is the very object of economic analysis. They blame selfish restraints on credit expansion imposed by bankers and other money lenders as the causes of scarcity and poverty, and therefore recommend unlimited public spending as the panacea. Their monetary pronouncements are built on a denial of economics.

But the two most popular bodies of monetary thought which shape contemporary monetary policies actually pay lip service to subjective economic theory while theorizing in acatallactic fashion. Both the income-expenditure theory of John Maynard Keynes and his numerous followers, and the quantity theory of Irving Fisher and his disciples, especially at the University of Chicago, completely ignore their catallactic premises when they arrive at the value of money. They deal with "price levels," "national economies as a whole," "levels of national output, employment, and income," and other holistic concepts that have no place in subjective economic thought. Such theories are as sterile and futile as their primitive acatallactic predecessors, but they are very popular with governments eager to indulge in deficit spending.

An integrated or catallactic explanation of the value of money starts

---

[6]Compare Arthur Eli Monroe, *Monetary Theory Before Adam Smith* (New York: Augustus M. Kelley, 1966), p. 26 *et seq.*

with the subjective valuations and actions of individuals. It never loses sight of the fact that a complete theory of money must rest on the subjective theory of value. In order to explain the determinants of the purchasing power of money and not only the causes of its changes, it endeavors to analyze the subjective significance or utility money has for individuals. For just as the price of an economic good is ultimately determined by the subjective valuation of buyers and sellers, so is the purchasing power of money.

The Demand for Money

Individual valuation of money is subject to the same consideration as the valuation of all other goods and services. People expend labor or forego the enjoyment of other economic goods in order to acquire money. At times they bid for money, at other times they offer money, and all this bidding and offering ultimately determines the purchasing power of money in the same way as it determines the mutual exchange ratios of other goods.[7] The individual demand for money springs from the fact that money is a very useful good, in fact, the most marketable good a person can acquire. While money made of precious metals (commodity money) may also render industrial services, paper money is not suitable to satisfy directly anyone's needs. But its possession permits us to acquire goods in the near or more distant future. People also want to keep a store of money to provide exchange power for an uncertain future. Some are satisfied with relatively small holdings, others prefer to hoard larger supplies. All may want to change their holdings in accordance with their changing situations and appraisals of future conditions. Money is never "idle," nor is it just "in circulation"; it is always in the possession or under the control of someone, affording economic utility to its owner.

The demand for commodity money thus consists of two partial demands: for use in consumption and production, commonly called the industrial demand; and that demand which flows from the intention to use the commodity as a medium of exchange, called the monetary demand. Obviously both demands affect the objective exchange value, or purchasing power, of the commodity. The explanation of economic value that flows from industrial uses is simple:

---

[7] For catallactic explanations see Ludwig von Mises, *Theory of Money and Credit* (London: Jonathan Cape Ltd., 1934), p. 97 *et seq.*, first published in German in 1912; also his *Human Action* (New Haven: Yale University Press, 1949), p. 395 *et seq.*; B.M. Anderson, *The Value of Money* (New York: Richard R. Smith, 1936), pp. 45-63, first published in 1917; Edwin Cannan, *Money* (Eighth edition, London: Staples Press, 1935), p. 20 *et seq.*, first published in 1918; F.A. Hayek, *Monetary Theory and the Trade Cycle* (New York: Augustus M. Kelley, 1966), p. 101 *et seq.*, first published in German in 1929; Murray N. Rothbard, *Man, Economy, and State* (Princeton, New Jersey: D. Van Nostrand, 1962), p. 661 *et seq.*

Usefulness and scarcity are the ultimate determinants of value. Both factors collaborate in what is commonly called the principle of marginal utility, according to which the importance of the want with the lowest degree of urgency among the wants that are covered by the available supply of goods determines the economic value of the goods. It is not the greatest degree of utility which a good affords, nor its average utility, but the smallest degree of utility for which a good can be expended that determines its value.

But how can this explanation be applicable to *fiat* money, the demand for which is purely monetary, and which has no economic uses other than as a medium of exchange? People seek money because it has purchasing power; and this purchasing power is greatly affected by the people's demand for money. But is this not reasoning in vicious circles? It is not! According to Ludwig von Mises' notable regression theorem, we must be mindful of the beginning of this monetary demand. Men's desires for cash holdings today are conditioned by yesterday's purchasing power of money, which in turn was affected by earlier purchasing power, and so on, until we arrive at the very inception of the monetary demand. At that particular moment the purchasing power of a certain quantity of gold or silver was solely determined by its non-monetary uses.[8]

Our search for the determinants of money value thus leads us back to the non-monetary uses of money, thereby avoiding the apparently circular argument. We trace back the value of money to that point where it was merely the value of a commodity. The subjective theory of value and its principle of marginal utility explain the value of the money commodity as they do in the case of every other economic good. This leads us to the interesting conclusion, already mentioned above, that the universal use of paper monies today was made possible only by their prior use as substitutes for real money, such as gold and silver, for which there was an industrial demand. Only when men grew accustomed to these substitutes, and governments deprived them of their freedom to employ gold and silver as media of exchange, did paper emerge as the only exchange medium. It has value and purchasing power, although it lacks industrial demand, because the people now direct their monetary demand towards government paper. If for any reason this public demand should cease or be redirected toward commodities as media of exchange, the *fiat* money would lose its entire value. The Continental Dollar and many other foreign currencies are excellent examples of this fact.

A source of countless errors is the popular notion that the demand

---

[8] Ludwig von Mises, *Theory of Money and Credit, op. cit.*, p. 110 *et seq.*; see also *Human Action, op. cit.*, p. 405 *et seq.*

for money is unlimited. Everyone can use more money. This idea mistakes the demand for wealth, which may be unlimited for most individuals, for the demand for money. They want money because of its purchasing power over real wealth, not more money *per se* with diluted purchasing power. Who needs more money that does not command more real wealth? On the market it is the effective demand that affects prices and production. This effective demand, as reflected by individual willingness to forego other goods and services, is always limited. It is strictly limited for economic goods as well as for money.

Particular Influences on the Demand for Money

Individual demand for money may vary for a great number of reasons. Personal aspirations may change, or the economic situation that warrants certain cash holdings. External factors may cause a person to revise his demand for money. In an advancing economy, for instance, more and more goods are offered for exchange, which tends to increase the demand for money. In a declining economy where productive capital is consumed and fewer goods reach the market, the demand for money will decline. In all such cases we speak of "goods-induced influences on the demand for money."

Let us assume we live in a medieval town that is cut off from all fresh supplies by an enemy army. There is great want and starvation. Although the quantity of money does not change, since no gold or silver has left the beleaguered town, its purchasing power must decline. Starving people place more value on food than on cash and seek to reduce their cash holdings in exchange for scarce food that is rapidly rising in importance.

The situation is similar in all cases where the supply of available goods is decreased although the quantity of money in the people's cash holdings remains unchanged. In a war, when the channels of supply are cut off by the enemy, or economic output is reduced for lack of labor power, the value of money tends to decline and goods prices rise even though the quantity of money may remain unchanged. A bad harvest in an agricultural economy may visibly weaken the currency. Similarly, a strike that paralyzes an economy and greatly reduces the supply of goods and services raises goods prices and simultaneously lowers the purchasing power of money. Imposition of price and wage controls that disrupt smooth market adjustments and create shortages has similar effects. In fact, every coercive intervention with economic production tends to affect prices and money value even though it may not be visible to many observers.

The level of taxation is also an important factor in the determination of the exchange value of money. When taxes claim between thirty to fifty percent of individual incomes as in most parts of the

15

world today, capital may be consumed and an incalculable amount of economic production may be prevented, which causes goods prices to rise and the purchasing power of money to fall. A new business tax, for instance, may necessitate production cutbacks, or even generate a general recession, which in turn may induce individuals to change their cash holdings. We are convinced that the ever rising burden of taxation by the federal, state, and local governments has contributed greatly to the depreciation of the American dollar.

Yet, this purchasing power loss of the dollar would have been far greater if a remarkable rise in industrial productivity had not occurred. In spite of the heavy burden of government and the phenomenal increase in the supply of money discussed further below, both of which exerted their influences toward lower dollar value, American commerce and industry managed to increase the supply of marketable goods and thereby retained or restored some purchasing power to the United States dollar. Under most difficult circumstances they managed to form more capital and improve production technology, and thus made available more and better economic goods which in turn helped to stabilize the dollar. Without this remarkable achievement by American entrepreneurs and capitalists, the United States dollar would have already followed the way of many other national currencies to radical depreciation and devaluation.

There are a great number of factors that directly affect the market demand for money. A growing population, for instance, with millions of maturing individuals entering the production process and eager to establish cash holdings, generates new demand, which in turn tends to raise the purchasing power of money and to reduce goods prices. On the other hand, a declining population with declining output would generate the opposite effect.

Changes in the division of labor bring about changes in the demand for money. Improvement increases it and disintegration reduces it. The nineteenth century frontier farmer who tamed the West with plow and gun was largely self-sufficient. His demand for money was very small when compared to that of his great-grandson who specializes in a single crop and buys all his food in the supermarket. As a participant in a highly advanced division of labor, the grandson bids for money for the satisfaction of all his wants through exchange. It is obvious that his demand has tended to raise the exchange value of money. On the other hand, deterioration of this division of labor and return to self-sufficient production, which we can observe in many parts of Asia, Africa, and South America, generates the opposite effect.

Development and improvement of a clearing system also exerts an important influence toward lower money value. Clearing means offsetting payments by banks or brokers. It reduces individual demand for money as only net balances are settled by cash payments. The American clearing system, which gradually developed over more than 130 years from local to regional and national clearing, slowly reduced the need and demand for cash and thus its purchasing power. Of course, this reduction of the dollar's exchange value was rather small when compared with that caused by other factors, especially the huge increase in money supply.[9]

Business practices, too, may influence individual demand for money and therefore its value. It is customary for business to settle its obligations on the first of the month. Tax payments are due on certain dates. The growing popularity of credit cards reduces the need for money holdings throughout the month, but concentrates it at the beginning of the month when payments fall due. All such variations in demand affect the objective exchange value of money. But we must never forget that all these factors exert their influences on individual valuation and attitude toward money. In the possession of certain cash holdings individuals may decide for one reason or another to increase or reduce their holdings. Reacting to the same external influences many people may act alike. If they increase their demand, the exchange value of money tends to rise; if they reduce their demand, the exchange value of money tends to fall.

This is so well understood that even some acatallactic theories emphasize the money "velocity" in their equations and calculations of money value. Velocity of circulation is defined as the average number of times in a year which a dollar serves as income (the income velocity) or as an expenditure (the transaction velocity).[10] Of course, this economic use of a term borrowed from physics ignores acting man who increases or reduces his cash holdings. Even when it is in transport, money is under control of its owners who choose to spend it or hold it, make or delay payment, lend or borrow. The acatallactic economist, who weighs and measures and thereby ignores the choices and preferences of acting individuals, is tempted to control and manipulate this "velocity" in order to influence the value of money. He may even blame individuals who refuse to act in accordance with his model for monetary depreciation or appreciation. Governments are only too eager to echo this blame, and, while they are creating ever new quantities of *fiat* and fiduciary money, restrain individuals in order to control money velocity.

[9]Compare Ludwig von Mises, *Theory of Money and Credit*, op. cit., p. 281 *et seq.*

[10]E.g. Richard T. Seldon, "Monetary Velocity in the U.S.," *Studies in the Quantity Theory of Money*, Milton Friedman, ed. (Chicago: University of Chicago Press, 1956), pp. 179-257; see also Irving Fisher, *Purchasing Power of Money* (New York: Macmillan, 1926), pp. 14-32, 164.

It is true that the propensity to increase or reduce cash holdings by many people tends to alter the purchasing power of money. But in order to change their holdings radically, individuals must have cogent reasons. For instance, they endeavor to raise their holdings whenever they foresee depressions ahead. They usually lower their holdings whenever they anticipate more inflation and declining money value. In short, they tend to react rationally and naturally to certain trends and policies. Government cannot change or prevent this reaction; it can merely change its own policy that brought forth the reaction.

The Quantity of Money

No determinant of demand is subject to such wide variations as the supply of money. During the age of the gold coin standard when gold coins were circulating freely, the supply of money was narrowly circumscribed by the supply of gold. But today, when governments have complete control over money and banking, when central banks can create or withdraw *fiat* money at will, its quantity changes significantly from year to year and from week to week. The student of money and banking now must carefully watch the official statistics of money creation in order to understand current economic trends.

Of course, the ever-changing supply of money must not be viewed as a factor that evenly and uniformly changes all goods prices. The total supply of money in a given economy does not confront the total supply of goods. Changes in money supply always act through the cash holdings of individuals who react to changes in their personal fortunes and in environmental conditions. It is through acting individuals that changes in supply exert their influences on various goods prices.

The popular notion that the demand for money is unlimited is related to the equally spurious belief that an increase of the stock of money is socially beneficial and desirable. Surely, if everyone can use more money, its creation must confer social utility. In the history of monetary thought from John Law to John Maynard Keynes few fallacies, if any, have caused greater economic and social harm than this. It lives on throughout the centuries, embraced by kings and dictators, politicians and statesmen, social reformers and revolutionaries. In its wake it has left shattered currencies, incalculable economic loss and individual tragedies, and last but not least, social and political upheaval. It springs forth, again and again, no matter how often economists may refute it, because an increase of the stock of money actually benefits some recipients at the expense of others. There is, first of all, the issuing authority, the central government with its monetary monopoly. When it covers its budgetary deficits with new money issues, it seizes real income and wealth from money holders. Its consumption is increased and that of the inflation victims reduced by a like amount, which explains the great popularity of inflation with monetary authorities, from Greek city tyrants to contemporary dictators and government officials. Of course, millions of recipients of government favors and the army of government employees readily support all measures that assure them higher incomes. In addition, inflation usually receives strong support from the class of debtors whose obligations are depreciated whenever the stock of money is greatly increased. And finally, labor unions usually are vocal supporters of inflationary policies, which tend to alleviate the stagnation and the unemployment caused by their own policies.

Nevertheless, the notion that an increase in the stock of money is socially beneficial and desirable is one of the great economic fallacies of our time. It is true that an increase in the supply of consumers' goods benefits some without detracting from the well-being of others. Similarly, an increase in the quantity of producers' goods has beneficial effects. But the only service rendered by money is that of medium of exchange. It cannot be consumed and cannot serve any productive end. Because of its exchange services it has a market demand that is directed toward a given supply. At any given time both the demand for and supply of money determine its exchange value. Whether the given stock of money is large or small, it renders the desired exchange services; there can be neither a surplus nor a shortage of money. Some 170 years ago David Ricardo eloquently expressed this very conclusion:

> If the quantity of gold or silver in the world employed as money were exceedingly small, or abundantly great . . . the variation in their quantity would have produced no other effect than to make the commodities for which they were exchanged comparatively dear or cheap. The smaller quantity of money would perform the functions of a circulating medium as well as the larger.[11]

When government changes the stock of money its purchasing power must adjust through individual valuation and action. An increase tends to lower the purchasing power, a decrease tends to raise it. Through changes in the money stock government affects individual valuations; it does not confer any social benefit by money creation. In fact, it causes economic upheaval and generates social and political strife. But regardless of its consequences, it is individual choices, actions, and reactions that always determine the value of money.

---

[11] Ricardo, "The High Price of Bullion," *Works,* Vol. III. Piero Sraffa, *ed. (Cambridge: Cambridge University Press, 1951),* p. 73.

II
The Causes of Inflation

It is not money, as is sometimes said, but the depreciation of money — the cruel and crafty destruction of money — that is the root of many evils. Inflation destroys individual thrift and self-reliance as it gradually erodes personal savings. It benefits debtors at the expense of creditors as it silently transfers wealth and income from the latter to the former. It generates the business cycles, the stop-and-go, boom-and-bust movements of business that inflict incalculable harm on millions of people. For money is not only the medium for virtually all economic exchanges, but also the very denominator of economic calculation. When money suffers depreciations and devaluations it invites government price and wage controls, compulsory distribution through official allocation and rationing, restrictive quotas on imports, high tariffs and surcharges, prohibition of foreign travel and investment, and many other governmental restrictions on individual activities. Monetary destruction breeds not only poverty and chaos, but also government tyranny. Few policies are more calculated to destroy the existing basis of a free society than the debauching of its currency. And few tasks, if any, are more important to the champion of freedom than creation of a sound monetary system.

Inflation is the creation of money by monetary authorities. In more popular usage, it is that creation of money that visibly raises goods prices and lowers the purchasing power of money. It may be creeping, trotting, or galloping, depending on the rate of money creation by the authorities. It may take the form of "simple inflation," in which case the proceeds of the new money issues accrue to the government for deficit spending. Or it may appear as "credit expansion," in which case the authorities channel the newly created money into the loan market. The government may balance its budget, but in order to stimulate business and promote full employment, it may inject new credit into the banking system. Both forms are inflation in the broader sense and as such are willful and deliberate policies conducted by government.

Ours is an age of inflation.[1] All national currencies have suffered serious depreciations in our lifetime. The British pound sterling, the shining example of hard money for one hundred years, has lost almost ninety percent of its purchasing power and suffered four devaluations since 1931. The powerful United States dollar of yesteryear has lost at least eighty percent of its purchasing power and continues to shrink at an accelerating rate. In the world of national currencies there have been more than one thousand full or partial devaluations since World War II. Many currencies have suffered total destruction and their replacements are eroding again.

To inquire into the causes that induce governments the world over to embark upon such monetary policies is to search for the monetary theories and doctrines that guide their policy makers. Ideas control the world, and monetary ideas shape monetary policies. Several distinct economic and monetary doctrines have combined their forces to make our age one of inflation. One doctrine in particular enjoys nearly universal acceptance, and every government the world over is guided by its principles. This is the doctrine that government needs to control the money.

Even champions of private property and individual freedom are reluctant to apply those principles to money. They are convinced that money cannot be left to the vagaries of the market order, but must be controlled by government. Money must be supplied and regulated by government or its central bank, they argue. That money should be free is inconceivable to twentieth century man. He depends on government to mint his coins, issue his notes, define "legal tender,"

---

[1] Compare Jacques Rueff, *The Age of Inflation* (Chicago: Henry Regnery Company, 964).

establish central banks, conduct monetary policy, and then stabilize the price level. In short, he completely relies on government to provide him with money. But this trust in monopolistic processes inevitably gives rise to monetary destruction. In fact, we are convinced that *money is inflated, depreciated, and ultimately destroyed whenever government holds monopolistic power over it.*

Throughout the history of civilization, governments have been the chief cause of monetary depreciation. It is true that variations in the supply of metallic money, due to new gold and silver discoveries, occasionally affected the value of money. But these changes were small when compared with those caused by government coin debasements or note inflations. Especially since the rise of statism and the "redistributive society," governments all over the world have embarked upon unprecedented inflations, the disastrous effects of which, though obvious, can only be estimated. To entrust our money to government is like leaving our canary with a hungry cat.

From the Roman Caesars and the medieval princes to contemporary presidents and prime ministers, governments have this in common: the urgent need for more revenue. The large number of spending programs, such as war or preparation for war, care of veterans and civil servants, health, education, welfare, and urban renewal, places a heavy burden on the public treasury, which is finally tempted to provide the necessary funds through currency expansion. True, government at first may merely endeavor to tax wealth and income. Without income of its own it may derive its spoils and benefits from wealthy producers. It may tax Peter to pay Paul. But this very convenient and popular method of government support is practically exhausted when Peter's income taxes reach one hundred percent. At this point any additional revenue is obtained either from raising everyone's taxes or from currency expansion. But the former is rather unpopular and therefore inexpedient politically. To win elections the taxes may even be lowered and the inevitable deficits covered through currency creation, *i.e.,* inflation.

The first step towards full development of this source of revenue was the creation of a government monopoly of the mint. To secure possession of the precious metals that circulated as coins, the sovereign prohibited all private issues and established his own monopoly. Minting became a special prerogative of the sovereign power. Coins either carried the sovereign's own picture or were stamped with his favorite emblems. But above all, his mint could now charge any price for the coins it manufactured. Or it could reduce the precious metal content of the coins and thus obtain princely revenues through coin debasemant. Once this prerogative of sovereignty was safely established, the right to clip, degrade, or debase the coinage was no longer questioned. It became a "crown right" that was one of the chief sources of revenue.[2]

An essential step towards gradual debasement of the coinage was the separation of the name of the monetary unit from its weight. While the original names of the coins designated a certain weight and thus afforded a ready conception of their gold or silver content — to wit: pound, libra or livre, shilling, mark, *etc.* — the new names were devoid of any reference to weight. The pound sterling was no longer a pound of fine silver, but anything the sovereign might designate as the national monetary unit. This change in terminology widely opened the door to coin debasement.

The next step towards full government control over the people's money was the passage of legal tender laws, which dictate to people what their legal money can be. Such laws are obviously meaningless and superfluous wherever the ordinary law of contract is respected. But where government wants to issue inferior coins or depreciated paper notes, it must use coercion in the form of legal tender legislation. Then it can circulate worn or debased coins side-by-side with the original coins, falsify the exchange ratios between gold and silver coins and discharge its debt with the overvalued coins, or make payments in greatly depreciated *fiat* money. In fact, once legal tender laws were safely established, debt repudiation through monetary depreciation could become one of the great thefts of our time. Contemporary jurisprudence was utterly paralyzed in its defense and administration of justice once it accepted legal tender laws. A debt of a million gold marks thus could be legally discharged with one million paper marks that bought less than one United States penny. And a government debt of fifty billion 1940 dollars can now be paid or refunded with a 1978 dollar issue that is worth less than twenty percent of the original amount. With the blessings of the courts of justice, millions of creditors can now be swindled out of their rightful claims and their property legally confiscated.[3]

But absolute government control over money was only established when money substitutes in the form of paper notes and demand deposits came into prominence. As long as governments had to make payments in commodity money, inflationary policies were limited to the primitive methods of coin debasement. With the advent of paper money and demand deposits, however, the power of government was greatly strengthened, and the scope of inflation vastly extended.

---

[2]Compare Elgin Groseclose, *Money and Man* (New York: Frederick Ungar Publishing Co., 1961), p. 55 *et seq.*
[3]Ludwig von Mises, *Human Action, op. cit.,* pp. 432, 444.

The Causes of Inflation

At first, people were made familiar with paper money as a substitute for money proper, which was gold or silver. Government then proceeded to withdraw the precious coins from individual cash holdings and concentrate them in its treasury or central bank, thus replacing the classical gold coin standard with a gold bullion standard. Finally, when the people had grown accustomed to paper issues, the government could deny all claims for redemption and establish its own *fiat* standard. All checks on inflation had finally been removed.

The executive arm of the government that conducts the inflation usually is the central bank. It does not matter who legally owns this bank, whether private investors or the government itself. Legal ownership always becomes empty and meaningless when government assumes total control. The Federal Reserve System, which is legally owned by the member banks, is the monetary arm of the United States government and its engine of inflation. It enjoys a monopoly of the note issue which alone is endowed with legal tender characteristics. Commercial banks are forced to hold their reserves as deposits with the central bank, which becomes the "banker's bank" with all the reserves of the country. The central bank then conducts its own inflation by expanding its notes and deposits while maintaining a declining reserve ratio of gold to its own liabilities, and directs the bank credit expansion by regulating the legal reserve requirements the commercial banks must maintain with the central bank. Endowed with such powers, the central bank now can finance any government deficit either through a direct purchase of treasury obligations or through open-market purchases of such obligations, which creates the needed reserves for commercial banks to buy the new treasury issues.

The final step towards absolute government control over money and money's ultimate destruction is the suspension of international gold payments, which is the step President Nixon took on August 15, 1971. When a central bank is hopelessly overextended at home and abroad, its currency may be devalued, which is a partial default in its international obligations to make payment in gold, or, in an outburst of abuse against foreigners and speculators, the government may cease to honor any payment obligation, as was the case in the United States default. All over the world, government paper now forms some 120 national *fiat* standards that are managed and depreciated at will.

Our age of inflation was thus ushered in. The decline of monetary freedom and the concomitant rise of governmental power over money gave birth to the age of inflation. Step by step government assumed control over money, which is not only an important source of government revenue but also a vital command post over our economy.

This is why we live in an age of inflation. Only monetary freedom can impart stability.[4]

The Transfer Society

We deny the popular contention that a managed money can ever be stable even when managed by honest, noble, and knowledgeable government agents. "If nations could somehow muster the will," writes the *Wall Street Journal* ("Review and Outlook," September 17, 1971), "there's no inherent reason why managed money can't be managed well, even if it's only paper." Surely the *Journal* and many other newspapers would not want to be managed by the United States government. But they do not hesitate to proclaim government-managed money as the "best monetary system," while denouncing the gold standard and monetary freedom as the "second-best." While we sympathize with hope that springs eternal even after forty years of continuous inflation and mismanagement, we do not share their great faith in the political management of money.

In fact, even the noblest politicians and civil servants can no longer be expected to resist the public clamor for social benefits and welfare. The political pressure that is brought to bear on democratic governments is rooted in the popular ideology of government welfare and economic redistribution. It inevitably leads to a large number of spending programs that place heavy burdens on the public treasury. By popular demand, weak administrations seeking to prolong their power embark upon massive spending and inflating in order to build a "great society" or provide a "new deal." The people are convinced that government spending can give them full employment, prosperity, and economic growth. When the results fall far short of expectations, new programs are demanded and more government spending is initiated. When social and economic conditions grow even worse, the disappointments breed more radicalism, cynicism, nihilism, and above all, bitter social and economic conflict. And all along, the enormous increase in government spending causes an enormous increase in taxes, chronic budget deficits, and rampant inflation.[5]

The "redistributive" aspirations of the voting public often induce their representatives in Congress to authorize and appropriate even more money than the President requests. Such programs as social security, medicare, anti-poverty, housing, economic development,

---

[4]Compare Ludwig von Mises, *The Theory of Money and Credit, op. cit.*, p. 413 *et seq.*; Murray N. Rothbard, *Man, Economy, and State, op. cit.*, p. 661 *et seq.*; see also his concise *What Has Government Done to Our Money?* (Colorado Springs: Pine Tree Press, 1963).

[5]Henry Hazlitt, *Man vs. the Welfare State* (New Rochelle, New York: Arlington House, 1969), p. 57 *et seq.*

aid to education, environmental improvement, and pay increases for civil servants are so popular that few politicians dare to oppose them.

The government influences personal incomes by virtually every budget decision that is made. Certainly its grants, subsidies, and contributions to private individuals and organizations aim to improve the material incomes of the beneficiaries. The loans and advances to private individuals and organizations have the same objective. Our foreign aid program is redistributive in character as it reduces American incomes in order to improve the material condition of foreign recipients. The agricultural programs, veterans' benefits, health, labor, and welfare expenditures, housing and community development, federal expenditures on education, and last, but not least, the social insurance and medicare programs directly affect the incomes of both beneficiaries and taxpayers. As the benefits are generally not based on tax payments, but rather on considerations of social welfare, these programs constitute redistribution on a nationwide scale. Foreign aid programs have extended the principle of redistribution to many parts of the world.

Whenever government expenditures exceed tax collections and the government deficit is covered by currency and credit expansion, we suffer inflation and its effects. The monetary unit is bound to depreciate and goods prices must rise. Large increases in the quantity of money also induce people to reduce their savings and cash holdings, which, in the terminology of mathematical economists, increases money "velocity" and reduces money value even further. It is futile to call these people "irresponsible" as long as the government continues to increase the money stock.

A very potent cause of inflation is the unrelenting wage pressure exerted by labor unions. It is true that labor unions do not directly increase the quantity of money and credit and thus cause the depreciation. But their policy of raising production costs inevitably causes stagnation and unemployment. This is why the union strongholds are the centers of unemployment. Being faced with serious stagnation, the labor leaders are likely to become advocates of all schemes for easy money and credit that promise to alleviate unemployment. The democratic government in turn does not dare to oppose the unions for political reasons. On the contrary, it does everything in its power to reduce the pressure which mass unemployment exerts on the union wage rates. It grants ever larger unemployment benefits and embarks upon public works in the depressed unionized areas. At the same time it expands credit, which tends to reduce real wages and therefore creates employment.

The demand for labor is determined by labor costs. Rising costs reduce the demand, falling costs raise it. Inasmuch as inflation reduces the real costs of labor it actually creates employment. When goods prices rise while wages stay the same, or prices rise faster than wages, labor becomes more profitable to employers. Many workers whose employment costs had exceeded their productivity value and who, therefore, had been unemployable now can be profitably reemployed. Of course, this employment-creating policy is then counteracted by the unemployment factors, such as rising minimum wage rates, higher unemployment benefits and welfare doles, and rising union wage scales and fringe benefit costs. In many industries the labor unions have introduced "cost-of-living clauses" that aim to prevent the decline of real wages through monetary depreciation. Or their wage demands take into consideration the rising rates of monetary depreciation. Their demands may become "exhorbitant," their strikes longer and uglier, and the economic losses inflicted on business and the public ever more damaging, until businessmen clamor for government wage controls. With wage controls come price controls and the whole paraphernalia of the command system.

Old Myths In Keynesian Garb

To give scientific justification to the policy of inflation, a host of economists have developed intricate theories. The most controversial, and undoubtedly the most influential, among them has been that of John Maynard Keynes. His economic doctrines have conquered the free world and now are shaping the economic policies of scores of governments. In Washington the policy makers of all administrations from Franklin Roosevelt to Jimmy Carter have used Keynesian principles to pursue their particular brands of a new and better society. Contemporary economists have reinterpreted and expanded the Keynesian theories, giving rise to a form of neo-Keynesianism, commonly called the New Economics. While Keynes was preoccupied with a depression-ridden world and with policies that would pull it to stability and prosperity, his modern disciples endeavor to make the national economies grow at more satisfactory rates. A mathematical economist may put it like this: Keynesianism + growth economics = The New Economics.

Keynes's doctrines rest on the assumption of the instability of the modern capitalist economy. Since the market system no longer works at top efficiency, government influence and intervention must raise it to that level. Keynes was convinced that government has not only the ability but also the responsibility to increase production, incomes, and jobs. Government must achieve general prosperity through the wise use of three important policy tools: taxation, government spending, and money management.

The Causes of Inflation

Keynes's discussion of money is found in his two major treatises: *A Treatise on Money*,[6] and *The General Theory of Employment, Interest and Money*.[7] The relationship between these two books is not very clear. Keynes himself admitted this in his preface to *The General Theory*. Nevertheless, in his later work, he announced successful emancipation from traditional thought:

> When I began to write my *Treatise on Money*, I was still moving along the traditional lines of regarding the influence of money as something so to speak separate from the general theory of supply and demand. When I finished it, I had made some progress towards pushing monetary theory back to becoming a theory of output as a whole. But my lack of emancipation from preconceived ideas showed itself in what now seems to me to be the outstanding fault of the theoretical parts of that work.[8]

In short, Keynes's *magnum opus* reflects his long struggle to escape "from habitual modes of thought and expression." Or as he put it: "The difficulty lies, not in the new ideas, but in escaping from the old ones which ramify, for those brought up as most of us have been, into every corner of our minds."[9]

The Keynesian system is a full employment recipe. It prescribes inflation as a remedy for chronic unemployment. Expansionary monetary and fiscal policies are said to work wonders. When the quantity of money in circulation is increased, interest rates will fall, investments increase, and income rise until full employment is reached. Aggregate demand, in the Keynesian system, determines employment, which in turn determines real wages.[10]

Unfortunately, according to Keynes, monetary policy may not be entirely effective. When the stock of money is increased, the "velocity" may decline as the people may be willing to hold the larger stock, merely preferring greater liquidity. Government must then invest directly in various public works in order to cure the unemployment. Fiscal measures, *i.e.*, government spending accompanied by tax cuts, are called for.

Government investments, Keynes theorized, enjoy the characteristic of the "multiplier," that is, they generate an increase in income that is a multiple of the original injection of government spending. As disposable income is raised, consumption, which is a

---

[6]New York: Harcourt, Brace & Company, 1930.
[7]New York: Harcourt, Brace & Company, 1936.
[8]*The General Theory, op. cit.*, p. vi.
[9]*Ibid.*, p. viii.
[10]*Ibid.*, pp. 113-131, 245 *et seq.*; cf. Alvin H. Hansen, *A Guide to Keynes* (New York: McGraw-Hill, 1953), pp. 2 -22.

function of income, is stimulated according to the marginal propensity to consume. Thus, if the government increases its investment by $1 billion, income will rise by $1 billion multiplied by the multiplier.

What a marvelous world of fancy! Government spending multiplies the people's income. But where is the money that government is supposed to spend coming from? From its own printing presses! The Keynesian remedies for unemployment can all be summarized in a single term: inflation. Of course, Lord Keynes denied that. Inflation means rising prices, he argued. It occurs only whenever the sum of consumption, investment, and government expenditures exceeds the full employment capacity of the national economy. In this case government would merely have to reduce aggregate demand through fiscal and monetary policy.

Among the American economists who pioneered the Keynesian cause and clarified and expanded the Keynesian framework is Alvin H. Hansen.[11] As one of the most outspoken opponents of balanced budgets, he developed the thought of compensatory finance through contracyclical debt expansion and tax reductions. Internally held government debt is no burden on the economy as interest payments are paid to ourselves. Government therefore should finance its compensatory full employment projects with debt rather than taxes. But the effects of this deficit spending would depend on who buys the government obligations. In the hands of the central bank that can print the money they are highly "expansionary"; in the hands of individuals who may forego other expenditures they may have little net effect on total spending. Therefore, Hansen generally preferred central bank financing.

The economist who mirrors the political and economic views of most American economists today is Paul Samuelson. His influence on American economic policy has been felt ever since he advised President Kennedy in the early 1960's. According to Samuelson, government has a clear responsibility actively to ensure full employment and economic stability. No given formula — simple or complex — can achieve it. Every situation must be judged within its own particular environment. His tool for the formulation of modern policy is the Phillips Curve, which shows the relation of increasing prices (inflation) and the unemployment rate, and the "menu" of alternatives for monetary and fiscal policy. Samuelson encourages governments to conduct "activist" fiscal policies. To stimulate a sluggish economy, government spending should be expanded and taxes cut. But when the inflationary pressures from government expenditures begin to

---

[11]*Monetary Theory and Fiscal Policy* (New York: McGraw-Hill, 1949); *Business Cycles and National Income* (New York: W. W. Norton & Co., 1951); and *A Guide to Keynes, ibid.*

The Causes of Inflation

be felt, the taxes should be increased again. Both the tax cut of 1964 and the surtax of 1978 were motivated by such considerations.[12]

Perhaps the most important contribution to the Keynesian system was made by Abba Ptachya Lerner. As author of the theory that government fiscal policy can be used to fine-tune the economy and thus assure full employment at all times, he became one of the most influential economists of our time. His theory of "functional finance" has become a standard tool in the armory of government finance, aiming to keep aggregate demand always on the full employment level. The theory reduces all government actions to one or more of six basic elements: to buying and selling, spending and taxing, lending and borrowing. If the rate of aggregate spending is deficient for assuring full employment, the government may buy goods or services, increase its spending, or lend money for either consumption or investment. If aggregate spending is excessive the process may be reversed.

When during the 1950's and '60's inflation existed side by side with unemployment, which obviously contradicted the Keynesian program, Abba Lerner came to the rescue. This is a "sellers' inflation and administered depression," he explained. Monopolies, trade unions, and government controls prevent the market from determining wages and prices. Where monetary and fiscal measures are thus rendered ineffective it is time to impose "price regulation." This regulation, which differs from price control, would manipulate wages and prices in accordance with productivity increases and the existence of surpluses or shortages.[13]

As the most popular of all Keynesian economists, John Kenneth Galbraith succeeded in bringing the New Economics to the New Frontier generation. Two of his books — The Affluent Society and The New Industrial State — are all-time best sellers in popular economics and are studied in hundreds of colleges. As the leading social critic of American life, he summarily rejects "conventional wisdom" and attacks nearly all the accepted doctrines of traditional economics. He insists that the basic values of society must be changed. As the state, which is essentially an arm of the industrial system, cannot be expected to provide the needed public goods, Galbraith calls on the intellectual community to effect the change. "What counts is not the quantity of our goods but the quality of life."[14] Therefore, price controls should be imposed not just to suppress managed prices, but also to

[12] The Collected Scientific Papers of Paul A. Samuelson Joseph Stiglitz, ed. (Cambridge: M.I.T. Press, 1966); Economics (10th ed., New York: McGraw-Hill, 1976), p. 205 et seq.; first edition published in 1947.

[13] Compare A.P. Lerner, Essays in Economic Analysis (London: Macmillan and Company, Ltd., 1953); "A Program for Monetary Stability," Proceedings of the Conference on Savings and Residential Financing (Chicago, 1962).

[14] The New Industrial State (Boston: Houghton Mifflin Company, 1967), p. 80; cf. also

assure the realization of more desirable social goals.

Modern inflation, the Keynesian epigones lament,[15] differs from that of the past in that prices and wages continue to rise while there is underemployment of capital and labor. When the monetary and fiscal brakes are applied and the rate of cost-push inflation is limited, the managed economy sinks into deep recession. Without the brakes, the inflation accelerates while unemployment remains high or goes even higher. The Keynesian tools of C +I +G (consumer, investment, and government spending) have lost their legendary power.

The Phillips Curve, which was hailed as the macro-manager's blueprint, has become a big question mark. Its quantification of the trade-off relationship between unemployment and wage rates obviously is more fiction than description. And its pictorial message that a low rate of inflation means high unemployment, and greater inflation less unemployment, is spurious. The fact is that the Keynesian formula for full employment through monetary and fiscal stimulation is finally yielding its foreseen results: rising rates of inflation together with growing unemployment.

The Keynesian system contains many errors, too numerous to analyze in this essay. But we must mention just a few that have a bearing on the issue. In particular, we must reject the basic psychological maxim that government can fool all the people all the time with easy money and credit.

Poor Psychology

Lord Keynes was banking on the economic ignorance and stupidity of wage earners and their union agents. He recommended deficit spending and credit expansion as an efficient method for gradually and automatically lowering labor costs. Admittedly, lower real wages raise the demand for labor and reduce unemployment. But the success of the Keynesian plan depends entirely on the ability to deceive the workers and their unions or, if this should fail, to persuade them to suffer voluntary losses in real incomes.

Deceit is always the false road to a solution. It weaves a tangled web, which in the end misleads one and destroys the confidence of others. While the Keynesians are weaving, the workers are marching in picket lines. They need no Ph.D. in Keynesian economics to understand how rising prices reduce the purchasing power of labor income. They are quick to demand wage boosts that compensate for the rise

---

The Affluent Society (Boston: Houghton Mifflin Company, 1958); *American Capitalism* (Boston: Houghton Mifflin Company, 1952); *Economic Development* (Cambridge, Massachusetts: Harvard University Press, 1962); *Money* (Boston: Houghton Mifflin Company, 1975).

[15]Paul A. Samuelson, *Economics, op. cit.*, p. 820.

in goods prices. Moreover, they may force rises in money wage rates that anticipate future purchasing power losses during the life of the contract. Both claims, together with the demand for higher real incomes because of "rising labor productivity," are foiling the Keynesian plan.

The post-Keynesians now admit that the customary dosages of monetary and fiscal policy no longer cause real wages to adjust to clear the labor markets. They speak of a great discovery of a new type of inflation in which labor does not want to be deceived, but continues to push for higher wages regardless of the recipe. In frustration and desperation, the Keynesian professors are developing new theories of "cost-push inflation" and charting new curves that are to explain the dilemma. Abraham Lincoln long ago answered the Keynesian cunning: "You cannot fool all of the people all the time."

Because economic reality does not conform with their doctrines, Keynesians now are joining many utopian and would-be reformers in urging the use of force to fit men into their special mold. To force economic life into the Keynesian mold they are discussing the use of government force in the form of an incomes policy, that is, wage and price controls, or governmental guide lines, or government getting tough with the unions, or some similar use of force.

Institutional Unemployment

We recall that all Presidents, from Franklin Roosevelt to Jimmy Carter, initiated their own programs for full employment. They all pledged top priority to the problem of mass unemployment. And yet, except for World War II years, unemployment has been our constant companion ever since 1930. In fact, it seems to grow ever more acute as it now makes its ugly appearance even in boom times. Almost eight million Americans are looking for jobs although the economy is said to be prosperous and growing.

The Carter Administration, like others before it, is not really coping with the causes of unemployment. Under the influence of post-Keynesian ideas, it seeks once again to stimulate the economy through deficit spending, credit expansion, tax rebates, public works, increased minimum wages, and increased unemployment compensation. It is resorting to the very measures that create unemployment rather than alleviate it.

Throughout the Keynesian and post-Keynesian era the inexorable laws of economics have not changed. Unemployment still is, and always has been, a cost phenomenon. A worker whose employment adds valuable output and is profitable to his employer can always find a job. A worker whose employment inflicts losses is destined to be unemployed. As long as the earth is not paradise there is an infinite amount of work to be done. But if a worker produces only $2 per hour while the government decrees a minimum wage of $2.50 an hour plus sizable fringe costs, he cannot be employed. For a businessman to hire him would mean capital loss and waste. In other words, any compulsion, be it by government directly or by a legally privileged union, which raises labor costs above those determined by the marginal productivity of labor, creates institutional unemployment.

The problems of unemployment are wholly obscured by a popular pseudo-humanitarianism according to which the demand for higher labor costs is a noble demand for the improvement of the conditions of the working man. Politicians and labor leaders who forcibly raise labor costs pose as the only true friends of labor and the "common man," and as the only stalwarts of progress and social justice. Actually, they are causing mass unemployment. Where there is neither government nor union interference with the costs of labor, there can be only voluntary unemployment. The free market offers jobs to all eager to work.

An administration that is genuinely interested in the well-being of the unemployed workers would aim at reducing their employment costs. In order to give new hope to our youth and promote on-the-job training and learning, a genuinely humanitarian administration would immediately repeal the minimum wage legislation. Or, as a beginning, it would exempt teenagers from its restrictions. But such a repeal would require great political courage, a courage which has adorned no President from Roosevelt to Carter. It is more expedient politically, and yet so cruel, to promise higher wages and more benefits, although the net result can be nothing other than unemployment.

The pseudo-humanitarian push for higher labor costs is reinforced by the popular drive for generous unemployment compensation and other benefits for the poor and "underprivileged." While we tax and discourage labor, we subsidize unemployment with great generosity. But we are harming millions of people economically and morally: the working population that is chafing under the growing burden of transfer taxation and, above all, the idle millions who are making the collection of public benefits a primary way of life. Unskilled workers whose earnings are relatively small can easily be caught in the intricate web of unemployment benefits. Why should a laborer seek employment at $100 a week if his unemployment benefits, supplementary compensations, severance pay and union support, food stamps, *etc.*, approach, equal, or exceed this amount?

The Causes of Inflation

Cyclical Unemployment

A particular brand of institutional unemployment is cyclical in nature. It swells the ranks of jobless workers during economic recessions and depressions. According to mainstream economic doctrine, this kind of unemployment is a chronic phenomenon of the individual enterprise order which from time to time suffers from fluctuations in investment or capital goods. Businessmen may make changes in investment which are amplified in a cumulative, multiplied fashion. They will add to the stock of capital, or make net investments only, when the level of national income is growing. Prosperity must come to an end and recession ensue when sales go down, or even when they merely level off or grow at a lower rate than previously. On the other hand, investment demand can be induced by growth of sales and incomes.

This explanation, known by the high-sounding name of the "acceleration principle," induces Keynesian governments to apply a great number of measures that aim at stimulating income. Wage increases, tax reductions and rebates for lower income earners, together with "expansionist" monetary policies, are to promote intended consumption, which they believe to be the moving force for full employment and economic growth.

The doctrine is as old as it is fallacious. It is built on the ancient myth that the stimulator and spender, *i.e.*, government, is an entity outside and above the economic process, that it owns something that is not derived from its subjects, and that it can spend this mythical something for full employment and other purposes. In reply we must again and again repeat the truism that government can spend only what it takes away from taxpayers and inflation victims, and that any additional spending by government curtails the citizens' spending by its full amount.

The business cycle with its phases of boom and depression is the inevitable consequence of inflation. When the federal government suffers a budget deficit it may raise the needed money through borrowing the people's savings or through the creation of new money and credit by the banking system under the direction of the Federal Reserve. To borrow and consume savings is to invite an immediate recession, for the Treasury now consumes the funds that had been financing economic production. As interest rates rise, business must curtail its operations. Therefore, lest all private industries contract as federal spending expands, the federal government resorts to inflation. It resorts to a method of deficit financing that completely muddles the situation. That is, while government is consuming more resources and capital funds, interest rates do not rise,

35

but actually decline on account of the creation of new money and credit. Declining interest rates now misguide businessmen who embark upon expansion and modernization projects, and mislead them to participate in an economic boom that must soon end for lack of genuine savings. Business costs, especially in the capital goods industries, soar until production becomes unprofitable or even inflicts losses. At this point the decline sets in. Projects are cancelled, output is curtailed, and costs are reduced. In short, the depression that is caused by a falsification of interest rates leading to structural maladjustments is alleviated through readjustment and repair of the damage inflicted by the credit expansion.

The Keynesians and their disciples in government are loudly proclaiming that they have learned to cope with the cycle. Actually they are not avoiding the cycle by refraining from deficit spending and inflation, they are merely "solving" the dilemma of stagnation and decline through ever larger bursts of deficit spending and money creation. Every administration is desperately spending and inflating in order to kindle another boom. Then, after a while, the boom is followed by another recession that necessitates an even larger deficit and more inflation. Unfortunately, this merry-go-round, which characterizes the administrations from Franklin Roosevelt to Carter, has debilitated the United States dollar and made individual savings an important resource for federal deficit financing.

During the economic boom, capital and labor are attracted by the feverish conditions in the capital goods industries. Here employment tends to rise as labor moves from consumers' goods industries to the booming capital goods market. There may even be some unemployed workers who now find jobs under boom conditions, which may temporarily reduce the general rate of unemployment. But the boom passes by the millions of workers who are condemned to idleness by minimum wage legislation, labor union policies, and the temptations of compensation and food stamps.

When the fever of the boom finally gives way to the chills of recession, the capital goods industries undergo a painful contraction. Capital and labor are set free. They now return to the long-neglected consumers' goods industries from whence they came. In an unhampered labor market the readjustment would be brief and direct. But in a market that is obstructed by 65 weeks of generous unemployment compensation and many other benefits, the readjustment process must be slow and circuitous. Unemployment rises and stays high for long periods of time.

In both boom and bust, prices rise as a result of the various injections of new money by the full employment planners. During the boom, capital goods prices lead the way. During the depression, when these retreat in contraction and readjustment, the prices of consumers' goods take the lead, which utterly confounds the Keynesians. The phenomenon of rising unemployment together with rising consumer prices painfully contradicts the acceleration principle and completely jumbles the Phillips Curve.

Hedge Unemployment

The Keynesian commitment to expansionary policies is a commitment to inflation that does not promote full employment. It does not achieve the "miracle . . . of turning a stone into bread," but generates the business cycle with periods of high unemployment. Continued application of the Keynesian recipe must finally lead to the complete breakdown of the monetary system and to mass unemployment.

Rampant inflation destroys the capital markets that sustain economic production. The lenders, who sustain staggering losses from currency depreciation, are unable to grant new loans to finance business. Even if some loan funds should survive the destruction, lenders shy away from monetary contracts for any length of time. Business capital, especially long-term loan capital, becomes very scarce, which causes economic stagnation and decline. To salvage their shrinking wealth, capitalists learn to hedge for financial survival; they invest in durable goods that are expected to remain unaffected by the inflation and depreciation. They buy real estate, objects of art, gold, silver, jewelry, rare books, coins, stamps, and antique grandfather clocks. Surely, this redirection of capital promotes the industries that provide the desired hedge objects. But it also causes other industries to contract. It creates employment opportunities in the former and releases labor in the latter. As the hedge industries are very capital-intensive, working with relatively little labor, and the contracting industries are rather labor-intensive, with a great number of workers, the readjustment entails rising unemployment. Of course, the readjustment process is hampered by labor union rules, generous unemployment compensation, and ample food stamps.

Similarly, double-digit inflation causes businessmen to hedge for financial survival. They tend to invest their working capital in those real goods they know best, in inventory and capital equipment. Funds that were serving production for the market become fixed investments in durable goods that may escape the monetary depreciation. Economic output, especially for consumers, tends to decline, which raises goods prices and swells the unemployment rolls.

Deficits Consume Jobs

Both federal deficits and the inflation that follows consume productive capital. The deficits of the United States government are consuming massive amounts of business capital that otherwise would produce economic goods, create jobs, and pay wages. During the 1950's total United States government deficits amounted to a mere $12.5 billion. During the 1960's, the total was only $57.235 billion. During the first half of the 1970's, deficits rose to $71.4 billion, and, as if they were following an exponential curve, in the second half of this decade will exceed $200 billion.

The inflation itself is a powerful destroyer of productive capital. It steals the savings of many millions of thrifty individuals for government consumption and redistribution. It weakens the capital markets and misleads businessmen into costly management errors. It causes businessmen to overstate their earnings, overpay their taxes, and consume their fictitious profits.

In the United States, government is attacking business capital from both sides: It is pressing continuously toward higher levels of consumption through spending schemes and extensive redistribution of wealth and income; and it is severely hampering economic production and capital formation through taxation and intervention. Environmental regulations alone are estimated to impose some $300 billion of cleanup costs on American industry during the 1970's. All such costs are unproductive, meaning that the expenditures consume business capital without generating new production and income. They will never build factories, stores, offices, and many other facilities of production. Above all, they will not afford employment to the jobless millions.

In a stagnant economy that no longer permits capital formation and business growth, the institutional pressures for higher labor costs are painfully felt in the form of rising unemployment. The job situation may even get worse when the net amount of productive capital begins to shrink as a result of excess consumption and declining production — that is, when the amount of capital invested per worker begins to decline and wage rates must readjust to lower levels. In such a situation, which in the judgment of some economists is already upon us, the institutional pressures for higher labor wages and benefits, to which labor has grown accustomed and believes itself to be entitled economically and morally, would generate even higher rates of unemployment. If, at the same time, government should "stimulate" the sagging economy with easy money and credit, goods prices will soar alongside the unemployment rolls.

Disintegration Unemployment

The ultimate folly which government may inflict on its people is the imposition of price controls, which are really people controls. When goods prices soar because monetary authorities are "stimulating" the economy through inflation, the administration conducting such policies desperately reaches for the control brakes. But there is probably no other measure that so promptly and effectively disrupts economic production and weakens the currency as comprehensive price controls. No other policy disaster causes more unemployment more rapidly than the imposition of stringent controls over prices.

Price controls instantly paralyze the labor market, hamper economic production, encourage consumption, and create shortages that invite an even more coercive system of rationing, allocations, and priorities. Obviously, where a central authority dictates all things, where millions of prices and wages are replaced by a single directive, chaos and darkness descend on economic life. Our splendid exchange system with its magnificent division of labor disintegrates and gives way to a primitive command system. The disintegration is accompanied by mass unemployment.

Even without price controls, rampant inflation causes such serious disarrangement of markets and disruption of production that both economic disorders, boom and depression, occur simultaneously. Consumers' goods industries tend to contract while capital goods industries that are producing the machines, equipment, and materials for business hedging, enjoy a feverish boom. But the labor market with all its institutional rigidities is unable to adjust to the rapid changes and therefore suffers the strains of rising unemployment. Moreover, the disintegration of the exchange system as a result of the failure of money, the medium of exchange, causes a general decline in real wages, which breeds widespread labor unrest. Individual productivity may fall, which in turn boosts business costs. Labor unions react with militant demands and ugly strikes which inflict losses on business and cause even more unemployment. With millions of idle workers searching for jobs, other millions march on picket lines in protest against the rampant inflation that is engulfing their jobs and livelihoods. Such are the symptoms of the finale of a currency that became a Keynesian stimulant and a medium for redistribution.

The Keynesian ship is sinking. The property loss is staggering, but the crew — the government — is safe. The passengers are not. Experience, which is the best of teachers, comes at a dreadfully high price. It teaches slowly, and at the cost of mistakes.

The Monetarists

In the diversity of contemporary American monetary thought the neoclassicism of the Chicago School has assumed an intellectual position that probably equals that of the New Economics. Chicago monetary thought has invaded in force not only the American Academy and the deliberations and actions of the Federal Reserve Board, but also the halls of Congress and the economic reports and policies of the President. This remarkable development is also reflected in the growing popularity and prestige now accorded to Milton Friedman, the most influential economist of the Chicago tradition.

We rejoice about this new trend in monetary thought and are appreciative of the effective Chicagoan challenge to the Keynesian orthodoxy. The analytical depth, scientific precision, and overwhelming empirical evidence offered by the monetarists have shattered many a cherished doctrine of the New Economics and thereby given new life to neoclassicism. In an age of Keynesian supremacy when the discussion of money had given way to debates on the techniques of fine-tuning through fiscal measures, the Chicagoans restored money to its rightful place. They successfully reconstructed a version of the quantity theory of money and re-emphasized the importance of monetary policy. And last but not least, they levelled devastating criticism at official monetary managers for having generated feverish booms and disastrous recessions through gross mismanagement of our money.

Despite all this, this writer casts doubt on the cogency and durability of this new neoclassicism. In our judgment, it is built on the quicksand of macroeconomic analysis; it misinterprets the business cycles and therefore is bound to fail as a policy guide for economic stability; and it is inherently inflationary because it makes government the guardian of our money. The intellectual forebears of this new neoclassicism were three Englishman and one American: William Stanley Jevons, Alfred Marshall, Ralph George Hawtrey, and Irving Fisher. As their tenets gave way to the New Economics of John Maynard Keynes, Alvin H. Hansen, and Abba P. Lerner a generation ago, so is the new neoclassicism itself destined to surrender to more statist doctrines. After all, it puts government in charge of economic stability and then prescribes monetary policies that will continue to generate business cycles. Inevitably, frustration and disappointment tend to breed demands for more government intervention.

Almost one hundred years ago William Stanley Jevons attempted to substitute exact inquiries, exact numerical calculations, for guesswork and groundless argument" in his analysis of quantitative data on prices and business movements.[16] In a paper on "The Variation of Prices, and the Value of the Currency since 1782," Jevons studied the

[16]*Investigations in Currency and Finance* (London, 1884), p. xxiv.

changing purchasing power of money between 1782 and 1865. He concluded his analysis with the following comment on gold: "In itself gold-digging has ever seemed to me almost a dead loss of labor as regards the world in general — a wrong against the human race, just such as is that of a government against its people in overissuing and depreciating its own currency."[17] Instead Jevons favored a "tabular standard of value" which his own work on index numbers was supposed to promote. He was convinced that some day this system would come into use and that gold coins would cease to be the principal media of exchange.[18]

Alfred Marshall lent his support to the Jevons plan. Mindful of the great changes in the purchasing power of money and their detrimental effects on contractual relationships, he searched for a stable monetary unit. In a proposal to the Royal Commission on the Depression of Trade and Industry in 1886, he urged the British government to publish tables showing changes in the purchasing power of money so that contracts could be made in terms of units of constant purchasing power.[19] Professor Marshall introduced the great dichotomy that continues to guide most contemporary economists, that is, the separation of the micro sphere in which individual prices are determined by supply and demand, from the macro sphere in which the total supply of money and its velocity determine the value of money and the price level.[20] Although Marshall did not draw the political conclusion from this doctrine, his followers in Great Britain and America later went the final step: They called on government for price level stabilization through manipulation of the quantity of money stock.

Sir Ralph George Hawtrey, an economist connected with the British Treasury from 1919 to 1937, developed a purely monetary theory of the business cycle on a macroeconomic concept of equilibrium.

---

[17]*Ibid.*, p. 104.

[18]Compare also "An Ideally Perfect System of Currency," *ibid.*, pp. 297-302; and "The Variation of Prices and the Value of the Currency Since 1782," *ibid.*, p. 120 *et seq.*

[19]*Official Papers* (London: Macmillan and Company, 1926), pp. 10-12; also *Money, Credit and Commerce* (reprint, New York: Augustus M. Kelley, 1960,), p. 36. According to Marshall, "An official index number, representing average movements of the prices of important commodities, might well afford the basis for a Unit of general purchasing power, in terms of which long-period obligations might be expressed; and in this matter the State might advantageously lead. The Unit would be derived from an official price list by adding together the prices of certain quantities of wheat, barley, oats, hops, beef, mutton, tea, coffee; together with staple timbers, minerals, textile materials and fabrics and so on. A new contract for interest on loans and other long-standing obligations might then be arranged by free consent of both parties to it in terms of the standard unit, instead of money."

[20]*Money, Credit, and Commerce, op. cit.,*p. 43 *et seq.* His theory was later put into the form of a quantitative equation by Professor Pigou in "The Value of Money," *The Quarterly Journal of Economics*, XXXII (November 1917), pp. 38-65.

According to this theory, changes in the flow of currency, in particular bank credit, cause instability in production and employment. At first, total bank credit expands as interest rates are reduced. Total demand for finished goods rises, which causes prices to rise. Businessmen use easy money to expand their inventories. The expansion of credit thus causes incomes to rise, which eventually leads to more currency passing into circulation. Under the gold standard this currency has to be either gold coin or paper money backed by gold. But such a demand encroaches on the available supplies of gold in all gold standard countries and especially in central banks. According to Hawtrey,

> . . . the flow of currency into circulation in such circumstances is very gradual, and lags far behind the expansion of credit which causes it. The result is that, if the authorities controlling credit are guided in their action by the adequacy of their stock of gold, their intervention is bound to be very tardy. And the expansion and contraction of credit are both likely to be very slow processes in a group of countries which are all made to keep pace with one another by the rather cumbersome expedient of gold movements.[21]

In short, the trade cycle, which is a credit phenomenon, is caused by the defects of the gold standard as a regulator of credit. Guided by their gold reserves, the monetary authorities intervene too slowly, first in the restriction of bank credit and then in the expansion during periods of recession. The Great Depression, according to Hawtrey, was the result of such defects. Throughout those baneful years he called for more credit expansion by the central banks as the only remedy for unemployment.[22] In 1962 Hawtrey restated his conclusion:

> When we look back on the monetary experience we have had since 1932, surely the moral to be drawn from it is above all the importance of maintaining stability of the money unit. The depression of the nineteen thirties was due to the doubling of the wealth-value of gold.[23]

---

[21] *The Gold Standard in Theory and Practice* (Fourth edition, London: Longmans, Green and Company, Ltd., 1939), pp. 101, 102, 121, 122; cf. also *Currency and Credit* (Third edition, London: Longmans, Green and Company, Ltd., 1927), p. 156 *et seq.*; *Monetary Reconstruction* (Second edition, London: Longmans, Green and Company, Ltd., 1926), p. 156; *Trade and Credit* (London: Longmans, Green and Company, Ltd., 1928), p. 82 *et seq.*

[22] *The Art of Central Banking* (London: Longmans, Green and Company, Ltd., 1932), p. 446 *et seq.*

[23] *A Century of Bank Rate* (Second edition, New York: Augustus M. Kelley, 1962), p. xxi.

The Causes of Inflation

Similar conclusions were drawn by Irving Fisher, the American economist who spearheaded the new neoclassicism. "The key to the business failure, and therefore the key to the depression," he wrote in 1933, "is the deflated price level; the key to the deflated price level is monetary deflation; the principal kind of money which deflates is our checking accounts at the banks." [24] This is why Fisher called for reinflation throughout the Great Depression. In particular, he urged President Roosevelt to devalue the dollar and later hailed him for having done so. In fact, Fisher went further: "We might even abandon gold altogether, and resort to a managed currency with no base but paper. Several other nations have done this to their distinct advantage.[25]

Professor Fisher had a simple explanation for business cycles. Credit currency perpetuates its own motion in a sort of vicious circle, or rather a vicious spiral — upward or downward as the case may be. But what determines the direction of the spiral? Fisher gave at least three different answers: (1) The motion springs from completely random, uncoordinated, inexplicable "frenzies of enterprise."[26] (2) "If something big enough hits humanity" the spiral may be set into motion. A war, for example, may trigger it. According to this explanation, "the depression grew out of a boom which started in a credit currency boom, which started from a debt boom, which grew out of the World War.[27] And (3), faulty monetary management by the central bank may redirect the motion. In 1928, for instance, the Federal Reserve Board brought the speculative movement to a stop through credit stringency, which then began to be felt in legitimate business.[28]

Fisher's crusading spirit led him to be active in many fields of reform, such as health, conservation, prohibition, the League of Nations, and many others. But throughout his active life he crusaded above all for economic stabilization and monetary reform. In numer-

---

[24] *Mastering the Crisis* (London: George Allen and Unwin, Ltd., 1934), p. 21.

[25] *Inflation* (London: George Allen and Unwin, Ltd., 1934), p. 91.

[26] *Mastering the Crisis, op. cit.*, p. 37. Professor Fisher apparently applied this version of trade cycle theory to his own financial transactions. He was caught unaware by the 1929 stock market crash and remained bullish throughout the decline. Although he enjoyed a great reputation as an economic forecaster he failed to foresee the depression and therefore lost his sizable fortune. Cf. Irving N. Fisher, *My Father, Irving Fisher* (New York: Commet Press, 1956). According to his son, "the 1929 stock market crash caught him unawares. Placing his faith unreservedly in the 'new economic era' he did not foresee that it was destined to collapse like a house of cards" (p. 242). Between 1929 and 1933 Fisher lost an eight to ten million dollar fortune which he had pyramided on his wife's blue-chip inheritance and was left with an ultimate debt to his aunt of three-quarters of a million dollars. A committee of a lawyer and two nephews finally handled his intricate debt relationship (pp. 264-267).

[27] *Inflation, op. cit.*, p. 80.

[28] *Stabilized Money* (London: George Allen and Unwin, 1935), pp. 259-262.

ous writings he presented his plan for the "compensated dollar," a
dollar of constant purchasing power, sometimes called the "commodity dollar." The conventional gold standard was to be replaced by a
standard that defined the dollar in terms of constant value, which
was to be determined by an index number of commodity prices of a
given basket of goods. This commodity standard was to be
strengthened further by "100% money," that is, a cash reserve of
100% against all demand deposits. A "Currency Commission" would
issue new money and turn into cash the assets of every commercial
bank so that the cash reserve of each bank would be increased to
100% of its checking deposits. The new money thus would provide
an all-cash backing for the checking accounts without either increasing or decreasing the total stock of money in the country. Thereafter
the banks would be required to maintain permanently a 100% cash
reserve against their demand deposits. According to Professor Fisher,
his plan would keep banks 100% liquid, prevent inflation and deflation, cure or prevent depressions, and wipe out much of the national
debt.[29]

The Chicago Tradition

The principal successors to this train of monetary thought from
Alfred Marshall to Irving Fisher were economists at the University
of Chicago. Frank H. Knight, Jacob Viner, Lloyd Mints, Henry Simons,
and Milton Friedman have made Chicago an important center of
contemporary economic thought. While Professor Knight greatly
strengthened the neoclassical structure with his analysis of the role
of profit in economic life, Henry Simons led a fierce attack on Keynes
and his American disciples.

Simons' theory of money deserves our attention because it is
clearly reflected in contemporary Chicago thought and it points up
the differences between the New Economics and the new neoclassicism, between the "fiscalists" and the "monetarists." In his attacks
on Alvin Hansen, the leading academic Keynesian, Professor Simons
not only restated the framework of the quantity theory but also
sharply criticized the various Keynesian schemes for recovery from
the Great Depression. A virulent critic of Keynes,[30] Simons nevertheless revealed a striking similarity in premise and analysis, which,
in our judgment, affords a common bond not only for Professors

---

[29] *100% Money* (New York: Adelphi Company, 1935), pp. 8-9.

[30] According to Simons, "attempting mischievous and salutory irritation of his peers
. . . he [Keynes] may only succeed in becoming an academic idol of our worst cranks
and charlatans — not to mention the possibilities of the book as the economic bible of a
fascist movement." Cf. "Keynes' Comments on Money," *Christian Century* July 22, 1936,
pp. 1016, 1017.

The Causes of Inflation

Keynes and Simons but also for all fiscalists and monetarists.[31] Surely Lord Keynes basically agreed with Professor Simons' analysis of the gold standard. In Simons' own words,

> The worst financial structure is realized when many nations, with similar financial practices and institutions and similar credit pyramids (and narrowly nationalist commercial policies), adopt the same commodity as the monetary standard. When one thinks of the total potential creditor demands for gold for hoarding, in and after 1929, it seems almost beyond diabolical ingenuity to conceive a financial system better designed for our economic destruction. The anomaly of such a system is perhaps abundantly evident in the strong moral restraints and inhibitions which dissuade many people from exercising their legal rights under it. Given the vagaries of commercial, fiscal, banking, and currency policies in the various countries, and given the character of national financial structures and price rigidities, it is to the writer a source of continued amazement that so many people of insight should hold unwaveringly to the gold standard as the best foundation of national policies. The worship of gold, among obviously sophisticated people, seems explicable only in terms of our lack of success in formulating specifications for a satisfactory, independent national currency. . . .[32]

Professors Keynes and Simons also were in basic agreement on the causes that generated the Great Depression. While Keynes lamented the increase in liquidity and lack of investments, Simons deplored the sharp fall in velocity, all of which, of course, are similar macroeconomic phenomena. To Simons, "aggregate turnover" needed stimulation; to Keynes, it was "aggregate demand." But when it came to the appropriate policies to overcome the depression, Messrs. Simons and Keynes differed noisily. Keynes favored stimulation of investment by immediate government spending, while Simons advocated "definite rules of the game." He called upon government to provide a stable framework of rules for monetary authorities to follow:

> In the past, governments have grossly neglected their positive responsibility of controlling the currency; private initiative has been allowed too much freedom in determining the character of our financial structure and in directing changes in the quantity of money and money substitutes.[33]

---

[31] See Milton Friedman, "The Monetary Theory and Policy of Henry Simons," *Journal of Law and Economics,* X, (October 1967), pp. 1-13.

[32] *Economic Policy for a Free Society* (Chicago: The University of Chicago Press, 1948), p. 168.

[33] *Ibid.,* pp. 161, 162.

To Professor Simons the rule of price level stabilization appeared "extremely attractive" either as a definite reform or as a transition expedient toward ultimate stabilization of the quantity of money. But no matter what rule of the game was to be adopted, ultimately "the power to issue money and near-money should increasingly be concentrated in the hands of the central government."[34] It is true that Professor Simons summarily rejected the numerous Keynesian schemes that require discretionary authority rather than "rules of the game." But in spite of his virulent opposition to the New Economics he took great pains in keeping even greater distance from the economic principles "to which reactionaries would have us return." For these principles "are perhaps worse than none at all."[35]

The Simons student who has captured the imagination of scores of economists and legislators is Milton Friedman. To do justice to such a colorful man, who, through his tireless work and great force of persuasion, set the agenda for most economic debates of the post-World War II era, is an impossible task. We must, therefore, limit ourselves, in the pages allotted to this essay, to a few observations on his monetary thought. After a brief presentation of his views, we would like to aim our observations at the essential differences between the monetary theories of the Chicago tradition, which Professor Friedman so brilliantly represents, and the subjective theories of the Austrian School of which Ludwig von Mises was the revered elder. For these differences are greater than the similarities, which we gladly acknowledge in so many other fields of economic analysis. Henry Simons clearly perceived the gap when he rejected the economic principles to which "reactionaries would have us return." It is true that Professor Friedman has rarely directed his critical pen at the literary efforts of subjective economists. His primary target has been the Keynesian orthodoxy that continues to rule the day. With massive empirical evidence he launched a many-pronged counterattack on the New Economics and demonstrated the futility of its policies. Above all, he restored money to a position of importance, which Lord Keynes and his followers had denied it in theory and policy. He emphasized the power of monetary policy and questioned the Keynesian faith in fiscal policy. He reconstructed a version of the quantity theory of money, and then reinterpreted the Great Depression in the light of his theory.

Friedman's position is at apparent odds with that of his Keynesian adversaries. Despairing about unpredictable changes in money velocity, they doubt the reliability of monetary policy. In contrast,

[34] *Ibid.*, p. 180.
[35] *Ibid.*, p. 176.

The Causes of Inflation

Friedman postulates a satisfactory stability of velocity, that is, a stable demand for money as a stable function of a limited number of variables that can be specified reliably. Therefore, he concludes, monetary policy can be an important factor of economic stabilization.[36] To Professor Friedman the quantity theory is as valid now as it was in the past.

> There is perhaps no other empirical relation in economics that has been observed to recur so uniformly under so wide a variety of circumstances as the relation between substantial changes over short periods in the stock of money and in prices; the one is invariably linked with the other and is in the same direction; this uniformity is, I suspect, of the same order as many of the uniformities that form the basis of the physical sciences.[37]

The problem of maintaining economic stability is far too complex to be left to fiscal fine-tuners. Therefore, Professor Friedman advocates a simple rule for steady monetary expansion, which could either be adopted by the Federal Reserve System itself, or be prescribed by Congress. For maximum price level stability he recommends a rate of increase of three to five percent per year for currency plus all commercial bank deposits. The particular rate of increase is less important than the adoption of a fixed rate that lies within this range.[38] It is the role of the monetary authorities to provide a stable monetary background that facilitates reasonable economic stability. Contracyclical actions as recommended by the Keynesians usually have destabilizing effects, for "there is likely to be a lag between the need for action and government recognition of this need; a further lag between recognition of the need for action and the taking of action; and a still further lag between the action and its effects.[39] But there are also considerable time lags between monetary changes and their economic effects. According to Professor Friedman,

> There is a connection which is, on the average, close but which

---

[36]Milton Friedman and David Meiselman, "The Relative Stability of Monetary Velocity and the Investment Multiplier in the United States, 1897-1958," *Stabilization Policies* (The Commission on Money and Credit: Prentice-Hall, 1963). See also Milton Friedman, "A Monetary and Fiscal Framework for Monetary Stability," *American Economic Review* (June 1948); reprinted in *Essays in Positive Economics* (Chicago: University of Chicago Press, 1953), pp. 133-156; and "Has Fiscal Policy Been Oversold?" *Monetary vs. Fiscal Policy, A Dialogue between Milton Friedman and Walter W. Heller* (New York: W. W. Norton and Company, 1969), pp. 43-62, 71-80.

[37]Milton Friedman, editor, *Studies in the Quantity Theory of Money* (Chicago: University of Chicago Press, 1956) pp. 20-21.

[38]*A Program for Monetary Stability* (Chicago: University of Chicago Press, 1956), pp. 20-21

[39]*Essays in Positive Economics* (Chicago: University of Chicago Press, 1953), p. 315.

47

may be quite variable in an individual episode. I have emphasized that the inability to pin down the lag means that there are lots of factors about which I am ignorant. That doesn't mean that money doesn't have a systematic influence. But it does mean that there is a good deal of variability in the influence.[40]

In fact, changes in the stock of money are mainly responsible for changes in money income, which characterize the business cycles. All major depressions from the 1870's to the 1930's are explained in terms of shrinking money stock. But while Professor Friedman presents massive statistical evidence, he is reluctant to develop a precise business cycle theory that would explain the causal relationships.

> It is one thing to assert that monetary changes are the key to major movements in money income; it is quite a different thing to know now in any detail what is the mechanism that links monetary change to economic change; how the influence of the one is transmitted to the other; what sectors of the economy will be affected first; what the time pattern of the impacts will be, and so on. We have great confidence in the first assertion. We have little confidence in our knowledge of the transmission mechanism, except in such broad and vague terms as to constitute little more than an impressionistic representation rather than an engineering blueprint.[41]

But Professor Friedman is fully convinced that the Great Depression was the inevitable result of a sharp and unprecedented decline in the quantity of money, for which the Federal Reserve System bears the main responsibility. It failed to create the necessary bank reserves that would have maintained price level stability and economic prosperity. The Reserve System did nothing, or even raised its discount rate, while hundreds of banks succumbed to bank runs and losses.[42]

One of the reasons for this deplorable failure of monetary authorities to create the needed reserves, according to Friedman, was their domination by "external forces," that is, by gold movements that dictated inaction or even contraction while the internal situation called for expansion. Therefore, national independence in monetary policy is desirable and should be achieved through immediate sus-

---

[40]*Monetary vs. Fiscal Policy, op. cit.,* p. 76. For further details on his lags hypothesis see *Essays in Positive Economics, op. cit.,* pp. 133-156.

[41]*The Optimum Quantity of Money and other Essays* (Chicago: Aldine Publishing Company, 1969), p. 222.

[42] Milton Friedman and Anna J. Schwartz, *A Monetary History of the United States, 1867—1960* (National Bureau of Economic Research: Princeton University Press, 1963), p. 300.

pension of gold payments and freely floating exchange rates. Let the price of gold be determined in the free markets of the world, and not by costly "price support" measures on the part of the United States government. If the free world were to adopt such a system, Professor Friedman assures us, the countries could enjoy independence of internal monetary policy and maximum international cooperation.[43]

An Austrian Critique

Although our space does not permit us detailed discussions of epistemological differences, we cannot ignore the chasm that separates the Chicago School from the Austrian School in all matters of epistemology. These differences leave their mark on many economic theories; in particular, on monetary theory. The Chicagoans, and especially Professor Friedman, represent variants of logical positivism, while the Austrians view monetary knowledge in the light of a general theory of human knowledge, called praxeology. The Chicagoans like to don the white robe of scientists whenever they deal with economic phenomena. They are seeking knowledge of which experience is the content. Professor Friedman's "positive" economics comprises descriptions of economic reality, which hopefully provide the tools for predictions. Disagreements usually are not over ends in view, but over predictions regarding the effects of policies aimed at certain ends. They can be resolved by empirical evidence.[44]

Austrian economists view economics in an entirely different light. To them it is a branch of praxeology which is purely theoretical and systematic. Its doctrines are not derived from experience, but are a priori like those of logic and mathematics, and antecedent to any comprehension of economic facts and events. Economics is not "quantitative" and does not measure human action because there are no constants in individual choice and preference. Austrian economists do not search for better technical methods of measurement because they realize its futility on ontological grounds. Statistical research into economic events offers interesting historical information on non-repeatable data, but provides no knowledge that is valid universally. It does not afford the material of which economic theories are made, nor does it permit predictions of future events.[45]

---

[43]"The Case for Flexible Exchange Rates," *Essays in Positive Economics, op. cit.,* pp. 157 203; also *A Program for Monetary Stability, op. cit.,* pp. 81-101.

[44]Milton Friedman, "The Methodology of Positive Economics," *Positive Economics, op. cit.,* pp. 3-43.

[45]Ludwig von Mises, *Human Action, op. cit.,* p. 30 *et seq.;* also his *Theory and History* (New Haven: Yale University Press, 1957), p. 240 *et seq.; Epistemological Problems of Economics* (Princeton, New Jersey: D. Van Nostrand Company, 1960); *The Ultimate Foundation of Economic Science* (Princeton, New Jersey: D. Van Nostrand Company, 1962); Friedrich A. Hayek, *The Counter-Revolution of Science* (Glencoe, Illinois: The Free Press, 1952).

The Causes of Inflation

To the Chicagoans the ultimate function of money is the measure of value. From Marshall to Friedman money has been criticized for its lack of stability, which frustrates accurate measurement and thereby precipitates grievous economic and social evils. Above all, monetary instability is held responsible for the business cycles that again and again have wreaked havoc on market economies. If only the price level could be stabilized and thus money be permitted to serve its true function! To the Austrians money is the most marketable good a person can acquire. It is never "idle", nor is it just "in circulation"; it is always in the posession or under the control of someone. The demand for money is subject to the same considerations as that for all other goods and services. People expend labor or forego the enjoyment of goods and services in order to acquire money. Thus individual demand and supply ultimately determine the purchasing power of money in the same way as they determine the mutual exchange ratios of all other goods. They reject the quantity theory of the "monetarists" as a manifestation of holistic thought and a tool for government intervention.

It is true that the Chicagoans are familiar with the principles that determine individual prices. But their conclusions are drawn from the sphere of macroeconomics in which the total money supply and a given velocity determine the price level. Here they call on government to take measures to stabilize the level and thus cure the business cycle. In this respect they are akin to the Keynesians who also seek stabilization through government manipulation. But while the Keynesians recommend compensatory fiscal policies, the Chicagoans realize the futility of continuous fine-tuning and therefore seek long-term stabilization through a steady three to five percent expansion of the money supply. In the light of Austrian theory such an expansion of the stock of money would suffice to generate some malinvestments and maladjustments that would later necessitate readjustments, that is, recessions. Professor Mises' trade cycle theory envisions economic booms and busts in every case of credit expansion, from one percent to hundreds of percent. The magnitude of expansion does not negate its effects, it merely determines the severity of the maladjustment and necessary readjustment. Even if most prices should decline while monetary authorities expand credit at a modest rate, the injection of fiduciary funds falsifies interest rates and thereby causes erroneous investment decisions. If by a discretionary decision of the monetary authorities the expansion should be directed at certain industries instead of being distributed widely over the loan market, the maladjustments would be even more serious in the industries favored. In short, if the monetary authorities expand fiduciary credit and thereby lower interest rates, the pattern of economic production is distorted. At first, it generates overinvestment in capital goods and causes their prices to rise while the production of consumers' goods is necessarily neglected. But because of the lack of real savings, the investment boom is bound to end. The boom causes prices to rise, including business costs. When profit margins finally falter, a recession develops in the capital goods industry. The recession is a period of readjustment, that is, the malinvestments are liquidated, and the long-neglected consumers' goods industries once again attract their proper share of resources in accordance with the true consumption-investment ratio.[46]

The monetarists actually have no business cycle theory, merely a prescription for government to "hold it steady." From Fisher to Friedman the antidote for depressions has always been the same: reinflation. The central banker who permits credit contraction is the culprit of it all. If there is a recession he must issue more money, and if there is inflation, that is, rising price levels, he must take some out. Professor Friedman himself seems to be aware of his lack of business cycle theory when he admits "little confidence in our knowledge of the transmission mechanism." He has no "engineering blueprint," merely an "impressionistic representation" that monetary changes are "the key to major movements in money income." His "gap hypothesis," therefore, is designed to fill the gap of theory and allow for the time it takes for maladjustments to be corrected. It endeavors to time the recession without explaining it.

Yet the Chicagoans proclaim in loud voices that business recessions in general, and the Great Depression in particular, are the result of monetary contractions. Mistaking symptoms for causes, they prescribe policies that would treat the symptoms. But the treatment, which is reinflation, tends to aggravate the maladjustments and delay the necessary readjustment. Thus, Chicagoan monetary policy, wherever practiced, would not only prolong the recession but also cause many goods prices to rise throughout the recession.

Austrian economists see the Great Depression in an entirely different light. They reject the simplicity of fiscalist and monetarist explanations and, instead, endeavor to analyze specific policies in the light of Austrian theory. In their view, the Great Depression was the inevitable outcome of a series of disastrous policies that first initiated the boom and later prolonged the depression. The first phase had its beginning in 1924 when the Federal Reserve System under the Coolidge Administration embarked upon massive credit expansion.

[46]Ludwig von Mises, *Theory of Money and Credit, op. cit.*, p. 365 *et seq.*; also *Human Action, op. cit.*, p. 535 *et seq.*; also F.A. Hayek, *Monetary Theory and the Trade Cycle, op. cit.*, and *Profits, Interest and Investment* (London: G. Routledge and Sons, 1939).

During a short business decline the System decided to create some $500 million in new credit, which led to a bank credit expansion of some four billion dollars in less than one year. The Federal Reserve System launched yet another burst in 1927 that lasted through 1928. Some $400 million in new Federal Reserve credit was created, discount rates reduced, and bank credit expansion invited. Consequently, total currency outside banks and demand and time deposits in the United States increased from $44.71 billion at the end of June 1924 to $53.4 billion in 1927, and $57.158 billion in October 1929.[47] The United States government thus was sowing the wind and the people were facing the economic whirlwind, which blows with the inevitability of inexorable economic law. The money and credit expansion by the Coolidge Administration made 1929 inevitable.

By 1930 the American economy had fallen into what today would be called a "recession." Under absence of new causes for depression, the following year should have brought recovery through readjustment as it did in all previous cycles. What then precipitated the abysmal collapse that was to follow?

Following a long tradition of Republican hostility toward international trade, the Hoover Administration began to curtail foreign imports. The Smoot-Hawley Tariff Act of June 1930 raised American tariffs to unprecedented levels, which practically closed our borders to foreign goods. According to many economic historians, this was the crowning folly of the whole period from 1920 to 1933 and the beginning of the real depression.

> Once we raised our tariffs, an irresistible movement all over the world to raise tariffs and to erect other trade barriers, including quotas, began. Protectionism ran wild over the world. Markets were cut off. Trade lines were narrowed. Unemployment in the export industries all over the world grew with great rapidity.[48]

But this was not all. The Revenue Act of 1932 doubled the income tax. It ordered the sharpest increase in the federal tax burden in American history. Exemptions were lowered; the "earned income credit" was eliminated. Normal tax rates were raised from a range from one and one-half percent to five percent up to four percent to eight percent; surtax rates from twenty percent to a maximum of fifty-five percent. Corporate tax rates were boosted from twelve

[47]Milton Friedman and Anna J. Schwartz, *A Monetary History of the United States, 1867-1960, op. cit.*, pp. 711-712.
[48]Benjamin M. Anderson, *Economics and the Public Welfare* (Princeton, New Jersey: D. Van Nostrand, 1949), p. 225.

percent to thirteen and three-fourths percent and fourteen and one-half percent. Estate taxes were raised and gift taxes imposed with rates from three-fourths percent to thirty-three and one-half percent. When state and local governments faced shrinking tax collections, they, too, joined the federal government in imposing new levies. Murray Rothbard, in his authoritative work on *America's Great Depression*, estimates the enormous increase in the fiscal burden of government during the depression as follows: The federal costs rose from approximately five percent to eight percent of gross private product, and from six percent to ten percent of net private product. The state and local government burden rose from nine percent to sixteen percent of gross product, and from ten percent to nineteen percent of net product. Total government burden rose from 14.3 percent to 24.8 percent of gross product, and from 15.7 percent to 28.9 percent of net product.[49] In short, the burden of government nearly doubled during the depression, which alone would bring any economy to its knees.

During the New Deal internal regimentation triumphed over freedom. Like Hoover before him, Roosevelt wanted the federal government in the driver's seat. He was not content with clearing away the economic barriers which his predecessor had erected. Instead, he untiringly built his own, such as a sweeping industrial reorganization by the National Industrial Recovery Act, higher income taxes, estate taxes, business taxes, the Wagner Act that greatly reduced labor productivity and raised labor costs, plus countless regulations and restrictions. The American economy thus would not recover from the abyss of depression into which it was first cast by the radical intervention of Republican administrations and then kept lingering by the Democratic New Deal. Individual enterprise, the mainspring of economic improvement, just did not have a chance.

In historical understanding as well as scientific method, theory, and policy the Chicago and Austrian Schools are worlds apart. To the Chicagoans money is a product of government, created and managed according to some rule of the game decided by a political process. To Austrian economists money is a marketable commodity, such as gold or silver, that has become a widely accepted medium of exchange. It is a product of trade voluntarily entered upon by individuals. Banknotes and demand deposits are merely substitutes that receive their value from the money proper. These economists deplore the seizure of commodity money by government and its replacement by *fiat* money which is characterized by rapid inflation and depreciation. They advocate the orthodox gold standard because it makes the value

---

[49] *America's Great Depression* (Princeton, New Jersey: D. Van Nostrand, 1963), p. 303.

of money independent of government, simply because the quantity of gold in existence is independent of the wishes and manipulations of government officials, politicians, parties, and pressure groups.

The monetarists are unanimous in their condemnation of the gold standard. But while they argue for government *fiat* "on purely scientific grounds," they pay lip service to monetary freedom. Professor Friedman would not deny us the freedom to buy, hold, and use gold in all economic exchanges, but paradoxically he would also impose a *fiat* standard. He seems to be unaware that monetary freedom would soon give birth to a "parallel standard" that permits individuals to make "gold contracts" and "gold clauses" calling for payment of measures of gold. Thus individual freedom alone, needing no reform law, no conversion or parity, no rule of the game, would lead us back to the gold standard, as free individuals would prefer gold over government paper.[50]

---

[50]Compare Hans F. Sennholz, *Inflation or Gold Standard* (Lansing, Michigan: Constitutional Alliance, 1970).

III
Age of Inflation

For more than 2500 years the civilized world used gold and silver for economic exchanges. These metals became valuable media of exchange not only because they were desirable for non-monetary uses, but also because they were durable, portable, and divisible. Silver was generally used for small transactions and gold in all larger exchanges. Throughout the ages their exchange ratios were determined by their purchasing power parities. If one ounce of gold bought a certain good that also could be bought for ten ounces of silver, the ratio between gold and silver was 1:10. If for any reason the exchange rate differed from this ratio, arbitrage would soon restore the exchange ratio to its purchasing power parity.

In all countries where gold was the standard money the exchange ratios between gold coins of different weights and finenesses were determined simply by this difference. If one coin weighed one ounce and another coin of equal fineness only one-third of an ounce, the exchange ratio obviously was 1:3. Under the gold coin standard, commonly called the orthodox or classical gold standard, gold coins were the standard money. National currencies represented a certain quantity of gold of a certain fineness. The United States dollar, for example, consisted of 25.8 grains of gold, nine-tenths fine, before the 1934 devaluation, and of 15 5/21 grains thereafter, or in troy ounces 1/20.67 and 1/35 of an ounce respectively. The United States $20 gold coin (Double Eagle) contained 30.09312 grams of fine gold; the $10 coin (Eagle) 15.04656 grams; and the $5 coin (Half Eagle) 7.52328 grams. The British Sovereign contained 7.322 grams; the Mexican 50 Peso coin 37.5 grams; the French 20 Francs coin, also called the Napoleon, 5.8 grams; and the Swiss 20 Francs coin 5.8 grams.[1] Exchange ratios between the various currency units consisting of gold thus were determined by their relative measures of gold.

The world had an international currency while on the classical gold standard. It evolved without international treaties, conventions, or institutions. No one had to make the gold standard work as an international system. When the leading countries had adopted gold as their standard money, the world had an international currency without convertibility or even parity problems. The fact that the coins bore different names and had different weights hardly mattered. As long as they consisted of gold the national stamp or brand did not negate their function as the international medium of exchange.

The purchasing power of gold tended to be the same the world over. Once it was mined it rendered exchange services throughout the world market, moving back and forth and thereby equalizing its purchasing power except for the costs of transport. It is true that the composition of this purchasing power differed from place to place. A gram of gold would buy more labor in Mexico than in the United States. But as long as some goods were traded, gold, like any other economic good, would move to seek its highest purchasing power and thereby equalize its value throughout the world market.

When gold was the world medium of exchange all shipments of gold were "interlocal." Some economists would describe this flow from country to country in terms of "import points" and "export points," which are the margins of movement determined by the cost of transporting gold. But as all coins and bullion were traded in terms of their weight in gold there were no "exchange rates" such as those between gold and silver, or various *fiat* monies.

The decline of the unadulterated gold standard, which was a gold coin standard, set the stage for the present exchange rate dilemma. At first, governments began to restrict the actual circulation of gold. They gradually established the gold bullion standard in which govern-

---

[1]Compare Franz Pick, *Currency Yearbook* (New York: Pick Publishing, 1970), pp. 13-15

ment or its central bank was managing the country's bullion supply. Gold coins were withdrawn from individual cash holdings and national currency was no longer redeemable in gold coins, but only in large, expensive gold bars. This standard then gave way to the gold exchange standard in which the gold reserves were replaced by trusted foreign currency that was redeemable in gold bullion at a given rate. The world's monetary gold was held by a few central banks, such as the Bank of England and the Federal Reserve System, that served as the reserve banks of the world.[2] But after World War II, the Bank of England, which was holding the gold reserves for more than sixty countries, commonly called the pound sterling area, gradually lost its eminent position. It began to hold most of its reserves in United States dollar claims to gold, which made the Federal Reserve System the ultimate reserve bank of the world, and the gold exchange standard a *de facto* gold and dollar standard. Finally, during the 1960's, a decade of accelerating inflation and credit expansion in the United States, the dollar itself gradually fell from its position of predominance. Several monetary crises which triggered world-wide demands for dollar redemption greatly depleted the American stock of gold and created precarious payment situations. In March 1968, when the demands were exceptionally heavy, the United States government introduced the "two-tier system," which meant default in gold payment to anyone but governments and central banks. But even these actually received very little gold after that. Finally, on August 15, 1971, in an atmosphere of utter international disarray, President Nixon abolished the last vestiges of the gold and dollar standard and repudiated all obligations to pay gold for dollars. After a brief restoration of order the system collapsed anew in March 1973, thus giving way to a managed float of managed *fiat* currencies.

Altogether, in some five years we experienced nine currency crises that signalled the coming end of the old monetary order. In November 1967 Great Britain devalued the pound and a number of other countries immediately followed suit. In March of 1968, under the pressure of massive pound sterling liquidation, the two-tier system was adopted. The third crisis occurred in France in May 1969, when political riots followed by rapid currency expansion greatly weakened the franc, which was later devalued. The fourth crisis erupted in September 1969 when massive dollar conversions to West German marks forced the German central bank to "float" the mark and then revalue it upward by 9.3 percent. In March and April 1971 a new flight from the dollar threatened to inundate several European cen-

---

[2] Compare Leland B. Yeager, *International Monetary Relations* (New York: Harper & Row, 1966), p. 251 *et seq.*

tral banks. In a concerted effort the United States Treasury and the Export-Import Bank endeavored to "sop up" the dollar flood. The sixth crisis began in May 1971, when a new flow of dollars into German marks, Swiss francs, and several other currencies caused the mark to float anew, the Swiss franc to be revalued upward by 7.07 percent and several other currencies to be allowed to float or be revalued. The seventh crisis was of such massive proportions that President Nixon was forced to announce the end of the old monetary order. After a realignment of exchange rates in December 1971, when the dollar was devalued 7.89 percent in terms of gold, the West German mark raised 4.6 percent and the Japanese yen 8 percent, a new exchange crisis of major proportions erupted in February 1973, leading to another 10 percent dollar devaluation. Again these adjustments failed to restore confidence, causing a new breakdown in March 1973. It led to the launching of a common float by all European Community countries except the United Kingdom, Ireland, and Italy, and a steadily downward drifting United States dollar.

Contemporary economic literature offers a great variety of explanations for this gradual deterioration of the international monetary order. There are official interpretations by monetary authorities who were managing the monetary system while it was disintegrating. Their answers must be expected to be self-serving and misleading as the blame is assigned invariably to anyone but themselves, to businessmen or speculators, and especially to foreigners. European monetary authorities, for instance, like to charge the United States with the monetary dilemma, while United States authorities tend to blame the Europeans.

Dr. Arthur F. Burns, Chairman of the Federal Reserve Board, probably reflected the official position of the United States government when, on May 20, 1971, he blamed foreign governments for the precarious situation. He urged them to release their restraints on imports and American investments and to help us with our foreign military operating expenses. Raising our interest rates, he asserted, was not the right way to improve the ailing dollar. He advocated more United States borrowing from the Eurodollar market through Treasury certificates and, in order to become more competitive in world markets, an "incomes policy" that would restrain the cost-push momentum of American labor.[3] Less than three months later President Nixon announced a ninety-day price and wage freeze, to be followed by some government control thereafter, and a ten percent surtax on imports to stem the flood of cheap foreign goods.

Academic theorists basically concur with Dr. Burns' explanation,

---

[3] *The Commercial and Financial Chronicle*, June 9, 1971, p. 16.

although some offer different solutions such as a crawling peg, a wider ban, flexible exchange rates, or the creation of new reserve assets, such as Special Drawing Rights by the International Monetary Fund.[4] But no matter what solution they proffer, their point of departure is the holistic national balance of payments theory. They believe that balance of payment surpluses and deficits cause imbalances of payment that are disruptive to international trade and commerce. Without any reference to individual actions and balances they build ambiguous structures that ignore the causes. Balances of payments of a country are merely a very small segment of the combined balances of millions of individuals, a segment that is limited to personal exchanges across national boundaries. Just as an individual may choose to increase or decrease his cash holdings, so may the millions of residents of a given country. But when they increase their holdings, that is called "favorable" in balance of payments terminology. When they choose to reduce their cash holdings, that is called "unfavorable." The fact is that drains of gold are no mysterious forces that must be managed by wise governments, but are the result of deliberate choices by people eager to reduce their cash holdings.

Wherever governments resort to inflation people tend to reduce their cash holdings through purchase of goods and services. When domestic prices begin to rise while foreign prices continue to be stable or to rise at lower rates, individuals like to buy more foreign goods at bargain prices. They ship some of their money abroad in exchange for cheaper foreign products or property. Thus an outflow of foreign exchange and gold sets in. The "unfavorable" balance of payments is the inevitable result of a rate of inflation that exceeds that of the rest of the world. It is simply Gresham's Law in operation.

During the 1960's, the decade of the "Great Society," and again during the years of the Nixon regime, money and credit were created at unprecedented rates prompted by record-breaking government deficits. Private demand deposits, bank credit at commercial banks, and Federal Reserve credit, which fueled the credit expansion, often rose at rates of ten or more percent. Therefore, in spite of countless promises and reassurances by the President and his advisers, the United States dollar suffered inevitable depreciation at home and abroad. The numerous monetary crises were the result of this depreciation.

---

[4] Compare William Fellner, *Maintaining and Restoring Balance in International Payments* (Princeton: Princeton University Press, 1966), Chapter 5; George N. Halm, "The 'Band' Proposal: The Limit of Permissible Exchange Rate Variations," *Princeton Special Papers in International Economics, No. 6* (Princeton: Princeton University Press, 1965); John H. Williamson: "The Crawling Peg," *Princeton Essays in International Finance, No. 50* (Princeton: Princeton University Press, 1965).

Age of Inflation

Pseudo-economic explanations of the disintegration of the world monetary order emphasize a growing worldwide demand for goods and services that chronically exceeds productive capacity. But the dilemma is explained without any reference whatsoever to money or monetary policy. World population, we are told, rose during the 1950's by five hundred million persons and during the 1960's by six hundred fifty million persons, all of whom are demanding more goods and services. Similarly, the eighty-odd new nations that emerged from the colonial possessions are said to be greater sources of demand for the world's goods and services than they were as colonies. Or, the cold-hot war is seen as the cause of worldwide inflation and monetary disintegration. The burdens of wars and armament contribute their demand pressures on productive capacity. Also, recent development may be blamed for a widening disparity between world demand and supply — the huge increase in the demand for fuels, particularly oil, for raw materials such as copper, tin, and rubber, for environmental protection, urban renewal and its related services. Finally, powerful labor unions are charged with pushing up costs and prices while giant firms resorting to monopolistic practices are said to "administer" ever rising prices.

In this confusion of "explanations" and accusations, prices, costs, and wages are rising at persistent rates. All over the world wholesale and consumer price indices are climbing steadily, with ever higher costs of living and lower standards of living, higher interest rates for loans, higher levels of government expenditures and receipts. In less developed countries currency depreciation rates of twenty percent are common, threatening all efforts at improving living conditions and precipitating repeated governmental crises. In Chile, Uruguay, and Argentina, the depreciation rates frequently exceed fifty percent per annum, causing military revolutions and take-overs as the economic situation becomes intolerable. In Europe growing inflationary pressures have caused prices to rise steeply in spite of some form of wage and price controls which most governments have introduced. The failure of the controls then leaves the countries wide open to rapid acceleration of their inflation rates. In November 1972 the Council of Ministers of the European Economic Community established, as a desirable goal, a four percent rate of currency depreciation. Since then, inflation in Europe has been running at more than twice the four percent target rate.

In the United States, Americans have always felt that serious inflation was a problem of other countries, especially those in Latin America. This attitude prevailed although goods prices throughout the 1950's and early 1960's rose steadily at the modest rate of two to three percent. But by the end of the 1960's the pace of price increases accelerated in spite of President Nixon's attempt in 1969 to cool the feverish economy through federal budget restraint and a tight Federal Reserve monetary policy. However, when the American economy soon fell into a mild recession his adminstration quickly reversed itself by resuming monetary expansion.

When goods prices rose at ever faster rates the administration, with great popular support, imposed price and wage controls. Through four successive phases of controls the American people lived with bureaucratic controls, production bottlenecks, and goods scarcities. But no sooner had controls been relaxed than prices began to soar — commodity prices more than fifty percent, wholesale prices of nearly all goods more than twenty percent, and consumer prices more than ten percent. Again both the public and the administration weaved unhappily between living with rising prices and wage-price controls. When prices soar the American public naively looks for relief through government controls. But when enmeshed in controls and chafing under goods shortages, black markets, shoddy quality of goods and services, industrial strife and conflict, and ever more comprehensive governmental power, the people wonder about the huge price they are paying for the suppression of prices and wages.

Americans are bewildered and dejected by the tenacity and severity of the inflation dilemma. Baffled and frustrated, many have lost faith in the political process that seems to be so helpless now. After all, their Presidents from Harry Truman to Jimmy Carter assured them numerous times that inflation would soon be overcome. Yet it rages with ever new fury and destructiveness to economic well-being and social stability.

Inflation and Deficits

Throughout two hundred years of American history inflation had been a wartime phenomenon that promptly came to an end with the cessation of hostilities. During the Revolution rapid depreciation of Continental and state paper moneys involved the country in difficult problems. But when the issues had lost their value in 1780, and the legal tender laws had been repealed, monetary stability was restored with the return of specie. At the close of the War of 1812 the finances of the federal government were in desperate straits, the currency was inflated and disorganized, and the banking system verged on collapse. But by 1820 a general return to specie redemption restored financial order and monetary stability. During the Civil War United States Treasury notes, commonly called "greenbacks," greatly depreciated, falling to thirty-five cents on the dollar in July 1864. Soon after the war the Treasury began to retire outstanding notes which caused them to appreciate. With the resumption of greenback redemption on January 1, 1879, they promptly returned to par.[5] During World War I the United States dollar depreciated steadily in spite of wartime price fixing policies. But in 1920 a readjustment set in that reduced the volume of Federal Reserve notes and restored monetary stability.

This was the last time in United States monetary history that the dollar recovered from wartime inflation. After World War II the dollar depreciation continued with irresistible force. According to the Bureau of Labor Statistics index (1967 = 100), consumer prices rose from 44.1 in 1941 to 53.9 in 1945, 72 in 1950, 80.2 in 1955, 88.7 in 1960, 94.5 in 1965, 116.3 in 1970, 161.2 in 1975, and 175.3 in January 1977.[6] It is true that the wars in Korea and Vietnam tended to accelerate the dollar depreciation, but peace did not bring stability. On the contrary, after the United States withdrawal from Vietnam the dollar depreciated even faster than during the war.

The worldwide depreciation of national currencies that characterizes our age differs fundamentally from the currency depreciations that plagued the western world during the last two centuries. In the past, the inflations were of relatively short duration, limited to periods of national emergency when the central government was called upon to finance extraordinary defense expenditures. After the end of hostilities monetary stability soon returned as the emergency financing was abandoned. Today, public demand for governmental services never abates, in wartime or peacetime, but seems to accelerate year after year. In fact, the more government spends on economic and social objectives the louder the public clamor for more services seems to become. Thus, the temporary emergencies that in the past gave occasion for extraordinary defense expenditures and inflationary financing have given way to a permanent emergency of social service and inflationary financing. It is true that inflation can never be permanent, for it must come to an end with the total destruction of the currency. But an age of inflation can last a long time, perhaps several generations, as new national currencies may be

---

[5] Gary North argues convincingly that the passage of the first legal tender act in February 25, 1862, marks a major transition from the Jacksonian position of laissez-faire to a general acceptance of the legitimacy of federal centralization in all spheres of economic life. The pro-greenback position during the Civil War lives on in contemporary monetary legislation and policy. Cf. his "Greenback Dollars and Federal Sovereignty, 1861-1865," in *Gold Is Money*, Hans F. Sennholz, ed. (Westport, Connecticut: Greenwood Press, 1975), p. 122 *et seq.*

[6] Federal Reserve Board, *Federal Reserve Bulletin* (Washington, D. C.: U. S. Government Printing Office), July 1974, p. A55; March 1977, p. A46.

emitted when the old issues disappear from the scene. From issue to issue the inflation can continue as long as the economic and monetary ideology that has given birth to the age of inflation continues to enjoy public credence and to shape monetary policy.

In the United States the ominous consequences of this ideological development are clearly visible. Today the American people no longer believe that they have to bear the expenses of government. They are quick to reject the old-fashioned notion that government is a necessary expense that assures law and order, that prodigality and largess are the vices of weak administrations, and that frugality and balanced budgets reflect the concomitant virtues of responsibility and strength. During the early 1930's this old fashioned philosophy of government and society began to change. At first the Hoover Administration and then the Roosevelt New Deal on a much larger scale embraced the principle of economic redistribution through the agency of government. The State now was called upon to benefit and support important segments of the electorate. The voter now asked the question, "What will government do for me?" The political parties began to vie with each other for votes and power through economic intervention and redistribution of property.

During the first generation of this new economic order, from Hoover to Eisenhower, the expenses of government benefits were covered largely by ever higher taxes on business and the rich. Income taxes were raised until they reached confiscatory rates of more than ninety percent. Estate taxes imposed by federal and state governments took between seventy-seven percent and one hundred percent from the heirs of wealthy individuals. Dozens of corporate and other business taxes extracted ever larger amounts from industry and commerce. By 1960, the last year of the Eisenhower Administration, confiscation of all incomes in excess of $25,000 per year would have yielded revenue for only ten more days of federal spending. In an atmosphere of stagnation and recession the Redistributive State was grinding to a painful halt.

The motto of the Kennedy Administration, "Let's get moving again," reflected the dilemma of the financial process. Since the public clamor for social services and benefits continued to grow, new revenue sources had to be found. The New Frontiersmen had several alternatives. They could proceed in the old direction of taxing the remaining income of the rich and then confiscate ever larger shares of their wealth and capital. In short, they could consume the substance of American business and enterprise. But in that direction obviously lay economic depression and chaos, which does not make taxation a viable alternative to more redistribution. Or the New Frontiersmen could embark upon taxing the majority of the American electorate for the new benefits and services that were promised and expected. The recipients of redistributive largess could be taxed to bear the expenses. But obviously this principle of payment of benefits by the beneficiaries negates the very principle of redistribution. In that direction lies welfare failure and political defeat.

Yet another financial method for the support of the Great Society needed to be discovered. As in all other statist societies, from Germany to Italy, France, and Great Britain, the needed funds for the statist redistribution of property were found in deficit spending and currency expansion. Thus in 1961, after one generation of taxes on Peter to support Paul, the Redistributive State entered a new stage of active inflation and currency destruction.

We need merely to compare the federal deficits during the 1950's with those of the 1960's. They amounted to a total of $12.508 billion during the 1950's. If it had not been for the 1959 deficit of $12.855 billion there would even have been a small surplus for the decade. But during the 1960's the net annual deficits totalled $57.235 billion. And from 1970 to 1977 they are estimated at $250.5 billion.[7] Do we need any further evidence for the conclusion that the United States has entered an age of growing deficits and accelerating inflation?

It is the mark of all demagogic politicians and weak statesmen to resort to inflation, which offers short-run solutions although it breeds disastrous remoter consequences. Lord Keynes summed it up rather well: "In the long run we are all dead." He could also have said, "After us, the deluge!"

And yet, in defense of the Keynesian doctrine it may be said that even its radical proponents envisioned budgetary surpluses in times of prosperity. But as we always have pointed out, the political forces for redistribution tend to accelerate once they are unleashed. A government that is called upon to embark upon deficit spending and credit expansion in bad years, i.e., during recession, cannot be expected to reduce its "benefits," influence, and power in good years. In fact, government benefits need to be continued lest their beneficiaries suffer again from the very evil the government spending was supposed to alleviate.

In the United States Keynesianism is reaping its bitter fruit as deficit spending has been elevated to a principle of political virtue and astuteness. To govern without a deficit is to be "blind to urgent social needs" and to commit political suicide. A balanced budget is a "naive superstition" and a relic of the past. Woe to the critic who points out that deficits usually mean inflation. Inflation, in popular and political

---

[7] *The Budget of the United States* (Washington, D. C.: United States Government Printing Office, 1978), p. 437.

terminology, is not the huge expansion of money and credit that is needed to finance the federal deficits, but merely the inevitable consequence of the expansion: the continuous rise in prices. It is not the government that inflates the currency, but businessmen and capitalists who greedily raise prices.

Obviously, such a definition of inflation permits government to continue its ominous policy while public blame is laid on some of its victims. The public may even call on government, the very source of the evil, to control and regiment American business. Thus, the individual enterprise system gives way to a government command system, commonly called socialism. Inflation destroys not only the currency but also the private property market order. Ultimately it places all democratic institutions in serious jeopardy.

The Three Stages of Inflation

Once deficit spending has been elevated to a principle of enlightened statesmanship, the inflation runs its natural course. Since most people have never experienced the phenomenon and blithely support the deficit spending in search of "social progress" and "equitable redistribution," they are slow in comprehending the situation. After all, government officials assure them again and again that the inflators, that is, greedy businessmen, will soon be restrained and that prices will come down again. And why shouldn't they trust their illustrious leaders who valiantly dispense billion dollar benefits? Because prices are rising slightly the people may save more money, buy more savings bonds and life insurance, and otherwise refrain from or delay consumption in the hope that prices will soon come down again.

This popular reaction, typical of an early stage of inflation, actually counteracts the price consequences of the deficit spending by government. When people increase their cash holdings while the government expands the money supply, the impact of the inflation on prices tends to be minimized. The prices of goods and services may rise quite slowly. This early stage of inflation, which we would like to dub "the stage of blissful ignorance," may last for a long time. The greater the public ignorance in economic and monetary matters, the longer this stage tends to be. In the United States it lasted from 1961 to 1973.

But a prudent man learns from personal experience, which teaches slowly and through costly mistakes. By 1973 many Americans had learned that inflation is a chronic disease of government and society. Especially businessmen learned to associate the growing deficits and the currency expansion with rising prices. Consequently they began to hedge against inflation by reducing their cash holdings. Many even sought to borrow more money, which was depreciating, in order to buy goods that were appreciating in price. They bought materials and supplies, machinery and equipment, buildings and land, precious metals and other durable goods. Now when business finally joins government in its rush for goods and services, their prices must necessarily rise. The mathematical economists call this psychological phenomenon "the rising velocity of money." We are calling it here "the second stage of inflation," in which goods prices climb at a faster rate than that of the currency inflation by government.

In 1973 the stock of United States money rose only eleven percent, according to official statistics. But wholesale prices and commodity prices soared by nineteen percent and eighty percent respectively. Obviously, businessmen were rushing to convert their cash, and their claims to cash, into real goods. Perhaps their learning was accelerated by the shortages and delays in goods deliveries which the four phases of price controls had generated since August 1971. But having learned the lesson of deficit spending and inflation, it is unlikely that businessmen will forget it again. On the contrary, knowledge tends to spread, especially if it is profitable. This is why we expect ever wider circles of business and commerce to join the rush out of money into real goods. Accordingly, we expect all goods prices to rise at an even faster rate.

Can this ominous process be stopped? In our opinion, the chances are negligible. The ideological prerequisites for balanced budgets and stable money are lacking. A large majority of the American public continue to clamor for "social improvements through federal spending." Public debate does not hinge around balanced budgets or spending cuts, but rather around such "urgent needs" as mass transit or national health care, which will increase the federal deficits by many billions of dollars. In case the American economy should evince symptoms of stagnation or recession, the President has already pledged the United States government to accelerate its spending in excess of the deficit already announced.

But even if the United States government, for unfathomable reasons, should suddenly balance its budget, the fear of further dollar depreciation would continue to lead businessmen to hedge against money and seek refuge in real goods. After more than a decade of massive deficit spending and four decades of economic redistribution, one, two, or even three balanced budgets would not convincingly establish a new trend. Furthermore, the very existence of a redistributive society depends on easy money and credit, without which it would soon sink into a deep depression. Again, the federal government would undoubtedly return to massive deficit spending in order to prevent such a decline. Finally, the pressures for further monetary depreciation from various attempts at price controls — which encourage consumption while retarding or preventing production — could be so great that one or two balanced budgets could not possibly contain the pent-up pressures. If prices should soar while government itself practices spending restraint, the public would surely demand more stringent price controls, which in time would precipitate ever higher prices.

If the second stage of inflation can no longer be aborted, how long can it last? All economists are pondering this difficult question. Obviously, the second stage with its many uncertainties and crises, great monetary instability, and radical government intervention, must be much shorter than the first stage of blissful ignorance and faith in government omnipotence. But no one can possibly foresee the future; its veil is forever woven by the hands of God.

We are convinced that this second phase of inflation which the United States entered in 1973 will be rather brief. After all, the American economy is much more vulnerable to the ravages of inflation than the economies of less developed countries such as Brazil, Chile, or Bolivia. They can endure, and actually have endured, high rates of inflation for many years. But they are "cash-and-carry economies" without any significant capital markets. Long-term debt in the form of government and corporate bonds, mortgages, life insurance, and pension funds that are payable many decades from now is virtually unknown. In the United States it is the mainstay of American productivity and high standard of living, the very structure of our economy and way of life. When it tumbles under the crushing burden of inflation, the economic, social, and political consequences will surpass all imagination. This is why we believe that inflation not only destroys the economic order but also weakens all democratic institutions.

The third and final stage of inflation in which the currency is completely destroyed must necessarily be short. It is characterized by a universal run from money and flight into real goods. When every housewife eagerly exchanges her money for any goods, when bank deposits are withdrawn for the purchase of real goods, life insurance policies are cancelled, and bonds and mortgages find no more buyers, the end of a currency comes in sight. In the sudden panic the inflation victims stampede in order to salvage their remaining belongings.

However, we trust that the United States will never reach this final stage. Since inflation is a world-wide phenomenon in this age of *fiat* money and economic redistribution, governments have had a great deal of experience with galloping inflation, and therefore may be able to prevent the final crack-up boom. Their favorite device is currency reform. When goods prices soar at ever faster rates because the people are finally losing all confidence in the currency, a reform may succeed in reversing the trend and returning the *fiat* system to the first stage of inflation, "blissful ignorance." Confidence and stability may thus return until the old forces of inflation generate new depreciation pressures. A currency reform endeavors to finalize the previous inflation losses in either one of two ways: (1) A new series of *fiat* money gradually replaces the old money at a given ratio such as 1:10 or 1:100. In terms of new money all prices and wages would tend to come down by a similar ratio. Since this kind of reform was first conducted in France in 1958, we would like to call it the "French method." (2) An entirely new currency is issued on the reform day; the old money is voided by law or decree. Since this method was applied twice in one generation in Germany, we may call it the "German method." The old money was replaced by new money at a ratio of 1,000,000,000,000:1 the first time this method was used, and at a ratio of 10:1 the second time.

But why should the people trust a currency reform and accept and hold the new money? In their desperation a new beginning is a welcome change that seems to deserve their support. Any new money must be better than the depreciated old money. Furthermore, a currency reform is usually accompanied by holy pledges and legal guarantees that the new currency will never be inflated, which restores in many victims the old faith in government money. The promises made by government officials and political leaders that it will never happen again may even be accompanied by serious attempts at balancing the federal budget. Taxes may be raised and spending slashed in order to avoid new deficits. Under such conditions it is understandable indeed that the people may hold on to the new money and thus give it new value.

We do not know the end that is awaiting the United States dollar. According to persistent rumors circulating in the popular press, the Federal Reserve System has already prepared for an emergency with an entirely new currency. If it actually exists, it will be used some day.

Double-Digit Inflation

It has been said that affliction is a school of virtue, that it corrects levity and interrupts the confidence of sinning. If this should be true, the rampant inflation which is our most serious public affliction should offer important lessons in virtue and hamper the confidence of economic sinning. But such lessons cannot be learned as long as ignorance deprives man of some basic understanding of his affliction and its remedies.

Age of Inflation

For hundreds of years the issue of excessive quantities of paper currency by government was called inflation. Rising goods prices were deemed to result inevitably from such issues and were thought to offer an indication or measure of the degree of monetary inflation. But in the semantic confusion of our age, we are calling the rise in prices inflation, and the issuer of the money, spendthrift government, we call an "inflation fighter."

How delightful and profitable for officials and politicians! They can spend and spend without much worry about budget deficits, which are covered by the issue of new currency. The new terminology implicitly lays the blame for rising prices on anyone who dares to raise his prices, on "greedy" businessmen, workers, speculators, and foreigners. But the confusion brings havoc and poverty to countless victims whose incomes are greatly reduced and savings destroyed. It impoverishes the "middle class," with its savings for the rainy day and retirement.

Inflation is sometimes described as a tax on the money holders. In reality, it is a terrible instrument for the redistribution of wealth. It is true that the government is probably its greatest profiteer, as its tax revenues are boosted by the built-in progression in higher income brackets, and its debts are lowered through the transfer of wealth from creditors to debtors. But in addition, the inflation shifts wealth from those classes of society who are unable, or who do not know how, to defend themselves from the monetary destruction, to entrepreneurs and owners of material means of production. It strengthens the position of some businessmen while it lowers the real wages of most working men and professionals. It decimates or destroys altogether the middle class of investors who own securities or hold claims to life insurance and pension payments. And finally, it gives birth to a new middle class of traders, speculators, and small profiteers of the monetary depreciation.

The magnitude of the present redistributive process in the United States can only be surmised. Let us estimate the total volume of public and private debt at $3.2 trillion (federal $800 billion, state and local government $250 billion, corporations $1,250 billion, farms $80 billion, residual mortgages $450 billion, commercial mortgages $75 billion, other commercial debt $55 billion, financial debt $65 billion, consumer debt $210 billion). A fifteen percent rate, which we may suffer in the future, would transfer $485 billion per year. If we estimate disposable personal income in the United States at $1,500 billion, the annual inflation income transfer or loss amounts to nearly one-third of annual income from productive services. In short, inflation is a powerful instrument of wealth redistribution.

The redistribution process is also a massive debt liquidation process in real terms. The nominal magnitude of dollar debt is rising, but in terms of real things and real values debt is being liquidated at the depreciation rate. A ten percent rate of currency depreciation reduces real debt by ten percent; total monetary destruction destroys debt totally. It transfers the ownership of real wealth from the people who have lent money to the people who have borrowed the money. Such are the profits and losses from only one source: the currency depreciation that gives to debtors that which it takes from creditors. In addition, several other inflation factors inflict huge losses on nearly all classes of society.

Rampant inflation destroys the capital markets which are the very well-spring of productive enterprise. Having suffered staggering losses through depreciation, few lenders are able to grant new loans to finance business expansion or modernization, or merely current business operation. Even if they had the funds, they are reluctant to enter monetary contracts for any length of time. Business capital, especially long-term loan capital, becomes very scarce, which precipitates economic stagnation and recession. Similarly, businessmen begin to hedge for survival, investing their working capital in inventory and capital goods. Funds that used to serve consumers become fixed investments in capital goods that may escape the monetary depreciation. Economic output, especially for consumers, thus tends to decline, which may raise goods prices even further.

A great deal of "unproductive" labor is needed to cope with the complexities of calculation and dealing with rapidly changing prices. Cost accounting faces the insoluble task of calculating business costs with a yardstick that is shrinking continually. Managerial decisions become very difficult and enterprise efficiency is greatly hampered, which raises business costs and reduces output. Finally, the greatest danger to economic production and well-being looms in sudden government intervention. Having recklessly depreciated the currency at two digit rates, the same government may want to legislate and regulate the economic actions of the people. It may suddenly impose price, wage, and rent controls, restrict imports or exports, levy new taxes, or commit some other folly, all in order to treat some symptoms of its own policies.

Real Wages Fall

Two-digit inflation tends to reduce the real wages of nearly all classes of employees, from unskilled laborers to chief executives. While many goods prices can be adjusted quickly to the monetary depreciation, wage and salary contracts are written for longer periods of time, often for a year or even longer. During this time employees suffer a continuous erosion of real incomes and standards of living. The reduction in real wages, which are business costs, tends to raise the demand for labor, which generally causes unemployment to decline. In addition, profitable enterprises that continue to compete aggressively for labor tend to review wages and salaries more often than before, perhaps every six months rather than two years. Others boost merit pay substantially to avoid rising costs through higher turnover.

Despite these measures, the general decline in real wages tends to breed widespread labor unrest. Individual productivity may fall substantially, raising business costs, reducing output, and thus boosting prices even further. Labor unions react by demanding large increases in nominal wages, and sometimes may succeed in restoring real wages at least temporarily, until the inflation again reduces real wages, followed by further union demands, and so on. Ugly strikes multiply, costing millions of dollars in lost work hours, inflicting business losses and raising costs, and thus generating ever greater pressures for higher prices. In desperation many millions of heretofore unorganized employees are led to joining unions or forming collective strike organizations in order to avert the loss of real wages. Labor unions seem to thrive on monetary depreciation and the economic conflict it generates.

Rampant inflation also affords growing popularity and public support for a system of wages based on a cost-of-living index, commonly called indexation. All wages may be fixed according to an index number calculated by a government bureau. Of course, even such a system cannot be expected to protect labor from the disastrous influences of monetary depreciation, for the index is calculated on the basis of past prices that differ from the prices prevailing when wages are paid and spent. General indexation of wages also works havoc upon those industries that suffer severely from the inflation, such as consumers' goods industries and service industries. They may contract further, reducing output and service, which again raises prices.

The poorest classes of society living closest to the subsistence minimum are hurt most severely by monetary depreciation. Especially those poor who live on fixed incomes, such as pensions and annuities or welfare gratuities that are slow to adjust to the rise in prices, may actually experience deprivation and hunger. Others may be forced to supplement their shrinking purchasing power by seeking employment if this should be possible. Thus, some unskilled laborers who used to prefer public support to working for a living will return to productive employment. Others may resort to vice and crime to bolster their falling incomes.

Real incomes of civil servants, military personnel, and salaried employees of commerce and industry may fall even faster than those of the poor. True, they may not immediately face deprivation and hunger, but they may be greatly reduced and impoverished by the rise in prices that tends to exceed their occasional salary adjustments. The situation may even be worse with professional men, such as physicians, dentists, attorneys, artists, writers, and professors at private institutions of learning. Rampant inflation may reduce them to a life of penury and misery as public demand for their professional services tends to decline significantly with the general impoverishment of the populace. After all, demand for their services is much more elastic than that for food, for instance, which explains why less money is spent on professional services in spite of ever larger government expenditures on health, education, and welfare.

The suffering of this professional class is compounded by the destruction of its savings through inflation. In general, the middle class generates the financial capital that affords productivity and expansion to commerce and industry. It holds a large share of national wealth in the form of financial capital, such as corporate stock and debentures, demand and time deposits, life insurance, pension funds, *etc.*, all of which suffer serious losses from the depreciation of the currency. In fact, rampant inflation expropriates the wealth and substance of this middle class.

Dangerous Stock Markets

The stock market offers great opportunities during periods of rampant inflation. Industrial shares especially are subject to extreme fluctuations in price, which astute traders will use to their advantage. This does not mean that the market offers investors a reliable hedge against inflation. On the contrary, the real value of shares tends to decline, which inflicts considerable depreciation losses on share holders. But alert traders can profit from the many chills and fevers that attack the market. The greatest factor of change that virtually shapes the price trends of stock is the monetary policy of the government. Large bursts of money creation and credit expansion are followed by sudden jerks of restraint or even stability, which trigger symptoms of economic recession and decline. Or the government may suddenly impose price, wage, and rent controls, or resort to other means of intervention that temporarily reverse the trend. To ignore the ever-changing signals of monetary policy and other government intervention can be very costly.

In terms of purchasing power, stock prices tend to decline because most business profits are more apparent than real. The sums set aside for maintenance of equipment, called depreciation, are inadequate. Replacement costs soar while depreciation that is allowable under the tax laws is based on past costs and therefore insufficient to cover present costs. In fact, many profits are fictitious, which causes companies to pay income taxes although there is no income, and declare dividends while working at a loss. Similarly, the inflation profits on inventory are mostly fictitious, for replacement costs may equal or even exceed the proceeds of a sale that was believed to be profitable. During periods of rampant inflation it is very difficult, even for experts, to ascertain the profitability of an enterprise. To interpret profit statements and balance sheets becomes nearly impossible, which affords companies an opportunity to hide their earnings or losses and show only what they want to show. For an investor to appraise the value of his corporate shares becomes an insoluble problem.

Occasionally the monetary authorities may slow down or even abstain from creating more currency and credit. Or the rate of money and credit expansion may fall short of that expected by buisnessmen. In each case the fevers of inflation are interspersed with the chills of recession and depression, which send stock and bond prices tumbling until, once again, the federal government comes to the rescue with record budget deficits and new bursts of currency expansion. After all, this is the basic recipe of the New Economics that has shaped federal economic policy since the 1930's and has given us "inflationary recessions," *i.e.*, simultaneous inflation and recession.

When one or several of these factors depress stock prices, the public may realize that even the purchase of industrial securities affords no safe means of investing their savings. Suffering heavy losses, they withdraw from the market and invest their remaining funds in goods or money market instruments, especially Treasury obligations. The public is the "middle class" of some thirty million stock holders and fifty million investors who indirectly own corporate securities through investment companies, pension funds, life insurance companies, credit unions, *etc.* They suffer heavy losses when they finally liquidate their stock investments for depreciated currency. It has been estimated that since 1965 most American stock investors have lost at least forty percent of their savings through price declines and another forty percent through currency depreciation.

From time to time the fever of inflation may cause stock prices to soar as the monetary authorities refuel the money markets in order to avoid depression and unemployment. The investor may rejoice about his long-awaited profits. Deluded by the apparently high prices he may be induced to sell his securities. Unfortunately he may not be aware of the real losses which the monetary depreciation is inflicting on him. Again he loses severely in purchasing power and real wealth, and yet may have to pay an income tax on the nominal profits he earned.

The speculator who observes the merciless drubbing of most investors has learned to distinguish "apparent profits" from "real" ones. He trades with the trends of the market, jumps from industry to industry, always seeking action and quick profits. But above all, he is basically a buyer of the securities that are liquidated by the middle class investor. The monetary depreciation, which greatly reduces their real price, makes it easier to acquire securities. Thus, we can observe not only a gradual shift of corporate wealth from the old class of capitalists and middle class investors, but also a concentration of industrial shares in fewer and fewer hands. A small new middle class of traders and speculators replaces the old middle class of investors, and huge new fortunes are created from the losses suffered by investors and capitalists.

The depreciation of public debt and the fall of industrial securities in terms of both price and purchasing power strike a devastating blow not only at millions of small investors but also at great capitalists whose wealth is invested in marketable securities. Wealthy stock brokers, bankers, financiers, *rentiers*, heirs, or retired businessmen, who before the inflation owned large fortunes — that is, the "old rich" — suffer serious losses. Old fortunes vanish, and eminent family names fade away. Similarly, the wealth of charitable institutions, religious societies, scientific or literary foundations, and endowed colleges and universities is destroyed by inflation.

Losses in Real Estate

While inflation inflicts havoc on monetary investments it has varied effects on the value of land and buildings. Agriculture, on the whole, survives a period of feverish inflation rather well. Farmers generally profit from the increase in prices of agricultural goods and from the depreciation of farm mortgages. Even small and middle-size operators whose debt may render their independence rather precarious in normal times can hold their own during rampant inflation. After all, they are the producers and owners of real goods, the prices of which rise, yielding ever higher incomes, while inflation reduces the real burden of their debt.

Ownership of residential housing offers a much poorer defense against inflation than is commonly believed. Although mortgage debt is greatly reduced by the inflation, which affords some inflation profits to owners, the market price of private residences and commercial property usually limps behind the rate of monetary depreciation. During rampant inflation, interest rates soar and mortgage loans are hard to find, which makes it rather difficult to finance a purchase. Thus, effective demand may be reduced, which tends to depress real estate prices. This is especially true for middle class housing whose owners feel impoverished and in need of retrenchment; it may not be true for beautiful mansions and large estates, which continue to sell at high prices to a new class of *nouveaux riches*. But even when real estate appreciates in price and the owner gains from a sale, a gain on which he must pay a capital gains tax, he may lose in terms of purchasing power. Deluded by apparently high prices, many owners may be induced to sell their homes, only to realize much later, perhaps, that they made a poor bargain.

The situation is most dangerous and precarious for apartment house owners. They are vulnerable not only to the imponderables of a feverish capital market, to the impoverishment of their working and middle class tenants, and to the price delusion mentioned above, but also to the ever-present danger of rent control. A desperate government may do desperate things. Drawing wrong conclusions from given facts and fighting symptoms rather than causes, it may by force arrest prices, wages, and rents. But rent controls imposed for prolonged periods of inflation reduce real rents significantly, which cause house prices to fall accordingly. With maintenance expenses rising, real rents falling, and losses looming, many owners may be forced to sell out — at very low prices. Again the class of old investors makes room for a new class of speculators who are buying a great many houses at bargain prices.

But even without controls rental property may be depressed because working and middle class demand for housing is shrinking as real income is declining. Many apartment house owners may not realize the significance of the monetary depreciation, and therefore are slow to adjust their rents, or they may be reluctant to raise rents for charitable reasons. In each case the yield from such property tends to decline, and therefore also the value of the property, which may inflict serious losses on its owners.

The Nouveaux Riches

Huge private fortunes and imposing concentrations of capital are formed by inflationary redistribution. But in contrast to the formation of capital under stable monetary conditions, when fortunes are built through productive changes and improvements, through technological inventions, and through efficient methods of production, the wealth derived from inflation is redistributive, from one individual to another. The new millionaires are not generally creators of new industries or reorganizers of production. They are mostly clever speculators with excellent understanding of monetary policy and its effects on stock prices, exchange rates, and high finance. They may even be industrialists who are turning away from the hard work of business management to the more rewarding fields of securities, commodities, and foreign exchange. But above all, they understand the phenomenon of inflation and use this knowledge in all their financial operations. As speculators they endeavor to render the most urgent economic service needed at the time. They are quick to adjust their resources to the rapid changes in prices and markets that suffer from perpetual maladjustments due to the ever-changing money supply and value. Thus they facilitate quicker and smoother readjustment and better allocation of economic resources to the most urgent needs of the public.

During rampant inflation one of the rules of good management is to contract as many productive debts as possible. The speculator borrows other people's money, which is repaid later with depreciated currency. Instead of keeping large bank deposits, he finds it more advantageous to incur the highest possible debt with his bank. Of course, at all times he must maintain his liquidity to meet current obligations, always guarding against sudden calling of loans by his bank in moments of extreme credit stringency.

Inflation not only destroys income and wealth, but also redistributes them from millions of creditors to many debtors. Some businessmen, especially the young, aggressive entrepreneurs, understand this principle and utilize it to their advantage. They expand their enterprises or acquire new ones, merge with others or form new business structures — always building on debt. The inflation losses suffered by banks and bond holders who finance the expansion accrue as profits to these entrepreneurs, who join the class of *nouveaux riches*. But occasionally when the government reverses its monetary policy, when it deflates rather than inflates, or when it merely reduces the rate of monetary depreciation, these entrepreneurs find themselves overextended. They may have to contract their operations or liquidate some of their holdings. In fact, some may lose their fortunes even faster than they made them.

Chills and Fevers

Financial survival is especially difficult as the fevers of inflation are interspersed with the chills of recession. Some industries may be seized by the inflation fever while others may suffer recession symptoms. Rampant two-digit inflation does not follow the simple pattern of earlier moderate inflation, which tends to generate economic booms that are followed by periods of recession. Instead, it causes such serious disarrangement of markets and disruption of production that both economic disorders occur simultaneously.

The rapid depreciation of the money virtually destroys the capital market. The supply of loan funds tends to shrink as lenders are fearful of suffering losses from the depreciation of the money. Capital-intensive industries and others that depend on long-term financing, therefore, lack the necessary capital for expansion, modernization, or maintenance of costly capital equipment. The strength and substance of such industries may deteriorate, they may expire quickly, which becomes visible in the deterioration or even breakdown of service. Obviously, the equity markets of these industries tend to be depressed throughout the rampant inflation.

Consumers' goods industries, in general, tend to contract throughout this period. After all, most consumers suffer losses of income and wealth and, therefore, are compelled to curtail the consumption of goods they deem the least essential. Vacations may be postponed or at least shortened. Expenditures on entertainment, amusement, and other "luxuries" may be cut. There may even be reductions in the quality of essentials, such as food, clothing, and housing. And instead of seeking education in private institutions, the children may attend public schools, and state or community colleges.

The only industries that thrive on rampant inflation are the capital goods industries. They are producing goods that permit business to hedge against the inflation through investments in new tools and equipment, or larger inventories of materials and supplies. As inflation reduces the real costs of labor, many businesses endeavor to accumulate capital in the form of durable assets, preferably those that are expected to appreciate in value while retaining some degree of marketability. Many companies use their own working capital or seek bank loans to increase their inventories or add to tools and equipment, which can be expected to rise faster in price than the interest costs on the capital invested. They sacrifice liquidity in the hope of higher profits from the expected rise in prices.

All these specific symptoms of rampant inflation tend to conceal the most important predicament that affects everyone: the boom-and-bust cycle that is generated by the inflation. When the monetary authorities first expand the money supply in order to finance deficit spending or stimulate the economy, they set into motion certain forces that seriously distort the allocation of productive resources. Specifically, the policy of easy money and credit temporarily reduces interest rates, which causes businessmen to invest more funds in new construction, machinery, equipment, and raw materials. It generates a feverish boom in the capital goods industries with rapidly rising prices of labor and resources. This boom, built on easy money and credit, must come to an end as soon as the rising prices of labor and resources, which are business costs, erase profit margins or even inflict losses. After all, the boom must end because it was artificially built on paper and credit only. The recession that follows permits the markets to return to normal; in particular, capital goods prices will decline; the industry will contract again; and the consumers' goods industries, which were neglected throughout the boom, will come into their own again.

But this cycle can be extended in duration and be made more severe in its fluctuations by new injections of money and credit. Merely the anticipation of new injections may cause businessmen to reduce their cash holdings and escape into real goods. Thus the boom may continue to rage even though the monetary authorities may cease temporarily to add new money to credit, because businessmen have come to expect an early resumption of monetary expansion. Once capital goods prices rise at two-digit rates, a temporary halt in the expansion process does not signal the end of the boom, for the boom continues to be fed by the businessmen's reduction in cash holdings. Although interest rates may soar and the costs of financing equipment and inventory may rise significantly, capital goods prices may rise at even greater rates. In that case, reason the businessmen, it pays to order and buy now rather than wait until prices have risen again.

The expectation of an early resumption of easy money and credit that keeps the fires of boom burning is solidly based on a political assumption: Government will soon inflate again in order to alleviate some consequences of its earlier inflation. Alarmed about the recession that is engulfing the consumers' goods industries, the government will want to stimulate those industries once again. When consumers are fast losing purchasing power during two-digit inflation, consumers' goods industries suffer symptoms of contraction and recession, especially unemployment of capital and labor. But by popular demand, government is expected to cope with this recession with all the means at its disposal. That is, it is expected to resume deficit spending and credit expansion in order to restore full employment. The economic boom thus burns on with new money and credit.

In today's ideological climate there can be no genuine reversal of monetary policy. The two-digit inflation must rage on, feeding an ever hotter boom of the capital goods industries and aggravating the recession in the consumers' goods industries. The purchasing power of the dollar must fall at ever faster rates, being depreciated by ever larger injections of money and credit and a growing expectation of further injections. Two-digit inflation only comes to an end with the advent of three-digit inflation, which signals the approaching demise of the paper currency. In the final convulsion of inflation fever, millions of housewives join businessmen in a panicky rush to exchange their rapidly depreciating money for real goods. When millions of consumers hurry to spend their monetary assets and use all their lines of credit in order to seek refuge in real goods, the end of the currency comes in sight. Consumers' goods prices that were rising at much lower rates than those of producers' goods then will soar to catch up with the latter, or even surpass them, in the final contortion of the crack-up boom. In the dusk of the paper system that springs from political power and economic redistribution, the dreaded depression that was so long delayed in coming will finally make its entrance with irresistible force. Thus, once again, the inexorable laws of economics will prevail over political intrigue and power.

Indeed, affliction is a school of virtue that may correct levity and interrupt the confidence of sinning. But how long and how often must man be afflicted before he learns his lesson?

Hyperinflation in Germany

The German inflation of 1914-1923 had an inconspicuous beginning, a creeping rate of one to two percent. On the first day of the war the German Reichsbank, like the other central banks of the belligerent powers, suspended redeemability of its notes in order to prevent a run on its gold reserves. Like all the other banks, it offered assistance to the central government in financing the war effort. Since taxes are always unpopular, the German government preferred to borrow the needed amounts of money rather than raise its taxes substantially. To this end it was readily assisted by the Reichsbank, which discounted most treasury obligations. A growing percentage of government debt thus found its way into the vaults of the central bank and an equivalent amount of printing press money into people's cash holdings. In short, the central bank was monetizing the growing government debt.

By the end of the war the amount of money in circulation had risen fourfold and prices some 140 percent. Yet the German mark had suffered no more than the British pound, was somewhat weaker than the American dollar but stronger than the French franc. Five years later, in December 1923, the Reichsbank had issued 496.5 quintillion marks, each of which had fallen to one-trillionth of its 1914 gold value.[8]

How stupendous! Practically every economic good and service was costing trillions of marks. The American dollar was quoted at 4.2 trillion marks, the American penny at 42 billion marks. How could a

---

[8]Constantino Bresciani-Turroni, *The Economics of Inflation* (Third impression, New York: Augustus M. Kelley, 1968), p. 440.

European nation that prided itself on its high levels of education and scholarly knowledge suffer such a thorough destruction of its money? Who would inflict on a great nation such evil which had ominous economic, social, and political ramifications not only for Germany but for the whole world? Was it the victors of World War I who, in diabolical revenge, devastated the vanquished country through ruinous financial manipulation and plunder? Every mark was printed by Germans and issued by a central bank that was governed by Germans under a government that was purely German. It was German political parties, such as the Socialists, the Catholic Centre Party, and the Democrats, forming various coalition governments, that were solely responsible for the policies they conducted. Of course, admission of responsibility for any calamity cannot be expected from any political party.

The reasoning that led these parties to inflate the national currency at such astronomical rates is not only interesting for economic historians, but also very revealing of the rationale for monetary destruction. The doctrines and theories that led to the German monetary destruction have since then caused destruction in many other countries. In fact, they may be at work right now all over the western world. In our judgment, four erroneous doctrines or theories guided the German monetary authorities in those baleful years.

No Inflation in Germany

The most amazing economic sophism that was advanced by eminent financiers, politicians, and economists endeavored to show that there was neither monetary nor credit inflation in Germany. These experts readily admitted that the nominal amount of paper money issued was indeed enormous. But the *real value* of all currency in circulation, that is, the gold value in terms of gold or goods prices, they argued, was much lower than before the war or than that of other industrial countries.

Minister of Finance and celebrated economist Helfferich repeatedly assured his nation that there was no inflation in Germany since the total value of currency in circulation, when measured in gold, was covered by the gold reserves in the Reichsbank at a much higher ratio than before the war.[9] President of the Reichsbank Havenstein categorically denied that the central bank had inflated the German currency. He was convinced that it followed a restrictive policy since its portfolio was worth, in gold marks, less than half its 1913 holdings.

Professor Julius Wolf wrote in the summer of 1922: "In proportion

---

[9]Karl Helfferich, *Das Geld* (Leipzig: C. L. Hirschfeld, 1923 [1910]), p. 646.

to the need, less money circulates in Germany now than before the war. This statement may cause surprise, but it is correct. The circulation is now 15 - 20 times that of pre-war days, whilst prices have risen 40 - 50 times."[10] Similarly Professor Elster reassured his people that "however enormous may be the apparent rise in the circulation in 1922, actually the figures show a decline."[11]

The Statistical Bureau of the German government even calculated the real values of the per capita circulation in various countries. It, too, concluded that there was a shortage of currency in Germany, but a great deal of inflation abroad.

	Gold value of monies in circulation, gold marks per person	
	1920	1922
Germany	87.63	17.92
England	84.40	110.73
France	180.05	229.90
Switzerland	89.49	103.33
United States of America	101.35	97.66

Source: Wirtschaft und Statistik, *1923, No. 1.*
(To arrive at U.S. dollar amounts these
figures should be divided by 4.2)

Of course, this fantastic conclusion drawn by monetary authorities and experts bore ominous consequences for millions of people. Through devious sophisms it simply removed the cause of disaster from individual responsibility and thus also all limits to the issuance of more paper money.

The source of this momentous error probably lies in the ignorance of one of the most important determinants of money value, which is the very attitude of people toward money. For one reason or another people may vary their cash holdings. An increase in cash holdings by many people tends to raise the exchange value of money; reduction in cash holdings tends to lower it. Now in order to change radically their cash holdings, individuals must have cogent reasons. They naturally enlarge their holdings whenever they anticipate rising money value as, for instance, in a depression. And they reduce their hold-

[10]Julius Wolf, *Markkurs, Reparationen und russisches Geschäft* (Stuttgart: F. Enke Verlag, 1922), p.10.
[11]Karl Elster, *Von der Mark sur Reichsmark* (Jena: G. Fischer, 1928), p. 167.

ings whenever they expect declining money value. In the German hyperinflation they reduced their holdings to an absolute minimum and finally avoided any possession at all. It is obvious that goods prices must then rise faster and the value of money depreciate faster than the rate of money creation. If the value of individual cash holdings declines faster than the rate of money printing, the value of the total stock of money must also depreciate faster than this rate. This is so well understood that even the mathematical economists emphasize the money "velocity" in their equations and calculations of money value.[12] But the German monetary authorities were unaware of such basic principles of human action.

For Health, Education, Welfare, and Full Employment

Immediately after the war the German government, under the leadership of the Socialist Party, embarked upon heavy expenditures for health, education, and welfare. The demands on the treasury were extremely heavy anyway because of demobilization expenses, the demands of the Armistice, the disorders of the revolution, and the staggering deficits of the nationalized industries, especially the railroads, postal services, telephone, and telegraph. Public administration by the new men raised to power by the revolution, nevertheless, was extravagant, as the resources made available by the creation of new money were apparently unlimited. A number of measures for the nationalization of certain industries (e.g., the coal, electrical, and potash industries) were introduced, but failed to become law. The eight-hour day was enacted, and labor unions were given many legal immunities and privileges. In fact, a system of labor councils was set up which authorized the workers in each enterprise to elect representatives who shared in the management of the company!

While government expenditures rose by leaps and bounds, the revenue suffered a gradual decline until, in October 1923, only 0.8 percent of government expenses were covered by tax revenues. For the period from 1914 to 1923 scarcely fifteen percent of the expenses were covered by means of taxes. In the final phase of the inflation the German government experienced a complete atrophy of the fiscal system.

The depreciation of the currency brought about the destruction of taxable wealth in the form of mortgages, bonds, annuities, and pensions, which in turn reduced government revenue. Some speculators reaped spectacular profits from the depreciation, but they easily evaded the tax collector. Moreover, the fiscal policies of the socialist government were openly hostile toward capital and frequently en-

---

[12]Compare Chapter I, The Value of Money.

deavored to impose confiscatory capital levies upon all wealth. Secretary of the Treasury Erzberger even vowed that "in the future Germany the rich should be no more."[13] Consequently a massive "flight of capital" from Germany developed as all classes of savers invested their money in foreign bank accounts, currencies, bills, securities, *etc.* Much taxable wealth was removed from the grasp of tax collectors.

Finally, the rapid depreciation of currency greatly reduced all tax liabilities during the time interval between the taxable transaction and the date of tax payment. The taxpayer usually paid a sum whose real value was greatly reduced by inflation. Nevertheless, government expenditure accelerated while revenue in terms of real value continued to decline. The growing deficits then were met with even larger quantities of printing press money, which in turn generated ever larger deficits. The German monetary authorities, in fact, were trapped in a vicious circle from which they did not know how, nor have the courage, to extricate themselves.

The leading monetary authority, Dr. Helfferich, even warned his people against the dire consequences of monetary stabilization.

> To follow the good counsel of stopping the printing of notes would mean refusing to economic life the circulating medium necessary for transactions, payments of salaries and wages, etc. It would mean that in a very short time the entire public, and above all the Reich, could no longer pay merchants, employees, or workers. In a few weeks, besides the printing of notes, factories, mines, railways, and post offices, national and local government, in short, all national and economic life would be stopped.[14]

The Balance of Payments and the Treaty of Versailles

Throughout the period of the inflation the most popular explanation of the monetary depreciation laid the blame on an unfavorable balance of payments, which in turn was blamed on the payment of reparations and other burdens imposed by the Treaty of Versailles. To most German writers and politicians, the government deficits and the paper inflation were not the causes but the consequences of the external depreciation of the mark.

The wide popularity of this explanation which charged the victorious allies with full responsibility for the German disaster bore ominous implications for the future. Its simplicity made it appealing to the masses of economically ignorant people whose chauvinism and

---

[13]Compare Costantino Bresciani-Turroni, *The Economics of Inflation, op. cit.,* p. 55.
[14]*Das Geld, op. cit.,* p. 650.

nationalism always make the idea of foreign intrigue and conspiracy so palatable. The intellectual and political leaders who actively propagated the doctrine were sowing the seeds for the whirlwind they reaped a decade later.

During those baleful years Germany actually procured gratuitously from abroad large quantities of raw materials and foodstuffs. According to various authoritative estimates, foreign individuals and banks bought at least sixty billion paper marks which the Reichsbank had floated abroad at an average price of one-fourth gold mark for a paper mark. The depreciation of the mark to one-trillionth of its earlier value repudiated these foreign claims to German goods. Thus foreigners suffered losses of some fifteen billion gold marks, or some $3.5 billion United States dollars, which was eight times more than Germany had paid in foreign exchange on account of reparations.

But even if it had been true that excessive burdens had been thrust on Germany by the Allies, there was no need for any monetary depreciation. Both phenomena are entirely independent. If excessive burdens are placed on a government, whether they be foreign or domestic, that government must raise taxes, or borrow some funds, or curtail other expenditures. Excessive reparation payments may necessitate greatly higher taxes on the populace, or large loans that reduce the supply of savings for industry and commerce, or painful cuts in government service and employment. The standards of living of the people thus burdened will probably be depressed — unless the reduction of bureaucracy should release new productive energy. But the value of money is not affected by the reparation burden unless economic productivity is impaired by the fund raising.

Once government has achieved the necessary budgetary surplus the payment of reparations is a simple matter of exchange. The treasury buys the necessary gold or foreign exchange from its central bank and delivers it to the recipient government. The loss of gold or foreign exchange then necessitates a corresponding reduction of central bank money, which in turn tends to depress goods prices. Lower goods prices encourage more exports while they discourage imports, that is, generate what is commonly called a "favorable balance of payments" or new influx of gold and foreign exchange. In short, there can be no shortage of gold or foreign exchange as long as the central bank refrains from inflation and monetary depreciation.

The German monetary authorities flatly denied this economic reasoning. Instead, they preferred to lament about the excessive burdens thrust onto Germany and the unfavorable balance of payments generated thereby. In 1923 they added yet another factor: the French occupation of the Ruhr district. The Central Statistical Office put it this way:

The fundamental cause of the dislocation of the German monetary system is the disequilibrium of the balance of payments. The disturbance of the national finances and the inflation are in their turn the consequences of the depreciation of the currency. The depreciation of the currency upset the Budget balance, and determined with an *inevitable necessity* a divergence between income and expenditure, which provoked the upheaval.[15]

Again I quote Dr. Helfferich:

Inflation and the collapse of the exchange are children of the same parent: the impossibility of paying the tributes imposed on us. The problem of restoring the circulation is not a technical or banking problem; it is, in the last analysis, the problem of the equilibrium between the burden and the capacity of the German economy for supporting this burden.[16]

Even American economists echoed the German theory. Professor Williams presented this causal order: "Reparation payments, depreciating exchanges, rising import and export prices, rising domestic prices, consequent budgeting deficits, and at the same time an increased demand for bank credit; and finally increased note-issue."[17] Professor Angell contended that "The reality of the type of analysis which runs *from* the balance of payments and the exchanges *to* general prices and the increased issue of paper seems to be definitely established."[18]

Speculators Did It

When all other explanations are exhausted, modern governments usually fall back on the speculator, who is held responsible for all economic and social evils. What the witch was to medieval man, what the capitalist is to socialists and communists, the speculator is to most politicians and statesmen: the embodiment of evil. He is said to be imbued with ruthless and fickle selfishness that is capable of wrecking the national economy, government plans, and, in the case of German inflation, the national currency. No matter how blatantly contradictory this explanation may be, it is most popular with government authorities in search of a convenient explanation for the failure of their own policies.

---

[15]Statistisches Reichsamt, *Deutschlands Wirtschaftslage* (Berlin, March 1923), p. 24.

[16]"Die Autonomie der Reichsbank," *Berliner-Bösen-Courier*, April 4, 1922, p. 1.

[17]John Henry Williams, "German Foreign Trade and the Reparations Payments," *Quarterly Journal of Economics,* Vol. 36, (May 1922), p. 503.

[18]James W. Angell, *The Theory of International Prices* (Cambridge, Massachusetts: Harvard University Press, 1926), p. 195.

The same German officials who denied the very existence of inflation lamented the depreciation caused by speculators, or they blamed the Allied reparation burdens and simultaneously denounced speculators for the depreciation. Dr. Havenstein, the President of the Reichsbank, embracing every conceivable theory that exculpated his policies, also pointed at the speculators. Before a parliamentary committee he testified: "On the 28th of March began the attack on the foreign exchange market. In very numerous classes of the German economy, from that day onwards, thought was all for personal interests and not for the needs of the country."[19]

In a chorus the newspapers chanted the charge:

> According to all appearances the fall of the mark did not have its origin in the New York exchange, from which it may be concluded that in Germany there was active speculation directed towards the continual rise of the dollar.
>
> We are witnessing a rapid increase in the number of those who speculate on the fall of the mark and who are acquiring vested interests in a continual depreciation.
>
> The enormous speculation on the rise of the American dollar is an open secret. People who, having regard to their age, their inexperience, and their lack of responsibility, do not deserve support, have nevertheless secured the help of financiers, who are thinking exclusively of their own immediate interests.
>
> Those who have studied seriously the conditions of the money market state that the movement against the German mark remained on the whole independent of foreign markets for more than six months. *It is the German bears, helped by the inaction of the Reichsbank, who have forced the collapse in the exchange.*[20]

In its broadest sense speculation is present in every economic action that makes provision for an uncertain future. The student who studies aeronautical engineering speculates on the future demand for his services. The businessman who enlarges his inventory speculates on a profitable market in the future. The housewife who hoards sugar speculates on the availability of sugar in the future. The buyer or seller of goods or securities hopes to make a profit from future changes in prices. All such actions reflect a natural motivation of free men to improve their material well-being or, at least, to avert losses.

When speculators observe or anticipate more inflation and monetary depreciation they naturally endeavor to sell the depreciating currency and buy goods or foreign exchange that do not depreciate.

---

[19] Quoted by Costantino Bresciani-Turroni, *op. cit.*, p. 63.
[20] *Das Abendblatt*, Berlin, May 22, 1923, p. 1.

They are preserving their working capital. Thus they are promoting not only their own interests but also those of society, which benefits from the preservation of productive capital. The government that is actively destroying the currency is injuring the national interest — successful speculators are safeguarding it. Surely the speculators who sold German marks and bought United States dollars were proved to be right in the end.

The worldwide inflation that is engulfing the western world now springs from similar doctrines and theories. There is no Treaty of Versailles and no reparation payments that can be blamed for the present inflation. But in many countries of Central and Western Europe the responsibility for monetary depreciation is squarely laid on American balance of payments deficits that are flooding those countries with United States dollars. While European monetary authorities are actively inflating and depreciating their own currencies — although at slower rates than their American counterparts — they are pointing at the United States balance of payments as the ultimate cause of their currency depreciation. As in the German hyperinflation, foreign intrigue and artifice are said to be at work again.

American officials and politicians are quick to lay the blame for United States difficulties on foreign intrigue, especially that of "the Arabs." Since the formation of the oil producers' cartel and the significant boost in oil prices, United States balance-of-payments deficits and the dollar weakness in foreign exchange markets are charged explicitly to the Arab countries. Lest any suspicion should fall on the United States monetary authorities, the American people themselves come in for some of the blame. Their use of "excessive" quantities of foreign oil is said to contribute to the balance-of-payments deficits and the dollar weakness. Therefore, our political leaders and economic authorities are debating the desirability of special taxes that would reduce the consumption of foreign oil. After the Arab blow at economic well-being the United States government is readying its blow for the sake of financial stability.

Again the speculators are charged for a share of the blame American investors who buy foreign securities or make direct foreign investments are said to be largely responsible for the outflow of United States funds and the loss of gold, which is creating an unfavorable balance of payments and weakening the dollar. Moreover, Americans who prefer foreign products over home-made products or choose to travel abroad rather than stay at home are decried as selfish and unpatriotic. Numerous regulations imposed by the very monetary authorities who perpetrate the inflation aim to prevent speculation in order to save the dollar.

The specious argument that denies the presence of any inflation in terms of purchasing power or gold value has, in our judgment, not yet been raised. But it must be expected to emerge in later phases of the inflation when our authorities will be desperate for any argument that promises to exculpate them.

The Second German Inflation and Destruction of the Mark, 1933-1948

The Great Depression in Germany provided a fertile soil for the tragic events that were to follow. Under the influence of certain social and economic ideologies, the governments of all Western countries were busily restricting world trade and commerce and strenuously raising taxes in order to maintain public expenditures. Between 1930 and 1932 the German President issued five emergency orders *(Notverordnungen)* that imposed drastic increases in tax burdens. Old taxes were raised, exemptions abolished, and new taxes piled on old levies. The percentage of public revenue to national income, which in 1928 exceeded thirty-five percent, rose to fifty-three percent in 1932.[21] The disintegration of world trade and finance, the disarrangements and maladjustments caused by previous policies, together with such drastic increases in fiscal burden, bore their bitter fruits.

Economic historians are aware of the startling similarity of the economic policies of the Hoover Administration in the United States to those conducted by the Brüning Administration in Germany. Both sprang from economic ideologies and yielded nearly identical effects. Today, nearly half a century later, most historians in both countries offer identical explanations. Mainstream economics, which is reviewing and rewriting economic history through Keynesian glasses, lays the blame for the economic disaster on the *deflationary policies* of both

---

[21]

German National Income and Government Revenue
(in billions of Reichsmarks)

Year	National Income	Taxes	Percent
1928	71.2	25.2	35.4
1929	70.9	26.6	37.5
1930	64.6	27.1	42.0
1931	52.1	25.3	48.6
1932	41.1	22.0	53.5

Source: Statistik der Bundesrepublik Deutschland,
Vol. 199 (Stuttgart 1958), p. 76, et seq.

administrations. But mainstream literature, so critical of the Brüning policies of 1930 to 1932, is enthralled and enthusiastic about the full-employment policies that characterized the period from 1933 to 1936. We should like to mention in passing that the German director of those contracyclical policies was Adolf Hitler. The manager was Hjalmar H. G. Schacht, whom Hitler re-appointed president of the Reichsbank in 1933 and installed as minister of the national economy in 1934. The intellectual architects were eminent economists, such as W. Lautenbach, H. Dräger, W. Grotkopp, R. Friedländer-Prechtl, H. Fick, and F. Bischoff. It is unlikely that they were influenced by John Maynard Keynes. But it is a titillating question how these writers and the German revival aided Lord Keynes in his "long struggle of escape" from orthodox economics, on which he reported so eloquently in 1936 in his *General Theory of Employment, Interest and Money.*

Full Employment Policy, 1933-1936

In just four years unemployment in Germany declined from 5.6 million in 1932, or 31 percent of the working population, to 1.6 million in 1936, or 8.5 percent of the working population. The number of gainfully employed rose from 12.5 million to 17.1 million. The index of industrial production, which is a significant yardstick for economic activity, rose from 58.7 in 1932 to 106.7 in 1936 (1928=100).

This remarkable revival of economic activity was achieved by an ingenious combination of dictatorial methods that greatly lowered the real costs of labor and otherwise reduced business costs. While the previous administrations had significantly raised their tax burdens in order to maintain the government apparatus, the new administration successfully shifted this burden to labor income. Immediately upon assuming power in 1933, the Nazis summarily abolished all labor unions and associations. A labor trustee *(Treuhänder der Arbeit)* assumed power over all collective bargaining and henceforth kept practically all wage rates and fringe benefits at depression levels. Similarly, all employer contributions to social security and other labor funds were frozen or even lowered throughout this period. By force and many insidious devices to achieve "voluntary" cooperation, the government successfully lowered production costs. This reduction in costs then helped to maintain goods prices despite the deficit spending and currency creation that began in 1933.

The adoption of expansionary credit policies was a gradual process that was hidden in a maze of devious devices. The Reichsbank was prohibited by law from financing government deficits. But it was possible to create and extend credit by special financial institutions, public and private, that were organized for the purpose of circumventing the legal restrictions. Their bills of credit could be freely accepted and discounted by the central bank. Furthermore, these credits and the expenditures they financed enjoyed the advantage that they did not appear in the government budgets and could be used to hide armament spending. In 1933 and 1934 some 4.6 billion marks were thus emitted, an amount which nearly equalled total tax revenues for the Reich in 1933. In 1935 and 1936 the new marks exceeded eight billion.[22]

The government thus created "financial intermediaries" whose acceptances could be discounted by commercial banks as well as the Reichsbank. In particular, it organized the Public Works Corporation (*Deutsche Gesellschaft für öffentliche Arbeiten*), which specialized in public housing. The Construction and Soil Bank (*Deutsche Bau- und Bodenbank*) invested in private housing. The Rent and Settlement Bank (*Deutsche Rentenkbank-Kreditanstalt und Siedlungsbank*) extended agricultural credits. And the Transportation Bank (*Deutsche Verkehrs-Kredit-Bank*) financed transportation investments. A businessman who received a government order would draw a draft on one of these "banks," ordering it to pay to the order of a person a designated sum of money. The bank would accept the draft, which made it eligible for immediate sale in the open market or to the Reichsbank. Or the bank would have its own bills accepted by other institutions in order to finance the project directly. The Reich government guaranteed it all, promising to repay

[22]

Reichsbank Credit (in billions of Reichsmarks)			
Year	Total	Bills Discounted	Full-Employment Bills
1932	3.448	2.806	1.904
1933	4.037	3.177	1.644
1934	4.977	4.021	2.955
1935	5.358	4.498	3.696
1936	6.108	5.448	4.643

Banker's Bills (Acceptances) (in billions of Reichsmarks)		
Year	Total	Full-Employment Bills
1932	9.27	—
1933	8.61	—
1934	9.79	2.42
1935	12.70	5.41
1936	15.05	8.32

Source: Heinrich Irmler, "Bankenkrise und Vollbeschäftigungspolitik (1931-1936)" Währung und Wirtschaft, 1876-1975 (Frankfurt am Main: Fritz Knapp, 1976), p. 322.

all bills and acceptances between 1934 and 1938. Long-term financing was then to be made available from government revenues, or from the capital market, or from repayment by the beneficiaries, *e.g.*, of a loan.

Together with this monetary expansion through short-term instruments came tax reductions that aimed at inducing a revival. The high rates imposed by the Brüning Administration were retained except for those levies a reduction of which would hopefully stimulate employment. Treasury Assistant Secretary for Tax Policy, F. Reinhardt, spearheaded the following reform:

1. As of March 31, 1933, all newly licensed motor vehicles were exempted from taxation. The owners of old vehicles were given the alternative of meeting all future registration fees and levies with a lump-sum payment. This measure was eminently successful in stimulating automobile production.

2. All capital replacement expenditures were made fully depreciable during the year they were made. In an economy that evidenced symptoms of "overcapacity" and therefore lacked proper capital replacements, a special stimulation of the capital goods industry seemed to be in order. Also this particular reduction in income taxation proved to be highly successful.

3. A ten percent income tax credit was granted for renovations and expansions of buildings.

4. All pre-1933 overdue income tax liabilities were cancelled provided the amount due was invested in renovations, expansions, and replacements.

5. Households employing domestic servants received additional income tax exemptions for dependents. This measure, which openly aimed at employment rather than redistribution, also had its desired effects.

6. In order to induce some three million women to leave the labor market of six million, loans of 500 to 800 marks were granted upon the establishment of new households. The loans were interest-free and repayable in monthly installments of one percent. Every birth of a child then cancelled one-fourth of the loan. To raise the revenue for this measure higher tax rates were imposed on bachelors.

7. Various other tax rates were lowered to benefit farmers, home owners, and wholesalers. Employer levies in support of the unemployment compensation fund were reduced as unemployment declined.[23]

This tax reform together with the credit expansion mentioned

---

[23]Willi Albers, "Finanzpolitik in der Depression und in der Vollbeschäftigung," *ibid.*, pp. 355, 356.

above, produced its foreseen effects. Since it lowered business costs, especially in favored industries, it raised the marginal productivity of labor and thereby stimulated the demand for labor. Hitler recognized the importance of full employment for the victory of his party and the foundation of his dictatorial regime. His "labor battle," as he called the reform program, met with the enthusiastic approval of most people.

Financial Policy During Full Employment (1936-1939)

At the end of 1936 German unemployment had fallen below one million, which in those years of worldwide depression meant full employment. The economic expansion together with the wage freeze since 1933 had significantly reduced labor costs, which had brought forth the desired demand for labor. Production increased substantially, boosting profits significantly. But goods prices began to rise, which prompted the administration in 1936 to impose comprehensive price controls. By 1939, at the beginning of the war, prices had risen merely nine percent in six years, which in modern terminology would be called remarkable stability. Of course, the German economy was no longer a market system, but a command order organized for war.

During this so-called "full-employment phase," labor income is estimated to have risen some seventy percent. Eighteen percent of this improvement is ascribed primarily to longer working hours raising average income. Fifty-two percent must be attributed to the expansion of employment.[24] The freeze of wage rates surprisingly did not generate popular dissatisfaction or create political problems. After so many years of unemployment or under-employment, the population was happy about the opportunity to work and grateful for the job security.

In 1936 the soaring profits led to the only prewar tax boost. The corporate income tax, which had claimed twenty percent of business income, was raised to twenty-five percent in 1936 and thirty percent in 1937. Revenue from this tax alone quadrupled in four years (from 593 million marks in 1935 to 2.417 billion marks in 1938), which indicates the remarkable rise in corporate profits.

Symptoms of excess demand made their first appearance in 1937. Shortages developed in a number of consumers' goods, especially in meats and dairy products. Long waiting lists appeared for many items of housing construction, and for tools and dies that were needed in the armament industries. The inexorable laws of the mar-

---

[24] *Loc. cit.*, p. 360.

ket, officially outlawed by an omnipotent regime, were revealing their effects to anyone able and willing to see, while the government moved ahead on the highways and byways of the command order. It introduced a comprehensive rationing system that allocated essential goods and services according to National Socialistic concepts of merit and adequacy. The distribution of important foods was organized by way of "customer lists," that is, consumers were requested to register with a grocer for goods allocation and redemption of ration cards and coupons. The sale of important raw materials as well as construction materials and tools and dies proceeded along similar lines. Thus a minutely regimented distribution system resembling that of an army garrison came into existence.

From 1935 on, armament expenditures exceeded one-half of all government expenditures. By 1939 they surpassed seventy-five percent, which meant that the economic expansion did not improve civilian consumption. Under the motto, "Cannons instead of butter," the government openly asked for sacrifices on behalf of national defense. The Reichsbank under Hjalmar Schacht lent its support by rediscounting armament bills and holding them for a number of years. The private bank that accepted such bills and then placed them with commercial banks or rediscounted them with the Reichsbank was a sham organization, Metal Research Inc. (Metallforschung GmbH), that made its appearance as early as 1933. Its acceptances were guaranteed by the Reich.

After 1938 the monetarization of debt for rearmament was supplemented by the issue of tax certificates that enjoyed limited legal tender qualities. Public institutions, such as the nationalized railroads and the postal service, paid forty percent of their construction orders with "tax certificates" (Steuergutscheine) that were acceptable for later tax payments. The certificates could also be used to pay subcontractors. One type bore no interest and matured in six months; another type paid four percent and matured in three years. Both types constituted not only a new kind of money but also new government debt.

The Reichsbank was to undergo a radical change that made it an integral instrument of government. The banking law of 1924 had created an autonomous central bank that was responsible for the integrity of the mark and the preservation of the gold standard. A law of October 27, 1933, authorized Chancellor Hitler to appoint the Reichsbank president and its board of directors. It also granted the bank the right to conduct open-market policies. A reform act of February 10, 1937, then placed the Reichsbank under the immediate command of the Führer and Chancellor and instructed it to attend directly and immediately to the fiscal affairs of the State. The bank thus became an integral administrative unit of government. Yet, the

bank's board of directors under Hjalmar Schacht showed remarkable
courage and independence when, in January 1939, it petitioned Hitler
for monetary discipline and restraint: "No central bank can safeguard
the currency from the inflationary expenditures of government."
This petition, together with other annoying attempts at restraint,
led to the immediate dismissal of Schacht and several board members.
A new banking law of June 15, 1939, then nationalized the bank and
reiterated that henceforth, "the German Reichsbank was to be managed under the supervision of the Führer and Chancellor according
to his instructions." The process of Reichsbank integration into the
command order that permeated all economic activities had now been
completed.[25]

War Economy and Inflation, 1939-1945

The German currency now was *de facto* and *de jure* a *fiat* currency,
free of any restraint and limitation. It had no ties to gold; political
authorities determined its rate of expansion and volume of circulation. The Führer held final authority over all money and credit transactions and, in particular, over the amount the Reichsbank could
discount. Thus all prerequisites were given for the "noiseless" war
financing that was to follow.

The economic command system of 1939 was already a "war economy." It needed no major readjustments or changes, merely a few
supplementary regulations. The rationing and allocation system was
extended to all important consumers' goods. The newspapers would
announce the available rations of food, such as bread, butter, meat,
sugar, *etc.* For clothing, shoes, bedding, *etc.*, coupons were issued
upon application and proof of need. Surely all allocated goods needed
to be paid for, but the coupon or ration card was the primary authority for purchase. The State, too, needed to pay for all its goods and
services. But throughout those years of total war it never suffered
from lack of money and purchasing power. Its economic problems
had been reduced to the application of persuasion and force for the
procurement of labor, raw materials, and facilities of production.

The German government made every effort to pay for most of its
war expenditures with tax revenues. The income tax was raised
immediately by fifty percent, but not in excess of sixty-five percent of
income. Excise taxes on beer, brandy, champagne, and tobacco were

[25]Bruno Schultz, *Kleine deutsche Geldgeschichte des 19. und 20. Jahrhunderts* (Berlin:
Duncker und Humblot, 1976), pp. 222-250; cf. C. W. Guillebaud, *The Economic Recovery of
Germany* (London: Macmillan and Company, 1939); J. Klein, "German Money and
Prices 1932-1944," *Studies in the Quantity Theory of Money*, Milton Friedman, ed. (Chicago:
University of Chicago Press, 1956); Hjalmar Schacht, *Abrechnung mit Hitler* (Hamburg:
Rowahlt Verlag, 1948).

94

boosted significantly. Since the corporate income tax had been raised shortly before the war, it remained unchanged until August 1941, when "war supplements" were imposed. For all manufacturing it was raised once more in March 1942. Dividend payments in excess of six percent of capital stock were prohibited.

To absorb private purchasing power and tap more sources of income, the State sought to collect future taxes in advance. A decree of July 1942 extracted a lump-sum payment from house owners, equal to ten years of real estate taxation, which was to discharge all future tax obligations. This device, which proved to be very productive of revenue, was presented as an opportunity for a suitable wartime investment that hopefully would induce individuals to spend less and save more.

A decree of October 1941 introduced the "iron savings account" offering certain tax advantages. Every employee could deposit twenty-six marks of his monthly income with a bank through payroll withholding, and half of his Christmas bonuses up to five hundred marks. The account was frozen throughout the war, *i.e.*, it was not transferable, but it was inheritable. It paid the same interest as other regular savings accounts. The deposits as well as their interest payments were exempt from income taxation and social security levies. He who failed to appreciate the opportunity of this savings program was persuaded through "voluntary force" to open his "iron savings account." In a similar manner, businessmen were induced to create credit accounts with the Internal Revenue Service through advance tax payments. Furthermore, they were invited to establish "commodity acquisition accounts" with the IRS. Both accounts, blocked for the duration of the war, created tax-free savings that were channelled directly to the government.

The Reich did not overlook the ancient device of extracting subsidies from the occupied countries. Bohemia, Moravia, Poland, and many others had to make war contributions. Even the German states, communities, and other public corporations were forced to bear their share. Altogether, the Reich managed to cover approximately one-half of its 1941-42 defense expenditures, or 75.6 billion marks, through taxation (32.3 billion) and other internal revenue (5.6 billion).[26]

Despite all efforts at extracting revenue from every conceivable source, huge deficits remained and grew bigger during the later years of the war. Once again the Reichsbank was called upon to grant short-term assistance through the purchase of Treasury bills. Its printing presses were rolling. Simultaneously the fiscal authorities developed an ingenious method of finance that noiselessly converted a large share of Reichsbank debt to middle- and long-term debt. This

Age of Inflation

method made all government appeals to public patriotism superfluous, and eliminated all public campaigns and drives for the subscription of war bonds and notes. The government simply placed its medium- and long-term obligations with the financial institutions that were accumulating the savings, *i.e.*, with commercial banks, savings banks, credit unions, and insurance companies. Because the

26

The Budget of the Reich
Receipts and Outlays 1938-1945
(in billions of Reichsmarks)

Fiscal Year	1938-39	1939-40	1940-41	1941-42	1942-43	1943-44	1944-March 7,45
Total Outlays	31.8	52.1	78.0	101.9	128.6	153.0	171.3
National defense	18.4	32.3	58.1	75.6	96.9	117.9	128.4
Family allowance	—	(a)	(a)	4.8	5.5	6.5	8.1
Interest	1.3	1.9	2.8	4.2	5.9	6.6	10.5
Amortization of debt and other obligations	1.0	1.3	1.7	1.9	2.1	1.8	2.8
Total Revenue	28.8	39.5	57.6	75.0	91.6	96.2	89.7
Taxes and tariffs	18.2	24.2	27.5	32.3	42.7	38.0	37.5
Contributions by states and communities	—	.8	1.4	1.4	1.6	2.0	2.5
Funded debt [b]	7.5	6.6	18.5	22.9	22.0	28.4	21.0
Other revenue	—	—	6.1	12.2	18.9	20.3	23.6
Deficit	3.0	12.6	20.4	26.9	37.0	56.8	81.6

(a) Data unavailable
(b) Including contributions by occupied territories to occupation costs

Indebtedness of the Reich
1938-1945
(in billions of Reichsmarks)

End of Fiscal Year	1938-39	1939-40	1940-41	1941-42	1942-43	1943-44	1944-end of war
Total Treasury Debt	30.7	47.9	86.0	137.7	195.6	273.4	379.8
Old debt incurred before 4/1/1924	3.4	3.2	2.9	2.7	2.6	2.4	2.1
New debt	27.4	44.7	83.1	135.0	193.0	271.0	377.7
(a) foreign	1.3	1.2	1.2	1.2	1.2	1.2	1.3
(b) domestic	26.1	43.5	81.9	133.8	191.9	269.8	376.4
Long- and medium-term	19.6	25.5	43.7	66.9	88.4	115.6	135.4
Short-term	6.5	18.0	38.2	66.9	103.5	154.2	241.0
Treasury bills	6.1	11.3	21.3	35.1	57.5	88.9	102.7
Acceptances	.4	6.5	14.9	26.0	37.3	61.2	116.0
Other debt [a]	.2	4.2	3.7	4.4	2.1	1.9	2.0
Private Bills Guaranteed by the Reich	11.9	11.4	10.8	10.1	9.5	8.8	8.1

a Tax credit certificates, production and supply debt, armed services certificates

Source: Statistisches Handbuch von Deutschland *(Munich: Länderrat of the American Occupation Zone, 1949), p.* 555.

quantity of available consumers' goods was shrinking throughout the war, making way for greater armament production, a rising share of personal income no longer found real goods and therefore was saved. Upon deposit of these savings with financial institutions they were immediately invested in medium- and long-term obligations of the Reich.

The public was hardly aware of this "noiseless" war financing. The gradual impoverishment of the people was accompanied by a rapid growth of savings that were generally mistaken for rising personal wealth. After all, everyone could watch his bank balance grow steadily, promising better living conditions in the future. Many bought new life insurance or greatly increased their coverage. Of course, those funds, too, were channelled directly to the treasuries of the Reich. When an insured amount was payable in case of death, it was deposited in a bank that would lend it to the Reich. The government thus managed to place almost one-half of its obligations in financial institutions. Unfortunately, national savings were smaller than the government demand for medium- and long-term loans, which necessitated Reichsbank financing of the balance through discounting of Treasury bills. The quantity of Reichsbank notes therefore continued to rise.

Emission of Reichsbank Notes (in billions of Reichsmarks)			
March 31		March 31	
1933	3.520	1941	14.188
1936	4.267	1942	19.774
1937	4.938	1943	24.697
1938	5.622	1944	33.792
1939	8.311	1945	56.400
1940	12.176		

Source: *Bruno Schultz*, op. cit., p. 246.

As can be seen from the table, the quantity of Reichsbank notes doubled between 1933 and 1939. During the first two years of the war it rose by less than six billion marks. Thereafter it rose very quickly. From 1941 to 1944 it more than doubled, and doubled again during the last twelve months. The total quantity at the end of the war can only be estimated. Some sources set the amount at sixty-five to seventy billion, others even higher.

The credit expansion by commercial banks kept pace with the Reichsbank note emission. Their total liabilities rose from 50.1 billion marks in July 1936 to 276.8 billion in September 1944, of which 97.2 billion were time deposits. Their assets, consisting of Treasury bills and acceptances, soared from 7.3 billion to 90.5 billion; market instruments and participations from 8.2 billion to 76.2 billion; and other loans from 12.9 billion to 63.1 billion.[27]

Contrary to all principles of economics, this vast expansion of money did not lead to higher prices. The state with its awesome power and coercion "stabilized" the purchasing power of money through stop orders and rationing systems. Daily spot checks of prices, followed by public prosecutions and severe punishments, brutally maintained the price structure. Wages were permitted to rise by a mere two percent in almost six years of war effort. However, total labor income rose by more than fifty percent because of the growing labor force and the longer workday. A decree of December 12, 1939, lengthened the permissible workday to ten hours.

A rising share of personal income no longer could buy anything and therefore was tramping about the economy. A "money surplus" came into existence that defied all government efforts at capture by the bank deposit system or the life insurance method. It formed the demand component of the black market that slowly grew in importance. Consumers' goods became available without coupons and ration cards at higher prices and with "Vitamin C," i.e., "connections" (in German popular usage, "Vitamin B" for *Beziehungen*). Severe fines and sentences failed to suppress the budding black markets.

Toward the end of the war the Allied bombing of German cities with its massive destruction of housing actually fomented the disarrangement of the monetary command order. The damage to personal property led to the withdrawal of more and more savings in order to replace the losses of furniture, household effects, clothing, *etc.* People used these funds to search, often desperately, for real goods, and when none could be found through official channels of distribution, traded on the black markets. Similarly, the "compensation funds" that were paid promptly for damages suffered often found their way to the black markets.

By 1940 the old coinage consisting of silver, nickel, and copper began to disappear. But before a great deal could find its way into private hoards the government was quick to replace the old coins with its own substitutes. The *Rentenbank*, which in 1923 had facilitated the currency stabilization, was reactivated and issued one and two mark notes replacing the silver coins. The fifty *Pfenning* coins were made of aluminum, and the ten, five, and one *Pfenning* coins of zinc. Hoarding of old coins was made punishable with fines and imprisonment.

---

[27]Bruno Schultz, *op. cit.*, pp. 246, 247.

The growing flood of paper money and the mountains of aluminum and zinc coins were further supplemented by special issues of paper *fiat* with limited legal tender standing. In the occupied countries and territories the armed forces issued at least three additional types of notes: "credit certificates" that were provided by a special bank, the *Reichskreditkasse;* "auxiliary media of payment"; and "clearing notes," which the armed forces created and issued without banking assistance.[28] During the final months of the war when money shipments were severely disrupted or completely prevented by air raids, the resulting shortages were alleviated through the issue of "emergency money." Reichsbank branches in Salzburg, Graz, and Linz simply manufactured photocopies of ten, fifty, and one hundred Reichsbank notes and emitted them in Austria and Southern Germany with full legal tender quality. Many of these notes were printed only on one side. Other branches in Northern Germany issued their own "credit certificates" or those of the *Reichskreditkasse* that were meant for occupied territories. The Provincial Bank of Saxony created its own notes for circulation in the east. Many cities and communities in the southwest desperately printed primitive shinplaster that took the place of the Reichsbank paper lost in transport from Berlin.[29]

The monetary disintegration paralleled the military collapse of Germany. Through conquest and capitulation the Reich ceased to exist. Its money lingered on for three more years, together with coupons and ration cards, until it was swept away along with so many other traces of the Reich.

Monetary Conditions During Occupation, 1945-1948

The chaos in money and banking that had spread over Germany during the last months of the war had a paralyzing effect on all economic life. It is difficult to estimate the great depth of the collapse. But it is probably no exaggeration to state that individual income in terms of purchasing power did not exceed ten percent of prewar income. By 1947, two years after the war, when economic production had been redirected toward consumers' goods and millions of former members of the armed forces and more millions of refugees had joined the production process, national income was estimated at barely one-half of the 1936 income.[30] But the quantity of money in the broader sense had grown more than sixfold, *i.e.*, from less than fifty billion marks to some three hundred billion (notes, seventy

---

[28]For a discussion of the inflation in occupied countries see A.J. Brown, *The Great Inflation 1939—1951* (London: Oxford University Press, 1955), p. 28 *et. seq.*

[29]Compare Günter Schmölders, *Geldpolitik* (Tübingen, Mohr, and Zurich: Polygraphisher Verlag, 1968), p. 344 *et seq.*

billion; savings accounts, one hundred and twenty-five billion; and other bank accounts, one hundred billion).[31]

In 1945 and 1946 the Allied occupation forces added some 12 billion "military marks" in denominations of one-half, one, five, ten, twenty, fifty, one hundred, and one thousand marks. They were equal to those issued by the Reich, and were used for the payment of troops and civilian employees. When the twenty mark note became the object of massive counterfeiting it was withdrawn from circulation.

The military government raised all tax rates to extraordinary levels, especially the individual and corporate income taxes, property and estate taxes, and all excise and sales taxes. Law No. 12, for instance, imposed progressive income tax rates up to ninety-five percent. The top rate applied to annual incomes of sixty thousand marks and higher, which at prewar exchange rates were worth $14,285. On the free money markets in Germany as well as in neighboring countries, the United States dollar was selling at two hundred marks and was rising. When calculated at these exchange rates the ninety-five percent income tax rates applied to all annual incomes of $300, or $25 per month. But few Germans admittedly earned such high incomes under the wage-control system.

The fierce taxation by the Allies reflected, among other things, their growing concern about the monetary situation. Surely, they could have continued to issue "military marks" until the German population as well as the occupation troops would have shunned them in a flight from all *fiat* monies, like that which occurred in 1923. But in 1946 the Western Allies chose to stabilize the siutation by refraining from expanding the money quantitites much further. Henceforth Allied troops were paid in their own national currencies, and military marks were issued sparingly upon special request only. Allied expenditures were borne by the Allies themselves or were covered by the revenue that flowed from German taxation. For the fiscal year 1946-47 they reported with pride that the occupation budget was in balance.[32] Yet the mark continued to depreciate, and the black markets assumed an ever greater role in the daily lives of the people. A number of factors contributed to this ominous development that gave the postwar period its most significant characteristics.

The Soviet Union had been in possession of duplicate American plates of the military marks since April 1944. By the time the Soviet

[30]F. Grünig, "Die Wirtschäftstatigkeit nach dem Zusammenbruch im Vergleich zur Vorkriegszeit," Die deutsche Wirtschaft zwei Jahre nach dem Zusammenbruch, (Berlin: Deutsches Institut für Wirtschaftsordnung, 1947), p. 70.

[31]Karl-Heinrich Hansmeyer und Rolf Caesar, "Kriegswirtschaft und Inflation (1936-1948)," Währung und Wirtschaft, op. cit.,p. 418.

[32]Bruno Schultz, op. cit., p. 252.

armies entered Germany they were supplied with large quantities of Russian-made marks, which they were spreading "like fall leaves over the country." Many billions of marks were distributed by the handsful with rations to millions of Russian soliders. Yet their impact on the German economy must not be overstated.[33] There was no market economy in which money could be freely exchanged for economic goods. But even if there had been such a system, the Communist troops neither traded nor bargained for whatever they needed or desired, nor did their victims who, fearing for life and limb, made themselves appear even more wretched than their Communist conquerors. Well-to-do Germans — especially businessmen, capitalists and landowners — were escaping to the Western zones, leaving behind everything they could not carry. The poor people who would not or could not make the hazardous trip across the zone border were hiding their few belongings. In short, under Communist occupation few Germans traded voluntarily with their masters. Even fewer Germans sought to deal with them illegally. To be dubbed a black marketeer had been dangerous under Hitler; it was fatal under Stalin.

The black market that nevertheless came into existence in Berlin and at the Soviet Zone border was created primarily by Allied occupation troops, civilians, and displaced persons. Russian soldiers with satchels of military marks were eagerly seeking American consumers' goods, especially cigarettes, clothing, watches, jewelry, and anything the American GI was willing to exchange for military marks. The Russian soldier thus acquired a pair of boots, a Mickey Mouse watch or two, while the American soldier received many thousands of marks, which he then converted into thousands of United States dollars through the medium of United States finance offices, and then invested in a beautiful home with a swimming pool, back in Florida. The United States Treasury, and ultimately the American taxpayers, financed it all.

Some of those Soviet marks undoubtedly found their way into the Western zones. Here, the end of the war had brought a radical readjustment of outlook from mere survival under wartime conditions to a new life aimed at restoring and rebuilding individual lives and economic well-being. The German veteran who during the war had been occupied solely with the daily task of survival had completely ignored his "iron savings account." But now he was eager to withdraw his savings to rebuild his economic life and make plans for his future. When official channels of distribution failed to provide the

[33]For an interesting discussion of some of the unintended ramifications of the delivery of duplicate plates to the Soviet Union, see Vladimir Petrov, *Money and Conquest* (Baltimore: The Johns Hopkins University Press, 1967), pp. 188-197.

desired economic goods his funds often turned to black markets. The situation was similar with every enterprise eager to repair and rebuild, resume operations, or just readjust from armament production to peacetime manufacture of consumers' goods. They all scrambled for liquid funds in order to finance the new beginning. In most cases the black markets offered the only opportunity.

Other changes also gave encouragement and support to the black markets. No matter how severe Allied law enforcement may have been, its fines and penalties for black market misdemeanors did not compare in severity with the punishment of economic crimes by the Nazi regime. Also, there were no more Nazis who would inform the authorities of illegal economic activities. Without much danger from informers and spies, practically everyone felt free to resume his economic existence to which the black markets could contribute so much. The fierce taxation imposed by the military government gave great impetus to black-marketeering. It led to massive tax evasion and thus created "hot monies" that had nowhere to go but to the black markets.

Despite all controls, ever more consumers' goods found their way from the official distribution system to the black markets where prices were much higher. In 1948 the flight into real goods began to accelerate. Nearly everyone now sought to convert as much money as possible into real goods in order to escape confiscation or cancellation through the expected currency reform. An American cigarette cost six to ten marks, a pound of coffee four hundred to six hundred, and a radio three thousand marks. It was often difficult to find such marketable goods, for the merchants themselves were hoarding them in the hope of selling them some day for better money.

Nearly all coins disappeared from use in exchange. Their metallic value as pieces of aluminum and zinc began to exceed their purchasing power as money. It was commonly assumed that a currency reform would not immediately provide a new coinage, and therefore would temporarily retain the old one with new purchasing power. Therefore, postage stamps, trading stamps, and other pieces of paper served to make change while the people were clinging to their coins. No picture could depict the conditions of 1948 more vividly than that of a wretched individual guarding his hoard of small pieces of aluminum and zinc.

While the monetary order was gradually disintegrating, a particular commodity emerged as the most marketable good, serving as the favorite medium of exchange: the American cigarette. The Allied troops used it in their dealings with the population, and the Germans among themselves. It could render all monetary services and as such could take its place as "cigarette currency" in most economic exchanges. It even served as the unit of calculation because its exchange value remained remarkably stable despite massive shipments from the United States. After all, a cigarette would serve as a medium of exchange just once or twice and then be withdrawn from circulation through consumption. It was an expensive currency, but more dependable and honest by far than the various issues of government *fiat* money. It was a free currency, free of all government regulations and controls that were throttling economic life and hastening economic disintegration.[34]

The Allied government helplessly watched official industrial output fall to twenty percent of the 1938 capacity and the shortage of consumers' goods reach catastrophic proportions. It reacted in a fashion that may be typical for military minds: It enforced with vigor and severity Eisenhower Proclamation No. 1, which had rigidly fixed all prices at the May 8, 1945, levels. It laid the blame for the economic disorder on the Reichsmark inflation and, with self-righteous condemnation, indicted the "economic immorality" of the people who were travelling about the countryside in search of black market supplies. It never occurred to the mighty authorities that their proclamation No. 1 and the continuation of Nazi economic controls were the primary causes of the disaster. Instead, they set out to launch ambitious "re-education programs," and on June 21, 1948, conducted a comprehensive currency reform.

The Currency Reform of 1948

For the man in the street, the currency reform, which the Western powers decreed suddenly without the cooperation of the Soviet Union, signalled a new beginning, the dawn of a new economic era. For an economist it was the command order's final operation that proved to be successful only because the German authorities under Ludwig Erhard simultaneously conducted an economic reform. They restored the freedom of markets and thus gave free play to the inexorable laws of human action. It was the competitive private property order that gave new hope and instilled new life in the German nation. It was capitalism that was to surprise the world as "the miracle of German recovery." The Allies watched the economic reform with great anxiety and misgiving. In fact, General Lucius D. Clay, the Allied Director for Economic Policy, sent a stern memorandum to Ludwig Erhard, the provisional German director, reminding him that the economic edicts of the military government could not be altered without prior permission. Professor Erhard's courageous answer de-

---

[34] Compare Günter Schmölders, "Die Zigarettenwährung," *Kölner Universitätszeitung*, Volume 5 (1947), p. 70.

serves to be repeated again and again: "I did not alter your controls, I abolished them."[35]

On Saturday, June 19, 1948, the military government announced three laws on the reorganization of the currency system: a Currency Law, an Emission Law, and a Conversion Law. The first two became effective the following Monday, the latter one week later. The Currency Law established the Deutsche Mark as the only legal tender currency and voided all other issues. In exchange for old marks each resident received sixty Deutsche Marks of which forty were paid immediately and twenty within two months. In order to avoid duplications and other irregularities, the ration card agencies were entrusted with the distribution of the money. All old money had to be deposited in a banking account. Businesses received an advance of sixty Deutsche Marks per employee. State and local governments were allotted an amount equal to their average monthly revenue. The military government allocated some twelve percent of the new issue to itself.

The Emission Law gave sole authority for the issue of notes and coins to the *Bank Deutscher Lander*. It imposed neither reserve requirements nor redemption obligations. The maximum amount of Deutsche Mark issue was set at ten billion. The Conversion Law provided for a conversion of all Reichsmark deposits with financial institutions. The basic exchange rate of old Reichsmarks to new Deutsche Marks was set at ten to one. Half of the converted amount was placed in "free accounts" and made available for immediate withdrawal. However, the "free account" was subject to a ceiling of 250 DM for individuals and families and 500 DM for businessmen and professional people. Greater amounts required review and authorization by the Internal Revenue Service, which sought to trace and tax retroactively illegal income from black-marketeering and other unauthorized economic activity.

Half of the converted amount remained frozen temporarily. Four months later, in October 1948, seventy percent was voided, twenty percent set free, and ten percent made available for certain investments in middle- and long-term obligations. In the final analysis, therefore, one hundred Reichsmarks deposited in financial institutions were converted to 6.5 Deutsche Marks. Bank deposits owned by public institutions were voided summarily, *e.g.*, those of the military government, the states and their subdivisions, the nationalized railroad, and the postal service. They received the original allocation mentioned above. The Conversion Law voided all Reich obligations

---

[35] Volkmar Muthesius, *Augenzeuge von drei Inflationen* (Frankfurt am Main: Fritz Knapp Verlag, 1973), p. 111.

and interbank deposits, but granted new government obligations, a cash reserve, and some capital stock to all financial institutions, thereby providing the necessary assets against new deposit liabilities.

All other debt obligations were converted at a ratio of 10 : 1. That is, all creditor claims were reduced by ninety percent. But in order to avoid any debtor profits from such a conversion, debtor obligations were reinstated fully in new marks, of which ten percent were payable to the creditor and ninety percent to the German government. Legislation that followed in September 1948 imposed the ninety percent levy for purposes of "equalization of war burdens" (Lastenausgleich).[36] In short, one thousand DM of an old ten thousand mark mortgage were payable to the creditor and nine thousand DM to the German government. The same conversion ratio applied to all corporate bonds, debentures, notes, annuities, and other financial obligations of private instititions. Wages, salaries, rents, pensions, and other recurring obligations were not converted. Similarly, obligations of partnership, inheritance, and divorce and obligations between marriage partners, parents, and children and social security contributions and benefits remained unaffected.[37]

The Deutsche Mark thus ventured upon its journey. In a conspicuous send-off and for lasting support the military government substantially reduced its tax levies. For lower income brackets the tax rates were cut in half while a steep progression was retained for higher brackets. The levy on annual incomes of thirty thousand marks, for instance, which had claimed 18,803 marks, or sixty-three percent, was reduced to 14,418 marks, or forty-eight percent. The corporate income tax was set at a uniform rate of fifty percent. Excise taxes on luxury items remained at prohibitive levels, e.g., fifteen DM ($3.57) on a pound of coffee.

A discussion of the currency reform of 1948 would be grossly deficient if no mention were made of the reform conducted by the Soviet military government in East Germany. In contrast to that in the West which brought forth an entirely new currency system, the Soviet reform merely reduced the stock of notes and coins and devalued certain bank deposits at various rates. This does not mean

---

[36]Between September 1948 and August 1952 Allied and German legislation established an "equalization of war burdens fund" that was to compensate refugees and victims of war damages. It paid a bonus to those owners of bank deposits, debt instruments, and life insurance contracts who had held them from 1939 and earlier. For them the bonus improved the conversion ratio to two DM for ten Reichsmarks. All profits from debt conversion were assigned to this fund. In addition, the equalization laws placed an indenture of fifty percent of market value on most personal and real property. It was payable over thirty years and carried an interest of four percent.

[37]Hans Möller, "Die westdeutsche Währungsreform," Währung und Wirtschaft, op. cit., pp. 433-483.

that the Soviet reform was less severe than that in the West. In fact, all bank accounts in the Soviet zone had been blocked since the summer of 1945. It is interesting to note that the West German reform caught the Soviet authorities by surprise. They, nevertheless, conducted their ten to one exchange within a few days after the Western reform by attaching validation coupons to old Reichsbank notes.

The Soviet government sought to extend its reform to West Berlin, which was occupied and governed by the Western powers. When they rejected the Soviet plan, the Soviets reacted strongly. They proceeded to enforce a blockade of West Berlin with its Allied garrisons and 2.5 million inhabitants, with the intention of driving out the Western powers. The prompt answer of the West was a counter-blockade of the Soviet zone and an airlift for the supply of Berlin. For fifteen months of confrontation American planes supplied the beleaguered city with needed food, fuel, and raw materials.

The Alternative Reforms

The currency reform of 1948 was probably the most comprehensive and incisive reform in the history of *fiat* money. In the ideological and institutional setting of its time it was welcomed by all. After all, a flight from the *fiat* Reichsmark had begun and several money substitutes were taking its place. Once such a flight is under way it tends to accelerate until in a mass stampede the currency is extirpated entirely. When a currency is irreparably damaged, like the German Reichsmark of 1948, it must be replaced as soon as possible with other media. This, then, raises all the problems and issues of a new beginning which a currency reform is to facilitate.

The Western Allies chose to re-establish another national *fiat* system with legal tender force. It proved to be rather successful in the eyes of most contemporaries because Professor Erhard and his German colleagues provided the free market setting in which the Deutsche Mark began to function satisfactorily. But it raises the gnawing question of how it would have functioned under the strictures and limitations of a command order as it was established first by the Nazi regime and then reinforced by the Eisenhower Proclamation. Would such a setting not have necessitated more currency reforms in order to reduce again and again the ratio of the growing quantity of money to the given supply of economic goods?

Surely the military government with its undisputed powers over the vanquished nation could have chosen several other alternatives of reform. When the Allied armies entered Germany, they could have repealed all Nazi regulations and controls, which would have restored the competitive market order and given rise to an immediate miracle of German revival. Goods prices would have soared and the Reichsmark would have fallen. But it probably would have "stabilized" with much lower purchasing power provided the military government refrained from emitting its own military marks. In fact, it is likely that after a few months of doubt and uncertainty the shrunken mark would have become exceptionally hard, as there was no Reich to inflate it. By now, in 1979, after many years of worldwide inflation, it could have been the most reliable currency in the world.

There were other intriguing alternatives for reform. The military government could have freed all economic activity from Nazi restraints and controls and continued to issue generous quantities of military marks. It could have repealed the Nazi foreign exchange controls and freed the foreign exchange markets which in time would have brought large quantities of United States dollars, British pounds sterling, and French francs to Germany. In a massive flight from the depreciating Reichsmark the Germans would have used these other currencies as their money. It is reasonable to assume that the United States dollar would have become the most important currency in Germany. Now, in 1979, the United States dollar probably would have had a sister currency, the German "Thaler."

In a nineteenth century setting, the conquerer would have repealed immediately all government controls and regulations, outlawed all paper issues, and permitted only gold and silver coins with his emblem to be minted. After a short transitional period in which monetary substitutes, such as cigarettes and coffee, would have facilitated economic exchanges, large quantities of gold and silver coins would have entered Germany from abroad, or been minted in huge quantities by the smelters of gold and silverware. A high purchasing power of coins would have made it most advantageous to reprocess objects made of gold and silver in order to create the needed currency.

If the Austrians had conquered Germany and Austrian economists had conducted the reform, they would have proceeded along similar lines. In his great classic *The Theory of Money and Credit,* Professor von Mises described how he would conduct a reform in "Ruritania." He would ban all money printing and permit gold to be traded freely. He would, once the market price of gold had been found, adopt this price as the new legal parity of the mark and secure its unconditional convertibility at this parity. A new "conversion agency" would sell gold bullion to the public against paper marks and buy any amount of gold offered at the legal parity. Thereafter, transition from this gold bullion standard would be achieved by an exchange of the mark notes for newly minted coins.[38]

When pressed for his proposal for a currency reform, this writer

[38]Ludwig von Mises, *The Theory of Money and Credit, op. cit.,* p. 435.

must confess that he would have conducted the simplest reform of all. He would pass no reform law, seek no conversion or parity, and offer no government cooperation. He would merely cease and desist from interfering with the inalienable rights of man. In particular, he would restore immediately all economic freedoms and repeal all legal tender laws. The freedom to trade and hold gold, the freedom to use gold in all exchanges, and the freedom to mint coins would bring forth the ideal currency to which all others could repair.

Of course, all such deliberations are idle speculations of an arm-chair economist. The victors of World War II chose to replace a defunct *fiat* currency with a new *fiat* system. It cannot surprise us, therefore, that the old forces of inflation and depreciation are gnawing again at the purchasing power of the Deutsche Mark. Since 1948 it has lost almost one-half of its exchange value. In comparison with so many other decaying national currencies it has performed rather well. But when compared with gold, man's money of the ages, it is a pitiful *ersatz*.

IV
THE FEDERAL RESERVE
SYSTEM

Banks are institutions for lending, borrowing, and caring for money. Bankers are the intermediaries between the grantors of credit and the grantees, the creditors and the debtors. They provide the organized markets for lendable funds and the demand for them. This basic function must be sharply distinguished from all other branches of their business that modern banks have assumed in recent decades. Bankers provide a fundamental economic service without which our high productivity, which flows from division of labor and capital formation, could not possibly be maintained.

Central banking is a manifestation of government control over the people's banking and money. It first developed in England during the eighteenth century when a private bank, the Bank of England, obtained special privileges through its dealings with the British government. During the last one hundred years the countries in Europe and America unfortunately followed the British example by adopting similar institutions of their own. The United States government followed in 1913. The Federal Reserve Act was Congress' answer to the phenomenon of the trade cycle that time and again had befallen the United States as well as Western Europe. The panic of 1907 and the subsequent lethargy of business and finance had given the last impetus to widespread clamor for banking and currency reform.

"We need a more flexible currency," the advocates of reorganization of the American banking system asserted, "a currency that can be made to expand or contract in accordance with the true needs and requirements of business." With a new central bank it was hoped that the recurring periods of financial stress and disorder could be avoided. They were pointing at the currency systems in Western Europe. There was the Bank of England. It enjoyed a monopoly of note issue and served the government as banker and agent. All other banks kept accounts with the Bank of England because its notes commanded greatest confidence and widest circulation. At the end of each clearing all banks settled their claims through transfers between their deposits with the Bank. It was the "lender of last resort." In times of financial crisis it was expected to stay liquid and grant accommodation to the most essential needs of credit. When it maintained its liquidity throughout the crises of 1873 and 1890 its reputation grew tremendously. In 1907 it merely had to increase its discount rate in order to allay public alarm.

Then there was the Reichsbank of Germany, which, like the Bank of England, conducted a discount policy for the protection of general banking liquidity. But the Reichsbank differed from the Bank of England in one important respect: the "elasticity" in its note circulation. In England, Peel's Act of 1844 had sanctioned a fixed amount of notes in circulation which needed to be covered only by government securities. All notes issued in excess of this amount had to be fully covered by gold. When Germany established the Reichsbank in 1875, a deliberate attempt was made to give the German banking system a greater degree of "elasticity" of note circulation. According to the German act, the Reichsbank had to maintain a minimum gold reserve of one-third of the notes in circulation, the remainder to be covered by discounted paper with a maturity of not more than three months. But beyond a certain fixed amount, the notes either had to be fully covered by gold or the Reichsbank was subject to payment of a five percent tax on the excess. These features were said to endow the system with elasticity.

In the years preceding the enactment of the Federal Reserve Act, most American writers on money and banking were clamoring for such a system. Eminent economists, such as M.L. Muhleman,[1] James Laurence Laughlin,[2] O.M.W. Sprague,[3] Edwin W. Kemmerer,[4] and

[1] *Monetary and Banking Systems* (New York: Monetary Publishing Company, 1908).
[2] *Banking Reform* (Chicago: The National Citizens League, 1912).
[3] *History of Crises Under the National Banking System* (Washington, D. C.: United States Government Printing Office, 1910).

many others[5] joined in the demand for banking reform. According to them, the United States, too, was in need of a bank that could weather or even alleviate the panics and depressions, a bank with an "elastic" note issue that would meet the needs of business. The outcome was the Federal Reserve System.

It differed from the German system in a few details. It comprised a number of regional reserve banks under central control. The minimum gold reserve amounted to forty percent against the notes in circulation. In addition to this gold reserve the notes were to be fully covered by discounted trade or agricultural bills. Against their deposits the Reserve banks had to maintain a cover of thirty-five percent in "lawful money." In an emergency the full reserve requirements could be suspended for thirty days with renewals of suspension for periods of fifteen days each. In this case the Federal Reserve banks were subject to a graduated percentage tax on the deficiency in reserves.

When seen in retrospect, the System's original purposes were rather modest in scope and objective. But since 1913 more than one hundred amendments to the Act have gradually shaped the Federal Reserve into a powerful arm of government that manages the people's money and credit. Today, its primary purpose is to finance federal deficits and conduct money and credit policies in accordance with the general plan of the administration in power.

Many popular conceptions about the Federal Reserve System flow from the fact that under the original Act the member banks were forced to bear the System's inaugural expenses through the purchase of System stock, yielding an annual return of six percent. But this Federal Reserve stock never included the right of ownership in the economic sense. Instead, it is akin to a perpetual bond without the customary creditor rights of the holders, a kind of forced loan on which the government consented to pay six percent interest. The control rests absolutely and undividedly in the hands of the United States President who received this power by legislation. The President of the United States appoints the seven members of the Board of Governors and the United States Senate confirms them. They are appointed for terms of fourteen years and their terms are so arranged that one expires every two years. The Board of Governors determines the System's money and credit policies in accordance with the legislation of Congress and the wishes of the President. The

---

[4] "Banking Reform in the United States," *American Economic Review Supplement,* Volume III. (March 1913).

[5] Compare the National Monetary Commission publications (Washington, D. C.: United States Government Printing Office, 1910-1912).

huge surpluses of the System are transferred to the United States Treasury.

For administrative purposes the System is divided into twelve districts. In each district there is one Federal Reserve Bank, and most of these have branches. Each district bank has nine directors, of whom three may be bankers, three are drawn from other industries in the district, and three are designated by the Board of Governors. One of this group acts as chairman and one as deputy chairman. The directors merely administer the district bank in accordance with the instructions of the Board of Governors in Washington. They are agents of the government, not corporate officials with the proprietorship rights and powers that customarily belong to stockholders of corporations.

It is quite important to emphasize the facts cited immediately above for widespread ignorance of them has constituted a common source of confusion. The Federal Reserve System is not now, nor has it ever been, a "private banking institution" engaged primarily in busily filling the pockets of the bankers. It is a product of the United States Congress, which originated it and has given it its present form. It is important to note, however, that some of the original sponsors of the System were German immigrants of both Christian and Jewish faiths; and these immigrants had friends and relatives in the old country, as immigrants usually do. They left their mark on the Federal Reserve System as they did on many other fields of scientific, economic, and political pursuit.

Many foes of the Federal Reserve System are rabid collectivists. They would like to replace the present System with one headed by the Secretary of the Treasury and thus "return the power over our money to Congress." They even quote the Constitution and then interpret it in radically socialistic fashion.

According to Section 8, Article I, of the Constitution, "The Congress shall have power . . . to coin money, regulate the value thereof, and of foreign coin, and fix the standard of weights and measures." This Constitutional power must be interpreted in the sense it was intended by the Founding Fathers and applied during the early years of the Republic. Congress defined the weight and fineness of the standard coin. As it fixed the standard of weights and measures so did it adopt the standard medium of exchange, the United States dollar. Monetary management in the modern sense was unknown, and would have been alien to the political and economic philosophy of the Founding Fathers. They still remembered the Continental dollar, which was issued in vast quantities by the Continental Congress until it became a symbol for utter worthlessness.

The ominous depreciation of the United States dollar during the last fifty years has been the work of the Federal Reserve System, which is the monetary arm of the federal government. It created large quantities of money and credit in order to cover the budgetary deficits of the United States Treasury or to stimulate the sagging economy. In short, the Federal Reserve System has become an indispensable and efficient tool of control in the hands of government.

In Search of Currency Elasticity

It all started rather inconspicuously with just one fallacious banking theory: the commodity bill doctrine. In the footsteps of the British Banking School of Tooke, Fullarton, and Wilson, the founders of the System were confident that they had discovered a method of banking that assures the most perfect adjustment of currency and credit to the changing demands of business. They were convinced that they could bring the quantity of money into a direct causal connection with the demand for it. We must create a central bank, they thought, that issues currency and credit solely on the basis of self-liquidating commodity bills. The quantity of these bills was said to be determined by the intensity of economic life. This automatic adjustment of the supply of currency and credit by way of the Federal Reserve's discounting of self-liquidating commodity bills then was thought to render money and credit neutral. Money would no longer affect prices, but would smoothly render the vital service of a medium of exchange.

Early amendments to the Federal Reserve Act then broadened the note and credit-issuing function of the Reserve Banks by accommodating not only business but also the government. The United States was at war with Germany. War was said to make for additional economic activity requiring additional money and credit. Therefore the amendments of June 1917 permitted the Federal Reserve Banks to extend credit on the basis not only of collateral consisting of commercial and agricultural bills, but also of promissory notes either by eligible paper or United States government securities.

Unfortunately, the British banking theorists and the American founders of the Federal Reserve System failed to understand the nature of bank credit. Credit is not elastic in the sense that its quantity can be made to increase or decrease with the intensity of economic life without influencing the purchasing power of money. But it is elastic in the sense that it arbitrarily can be made to expand or contract, which brings about a decrease or increase in the purchasing power of money. The outcome depends entirely on central banking policy.

The famous scholars of the British Currency School led by Sir Robert Peel had correctly recognized the causal connection between the extension of bank credit by way of uncovered bank notes and the monetary crises that had occurred up to the middle of the nineteenth century. They had observed that in years of great confidence the banks slowly expanded the volume of uncovered bank notes through reductions in interest rates. During the economic boom that followed, commodity prices rose and the purchasing power of money declined. This fact then led to an "external drain" of the gold reserves to countries where there were no banks expanding credit. At this point the banks began to feel uneasy about their waning gold reserves and the expanded volume of uncovered note circulation. When they began to restrict their loans and contract the volume of notes in order to protect their liquidity, the crisis set in.

In England, Peel's Act set out to remedy this evil of uncovered credit expansion. It prohibited all future expansion of notes without one hundred percent gold backing. But it sanctioned the volume of uncovered notes in circulation at the time of enactment in order to avoid a drastic credit contraction. The Act contained a tragic oversight, however. While it prohibited the expansion of uncovered bank notes, it failed to close the other road of credit expansion: by way of demand deposits subject to checks. Thus credit expansion and contraction, external drains and financial panics, booms and busts, continued to plague the country.

In the United States, expansion of credit by way of uncovered notes was severely limited by a series of Congressional Acts. An Act of 1865 had levied a tax of ten percent on state bank notes in circulation, which eliminated them entirely. The maximum circulation of national bank notes was at first limited to $300 million. When this limitation was removed in 1875 another check began to play a more important role. This was the provision that notes had to be backed by United States government bonds. But inasmuch as the federal government called in its debt as rapidly as its surplus revenues permitted after the Civil War, the basis provided for note issue continuously diminished. Moreover, an Act of May 1873 had limited the volume of greenbacks in circulation to $346 million, which thus became a permanent part of the American currency. Finally, the Gold Standard Act of 1900 had limited the volume of silver dollars and silver certificates by making them redeemable in gold coin at the option of the bearer.

Throughout this period the demand deposits subject to checks increased manyfold. The larger part of this expansion was uncovered. In periods of public confidence in the soundness of the banks, they expanded the volume of uncovered loans to the very limit of liquidity or to the limit of legal reserve requirements which, however, were so low that they gave ample leeway for expansion. Then when the external drain of gold set in on account of the monetary depreciation, amounting to one or two percent, or when the bankers became concerned about their uncovered expansion, the contraction got under way. A depression followed. It lasted until all the malinvestments of the preceding boom period were eliminated and goods prices had readjusted to the true state of markets.

Obviously the problem urgently needing solution was the jolting expansion or contraction of uncovered bank credit which time and again interrupted the economic development. This solution could have been found in an unconditional application of the legal restrictions on the issuance of notes to the expansion of demand deposits also. In order to avoid a serious contraction of credit, the volume of uncovered loans on the day of stabilization would have had to be sanctioned. This is the very core of every currency reform and true anticyclical policy.

The Federal Reserve System and all similar central banking systems must be evaluated in the light of this knowledge. The lowering of the reserve requirements as provided by the Act clearly meant an encouragement of further credit expansion. That is to say, the evil that caused the booms and crises was to be continued and the readjustment postponed. This can certainly be done temporarily. But it merely leads to an aggravation of the economic maladjustment. When the day of crisis and readjustment finally arrives the adjustment will be all the more painful and severe. It was no coincidence that the depression of 1920-1922 was more severe than all preceding depressions. The depression of 1930-1940 again was deeper than any in the past. The hostility of government towards business greatly contributed to the prolongation of the Great Depression. In both cycles the bank credit expansion would have come to a halt much earlier and with less painful effects if the Federal Reserve had not postponed the readjustment through tremendous expansion of its own. The fact that the recessions of 1948-1949, 1953-1954, 1957-1958, 1960-1961, 1970-1971, and 1973-1975 did not develop into full-scale depressions must be explained similarly. In all cases the Federal Reserve averted the depression by rekindling the economic boom through accelerating the credit expansion. The inevitable depression was postponed at the cost of further economic maladjustment and further depreciation of the dollar.

The very formation of the Federal Reserve was an act of credit expansion. The new system was superimposed on the existing banking structure. The Federal Reserve notes that were issued in ever increasing volumes did not supplant an equal amount of bank notes, but rather constituted additions to the money supply. The expansion of member bank deposits with Federal Reserve Banks was even more portentous. When the member banks had deposited their gold reserves with the Reserve Banks, they naturally employed their reserve accounts the same way they formerly had used their gold: as the basis for their volume of credit. Consequently the member banks used additional Reserve Bank credit, which they could obtain through rediscounting commercial or agricultural bills, as if they had acquired additional gold reserves. In other words, Federal Reserve credit, which itself was newly created, was employed as the basis for further credit creation by commercial banks. This explains why Federal Reserve money is "high-powered money" that serves as the basis for a multiple expansion of credit by commercial banks.

The original channel through which this new high-powered credit enters the money market was very narrow in the beginning. It is the channel that allegedly made the currency more elastic: the discounting of commercial and agricultural bills by the Federal Reserve. However, as mentioned above, the discounting of bills does not depend on the intensity of economic life, but rather on the interest rate charged by the discounting bank. If it lowers its rate, the demand for credit will increase. The bank then can satisfy this increased demand only through the expansion of uncovered credit which enhances the money supply, lowers its purchasing power, and leads to an intensification of economic life. In other words, the intensity of economic life depends on the volume of discounted paper, which in turn depends on the discount rate.

The provision that Federal Reserve credit had to be covered only by bills was of great significance, however. It constituted a limitation of Federal Reserve credit not covered by gold. When the Federal Reserve lowered its discount rate below that warranted by the state of the market, the demand for credit increased correspondingly. But the requirement of commercial bills as collateral disqualified a considerable part of the potential credit demand, such as for real estate, business investments, government spending, consumer loans, *etc.* However, no matter how narrow and onerous this channel for Federal Reserve credit expansion was, it constituted the very channel through which inflationary funds flowed into the economy. The next fifty years of Federal Reserve evolution witnessed a continuous widening of this first channel, which today is a huge pipeline capable of facilitating a complete inundation of the American economy.

In Search of Economic Boom and Full Employment

The Great Depression ushered in a new era of government leadership in all economic matters. The federal government, which for several decades had injected its will and power into a few isolated areas, now became a back-seat driver who was to become more vocal and commanding year after year.

The original Federal Reserve Act of 1913 had granted the System the power to buy and sell obligations of the United States, and of any state, county, district, political subdivision, or municipality in the United States. By the 1920's it was recognized that such open-market transactions by the Reserve Banks offered an important method of central credit control. Therefore, many writers were advocating a concentration of this control into the hands of one regulatory body. Legislation enacted in 1933 provided that no Federal Reserve Bank should engage in open-market operations except in accordance with regulations adopted by the Federal Reserve Board. To improve and formalize this centralization the Open Market Committee was organized. In 1935 an amendment to the 1933 Act finally provided that "no Federal Reserve Bank shall engage or decline to engage in open-market operations . . . except in accordance with the direction of, and regulations adopted by, the Committee."

Possessing this tool, the Federal Reserve System no longer had to wait for member banks to ask for discounts and advances. It could make them directly, on its own initiative, by buying or selling securities to make money and capital markets more liquid or more tight, as it might wish. For in payment for securities the Federal Reserve merely draws on itself a check which constitutes newly created money. Then, as this check is deposited by the recipient in his bank, and redeposited by that bank, it winds up as an addition to the reserve account of some bank with the Federal Reserve. Open-market operations of the Federal Reserve may involve long-term securities. Thus they may affect, directly, long-term interest rates and yields; and this is immediate. They are, therefore, a quite comprehensive instrumentality of control. For this reason such operations have high prestige and preference in the plans of the money managers.

Another powerful instrument of credit control in the hands of the Federal Reserve System is its authority to change the reserve requirements of its member banks. Both the rediscount process and the open-market transactions either increase or decrease member bank reserves, and hence the amount of credit which commercial banks can make available. But changing the percentage of reserves which banks must keep is an even more drastic form of influence over the stock of money and credit.

Suppose a bank holds one million dollars of demand deposits. If the reserve requirement is ten percent, the bank must keep one hundred thousand dollars in its regional Reserve Bank. It may loan out or invest the rest. But if the reserve requirement should now be lowered, let us say, to five percent, our bank would need only fifty thousand dollars as a reserve against its demand deposits. It can lend or invest the remaining fifty thousand dollars.

If this were the only effect, only fifty thousand dollars of additional money would enter the economy. In reality, however, this is merely the beginning of a chain of fiduciary money creation. Possessing "excess reserves," the bank may extend more credit to its customers. Of course, it would have to proceed very slowly lest it lose its reserves to other banks or customers demanding cash. It cannot proceed any faster than other banks that are also expanding their credits on the basis of their new excess reserves.

This is an oversimplification, of course. But the impact on the capital and money markets of changes in reserve requirements is extremely potent. It is estimated that at present a fluctuation of only one percent tends to increase or decrease the total volume of bank credit by more than six billion dollars. This authority to vary reserve requirements was given to the Federal Reserve System in 1933, as a special emergency power. Since 1935 it has been a permanent instrument of credit control.

The Great Depression led to many other extensions of Federal Reserve control over money and banking. The Glass-Steagall Act of 1932 permitted the Reserve Banks to extend credit on any securities acceptable to them. It also authorized the Reserve Bank to use not only commercial bills and gold, but also government securities, as collateral for Federal Reserve Notes. The Reserve Banks were supposed to conduct contracyclical policies through monetary intervention. The Banking Acts of 1933 and 1935 and the Securities and Exchange Act of 1934 authorized the Reserve Banks to make loans directly to business enterprises. Moreover, the System received the power to vary greatly the member banks' reserve requirements against their liabilities and regulate margin requirements for trading in securities. During World War II, the monetary needs of the government again became the paramount concern of the Federal Reserve. For this purpose Congress created new Federal Reserve powers to regulate the use to which bank credit is put and to extend more direct loans to business. Provided with all these powers the Federal Reserve embarked upon the financing of World War II through massive creation of new money and credit.

Today, the Federal Reserve System is supposed to use all these powers and its vast resources for "creating conditions favorable to sustain high employment, stable values, growth of the country, and a rising level of consumption."[6] Unfortunately, it has achieved no such objective; instead, it has given us rampant inflation and unprecedented economic instability.

An appraisal of the good points of the Federal Reserve System depends on the political and economic philosophy of the appraiser. If one favors government control over our economy he will regard the Federal Reserve most favorably, for it actually holds absolute power over the people's money and credit. If one is convinced of the beneficial nature of an individual enterprise economy, he will unconditionally reject the Federal Reserve System. He will condemn it as the controlling body of an important industry. He will blame it for having shattered the American dollar; for having caused booms, busts, recessions, and depressions; and for having given the sixty-three years of its existence the period's fundamental characteristic: an unprecedented economic instability.

In the opinion of this writer this instability has fostered the growth of ideologies that are hostile to individual liberty. The Federal Reserve, through its policies of "boom and bust," helped to usher in the New Deal. It now acts as midwife to ever more extensive government controls. First, our economic planners in Washington clamor for an expansion of the volume of money and credit, in order to bring about — or sustain — a boom, prosperity, and full employment. They rejoice over wage boosts, but dislike parallel price rises and the hardships caused those with fixed incomes. They approve of additional housing construction, but disapprove of higher prices for houses. They like one set of inflationary effects, but denounce other effects of inflation. Our economic planners are always most anxious indeed to do something about these undesired effects. In order to "fight" inflation they propose to curb our economic actions with a series of controls. They want credit controls, price controls, wage controls, and all kinds of other government controls over our economic lives.

Under these conditions the Federal Reserve System is the most important tool in the armory of economic interventionism. But in the Governors' own words, it is the system's objective "to help counteract inflationary and deflationary movements, and to share in creating conditions favorable to sustain high employment, stable values, growth of the country, and a rising level of consumption." This is interventionism at its baldest, with all of the planners' usual assumption of benevolent omniscience. An institution which was established as a cooperative undertaking

---

[6] Board of Governors, *The Federal Reserve System, Purposes and Functions* (Washington, D. C.: United States Government Printing Office, 1954), p. 1.

by the banks of the country to pool their resources has developed into the right hand of the government in promoting its transfer objectives. The fallacies of "central planning" are being substituted for the hard, but lasting and productive, truths of a free market. The Federal Reserve System supplies the magician's cloth under which the substitution is made.

Its part in the colossal metamorphosis of our country is not limited to the maintenance of cheap money in order to prolong or create a boom. It also provides the government itself with the money the planners think they should have, beyond the amount they dare take directly in taxes. The Federal Reserve System facilitates the government's own inflationary financing "in periods of emergency." It makes easy the inflationary financing of budget deficits and the inflationary refunding of government loans. It supports the government bond market to the advantage of the government. It does all of this by wrecking the purchasing power of the dollar; by subtly taking from the people of this country what it thus provides for the government through a process exactly on a par with the coin-clipping of ancient kings — but much more diabolical because so much less visible.

A Ready Instrument of Tyranny

The minds of men are most easily molded in periods of emergency when adversities demand immediate solutions. In haste new ideas are readily accepted, new policies adopted, and new powers granted to the government that declared the emergency. Individual freedoms may be permanently lost, or, at least, difficult to retrieve upon return to normalcy. Also, new evils require new remedies. As every emergency appears to be new and unprecedented, popular opinions and feelings are drawn to accept new policies that are to remedy the evils. Thus great changes are made in human affairs.

If we accept such changes in a moment of emergency we may favor them also in periods of near-emergency, semi-emergency, or even normalcy. If they are desirable under adverse condtions they may also be superior under normal conditions. This rationale has influenced American policies for more than forty years of nearly uninterrupted national emergency, from the Great Depression to the war on poverty, from World War II to Vietnam. In fact, emergency regulations are early symptoms of the changes to come. He who would dare to oppose such changes on grounds that they are made in haste, are destructive of the inalienable rights of man, conducive to tyranny, or merely that they cannot achieve the desired objectives, is quickly thrust aside. In fact, he may be decried as perverse and obstinate in the face of a national emergency, a traitor to his country.

To prepare for an eventual emergency, the Secretary of the United States Treasury, on January 10, 1961, issued the Emergency Banking Regulation No. 1, which probably is one of the most alarming orders ever issued by an American official.[7] No voices of protest were heard, for no one would dare to oppose government preparations for a national emergency.

Emergency Banking Regulation No. 1 is just one of a number of emergency measures that would impose government control over rents, prices, salaries, and wages, and introduce rationing. The Regulation orders the instant seizure of most bank deposits "in the event of an attack on the United States." The Regulation is based on the Trading with the Enemy Act of October 6, 1917, and covers all banking institutions, including every commercial bank, trust company, private bank, savings bank, mutual savings bank, savings and loan association, building and loan association, cooperative bank, homestead association, credit union, and United States postal savings office.

Section 2 of Chapter V of the Regulation is most shocking in its wanton denial of individual freedom and private property. Lest we be suspected of misinterpretation we quote:

> (a) No depositor or share or savings account owner may transfer in any manner or by any device whatsoever any balance to his credit on the date on which this Regulation becomes effective, except for the payment of (i) expenses or reconstruction costs vital to the war effort, (ii) essential living costs, (iii) taxes, (iv) payrolls, or (v) obligations incurred before the date on which this Regulation becomes effective, to the end that the best interests of the war effort and the public will be served.
>
> (b) Banking institutions shall prohibit the transfer of credit in any case where there is reason to believe that such transfer is sought for any unauthorized purpose.
>
> (c) After this Regulation becomes effective, banking institutions shall retain until released by Federal authority the original

---

[7] It was issued by the Secretary of the Treasury pursuant to the authority vested in him by Section 5 (b) of the Trading with the Enemy Act of October 6, 1917, as amended (50 U. S. C. App. 5 [b]), and Executive Order No. 9193.

President Nixon's Executive Order 11490 (cf. *Federal Register*, Vol. 34, Number 209, [October 30, 1969]) was similar to President Kennedy's Executive Order 9193. In many cases it is a copy of the latter, but was issued probably because of organizational changes that had taken place since Kennedy's Order was written. As of this date (May 21, 1977) Emergency Banking Regulation No. 1 seems to be in effect. For an excellent collection of Emergency Power Statutes see the *Report of the Special Committee on the Termination of the National Emergency*, United States Senate (Washington, D. C.: United States Government Printing Office, September 1973), pp. 98-406.

or a photographic copy (face and reverse sides) of each check and other evidence of transfer of credit in the amount of $1,000 or more.

In short, your money in the bank is blocked unless you propose to spend it toward the war effort, *i.e.*, to buy United States Treasury obligations or to finance expenditures deemed "vital" by the government. You may withdraw your money for living expenses, but only sums deemed "essential." You may pay taxes and wages, and discharge old obligations. But any other use of your money is prohibited. Let us assume that you were saving for another car, new furniture, or a house, or for your children's college education. As such objectives can hardly be called "essential" either for the war effort or for individual living, your money would be blocked.

The Emergency Regulation would permit business to pay taxes and wages, but deny all other expenses without which there can be no business. After all, manufacturers need materials, tools, and equipment in order to produce goods and services. Merchants continually need new supplies of merchandise in order to stay in business. Even professional people, such as doctors and dentists, have expenses other than taxes and wages. This is why the Regulation would halt all economic activity but that of the government. In fact, no enemy attack, no matter how devastating to human life and property, could conceivably have a more disruptive effect than the Emergency Banking Regulation.

Chapter VI, Section 1 of the Regulation would radically change the very nature of banking:

> No banking institution may make any loan, extend any credit, or discount or purchase any obligation or evidence of debt, unless it is established and certified in writing by the borrower and a banking institution that the purpose is to pay (i) expenses or reconstruction costs vital to the war effort, (ii) essential living costs, (iii) taxes, or (iv) payrolls, to the end that the best interests of the war effort and the public will be served.

It is ironic that the stated purpose of the Regulation is "continuance of operations and functions" of all banking institutions. Indeed, banks would be required to "remain open and continue their operations and functions" (Chapter IV, Section 1). In reality, the stated purpose should properly read "cessation of all banking operations and assumption of the exclusive function of government finance." After all, what is banking? It is negotiating credit between lenders and borrowers, and maintaining cash balances for the convenience of depositors. It is obvious that banking ceases to exist if credit can no longer be negotiated and cash no longer be paid upon demand by the depositors. The Emergency Regulation would make all financial institutions agencies of the United States Treasury.

In order to facilitate the transition from banking to Treasury financing, the banks are ordered to retain all checks, or photographic copies thereof, in the amount of $1,000 or more. Obviously this provision aims to coerce the banking personnel fully to execute the Regulation, and to preserve the evidence for official inspection and approval. It not only breaches all individual rights to privacy for depositors, payees, and bankers, but also provides official records for banker incrimination. The great principle of law that no one can be forced to incriminate himself is replaced by the motto: The interests of the State negate all individual rights and deny due process of law. Of course, if banking is merely a division of government finance and every individual action is a function of the state, all checks must be held as records of public finance.

The Emergency Banking Regulation violates nearly every principle of law. In fact, it presumes to supersede or set aside federal and state law. Section 4 of Chapter IV expressly states that Federal Reserve Banks, Federal Home Loan Banks, or banking institutions will maintain operations and functions "without regard to the restrictions of Federal or State law." Law, which is the body of principles that govern human conduct, is cast aside by simple regulation. Administrative regulation negates the common law, which is our age-old body of legal principles based on custom and observed so long that the courts recognize them and enforce them. It denies constitutional law, in particular the Constitution of the United States and those of its fifty sovereign states. Amendments IV and V of the Constitution stand in open contradiction to the Emergency Banking Regulation. The Fourth Amendment:

> The right of the people to be secure in their persons, houses, papers, and effects, against unreasonable searches and seizures, shall not be violated, and no Warrants shall issue, but upon probable cause, supported by Oath or affirmation, and particularly describing the place to be searched, and the persons or things to be seized.

The Fifth Amendment:

> No person . . . shall be compelled in any criminal case to be a witness against himself, nor be deprived of life, liberty, or property, without due process of law; nor shall private property be taken for public use without just compensation.

The Regulation clearly violates contract law, which is an essential part of our individual enterprise order. The rights created by contract are protected and the duties enforced by the courts. Bank deposits, loans, and other bank transactions are circumscribed by contract which cannot unilaterally be impaired by bank or customer without the responsibility for damages and penalties stipulated by the contract. Few fields of law are more important to business and our economic order than that of negotiable instruments, which are written promises or orders to pay money. A uniform law governing negotiable instruments such as promissory notes, bills of exchange, and checks is in force in every state of the United States. The Emergency Banking Regulation repeals the law without even mentioning it.

Similarly, the law of trust is denied by the Regulation. Trust departments of banks hold and manage property for the benefit or use of individuals. The Regulation, which makes banks agencies of the United States Treasury and stops payment for all purposes but taxes and payrolls, obviously prevents the trusts from managing the properties for their beneficiaries.

Finally, the law of bankruptcy of the United States and the insolvency laws of the States are violated. According to the Bankruptcy Act, banks commit an act of bankruptcy whenever they cease payments and then transfer their assets to one or more of their creditors with the intent to prefer such creditors over all others. The Emergency Banking Regulation orders all banks to commit such acts of bankruptcy and then to keep their doors open as usual.

But no matter what the legal aspects of the Emergency Regulation may be, its political and economic implications are ominous. It implies an economic order that is diametrically opposed to the American individual enterprise system. There is no room for individual initiative and independence, for private property in economic production, for competition, markets, prices, and profits; even the role of money is severely limited. A completely regimented economy with government control over all production, with rationing, allocations, and priorities, with central planners and commanders, would replace our traditional order. We wonder whether our political system could survive such a dictatorial economic order.

Government finance is all comprising; business and individual finance merely are subdivisions of public finance. Every financial concern of the individual becomes a state matter. In a national emergency the supreme efforts, including the financial resources of every individual, of such a society are to be directed towards defense. This is why the Emergency Banking Regulation proposes to seize all financial reserves. But this regulation represents merely the visible tip of the financial iceberg that grows in such a system. After all, national emergency financing is likely to require our maximum efforts for many months, or even years. The initial seizure of all demand and time deposits cannot be expected to cover the huge expenses of government for more than a few months. How does the federal government raise its needed revenue thereafter? And how much more would be needed?

We may get the proper perspective of the magnitude of future emergency financing by reviewing the growth of federal financing during the last national emergency, World War II. Between 1940 and 1945 federal expenses grew from $9.5 billion to $95.2 billion, or 900 percent. The federal debt leapt from $48.5 billion to $259.1 billion, or some 430 percent. If we apply the same growth rate to future national emergencies, which in the light of the Banking Regulation is a rather conservative assumption, we must anticipate expenses rising quickly to many trillions of dollars annually. In case of a nuclear holocaust these estimates must, of course, be raised by multiples.

But how can anyone anticipate a magnitude of government expenditures that exceeds today's Gross National Product? As in World War II, the Korean War, and the Vietnamese War, we must anticipate massive injections of new purchasing power directly from the federal printing presses, that is, massive inflation. Furthermore, we should bear in mind that the Gross National Product, as the federal government calculates it, is the sum of various expenditures including those of government. If the federal government boosts its spending by two trillion dollars, the Gross National Product will rise by this very amount.

Future emergency financing will differ from past financing in one important respect: the measure of coercion applied to the citzenry. As the Emergency Banking Regulation clearly indicates, the federal government must be expected to resort to new radical measures of financing that are unprecedented in American history. But we can learn from the financial histories of other nations with total government control, such as Soviet Russia, Nazi Germany, and Communist Cuba.

The massive creation of new money for emergency financing wreaks havoc on all price and cost relations, renders economic calculation virtually impossible, and therefore disrupts production and distribution. This is why the central government immediately imposes price and wage controls in an attempt to suppress the disastrous effects of the inflation. Furthermore, government resorts to a comprehensive system of rationing, allocation, and priority distribution, the objective of which is the curtailment of individual consumption and maximum allocation to government. The rationing system reduces individual consumption to the very minimum, thus generating a cash surplus in the hands of individuals. Special "anti-hoarding laws" that threaten heavy fines and long imprisonment then force the people to deposit their surplus cash in banks that lend them to the government. In short, the initial seizure of bank deposits is followed by continuous seizures through the banking system.

Such a policy siphons off the people's savings generated by the rationing system and forced into the banks by anti-hoarding laws which make it unlawful for individuals to hold cash in excess of a certain amount, for instance, $1,000. In World War II Germany, a cash holding in excess of one thousand marks was a crime that was punished with confiscation of the "hoard" and two years of imprisonment.

The financial means thus seized by the federal government are likely to be sizable. Forced savings and deposits become as important a source of revenue as taxation and inflation. By drawing into the federal treasury all individual savings left after taxes, voluntary war loan subscriptions, and vital living expenses, the federal government conceivably may consume two-thirds or more of our national product. And although the budgetary deficits are huge, inflationary financing is kept at a minimum. That is to say, only those financial requirements of government that are not covered by taxation, voluntary loan subscriptions, and bank account seizures are met with new money creation.

But such financing creates a new problem that must be faced in the end: the huge accumulation of private bank deposits. Although their payment is blocked by the Emergency Banking Regulation, they represent legal claims that must ultimately be settled. Payment is out of the question as the release of trillions of dollars accumulated during several years of "emergency" would severely disrupt the economy. After all, the bank deposits represent no economic goods, merely government debt. In case of release, goods prices would soar and the value of the dollar drop precipitously. This is why government then must be expected to conduct a "currency reform" that cancels and repudiates most private bank deposits. It may exchange "old" deposits for "new" deposits at a ratio of one for ten, or one for a hundred, or whatever ratio may be appropriate. In the end, the private deposits that were seized or made by force, and depreciated by rampant inflation, are repudiated legally through currency reform. Government is consuming the people's savings: Currency reform cancels its debt. In all its financial and economic policies the United States government relies on the Federal Reserve System as an important instrument of control, inflation, and repudiation.

V
THE AMERICAN
ECONOMY IS NOT
DEPRESSION-PROOF

Most contemporary economists are fully convinced that a major depression of the 1929-1941 variety cannot happen again. It is inconceivable, they say, that the American economy should fall again into such an abyss of despair as that one, in which more than thirteen million Americans were unemployed, banks and businesses failed by the scores, countless farmers lost their land, and nearly everyone suffered painful losses of wealth and income. The tragedy of the Great Depression lives on as a nightmare that frightens everyone, especially during periods of recession or stagnation. But our politicians and their learned advisors, the economists, assure us almost in unison that they will not let it happen again. They are solemnly pledging the awesome power of government to prevent another depression.

We do not question the sincerity of their intentions, as we cast no doubt on the good will of the policymakers of the Hoover and Roosevelt era who were engulfed by the Great Depression. But we wonder whether we have learned to avoid the dreadful errors of policy that caused and prolonged the disaster. If we repeat the errors that generated the Great Depression, inexorable economic law determines that it must happen again. In fact, we doubt that our policymakers have learned the lessons of the Great Depression. Their explanations and interpretations of economic decline differ little from those offered by the politicians of the 1920's and 1930's. Contemporary economic policies, although far more comprehensive and massive in scope and import, are similar to those conducted by the Hoover and Roosevelt Administrations.

It is true that the Hoover Administration applied several impediments that greatly contributed to the economic dilemma. The Smoot-Hawley Tariff Act of June 1930 raised American tariffs to unprecedented levels and practically closed our borders to foreign goods. According to most economic historians, this was the crowning folly of the whole period from 1920 to 1933, and the beginning of the real depression. Then, in the dark hours of economic decline and human suffering that followed, the federal government struck another blow. The Revenue Act of 1932 ordered the sharpest increase in federal tax burden in American history. When state and local governments faced shrinking tax collections they, too, joined the federal government in imposing new levies. In short, the burden of government nearly doubled during the Hoover Administration, which alone would have caused a deep depression.

Today, under the influence of Keynesian economic thought, contemporary administrations surely would avoid these two disastrous errors of policy. But Keynesian monetary policies do not differ fundamentally from those conducted in 1924-1925 and again in 1927-1928. The credit expansion that preceded the crash of 1929 was approved and applauded by the New Economics. Early in 1930, the Federal Reserve purchased large quantities of government securities, which made money cheap and led to further expansion of bank credit. But when in September 1931, following England's cessation of gold payment, a foreign run on American gold developed, the Federal Reserve System could no longer prevent great liquidation of bank credit through massive credit expansion of its own because it had previously reached the legal limits of its expansionary powers. Surely, a Keynesian administration would immediately have reduced the forty percent gold and lawful money against bank deposits. But we doubt that even huge injections of credit could have prevented the contraction, as the forces of maladjustment, trade disruption, and the growing burden of government were extremely strong. More credit, if administered in massive doses, might have delayed the decline, but it could not have avoided it. After all, one more application of the very cause of maladjustment and depression could not possibly correct the inevitable consequences of previous applications.

The Hoover and Roosevelt Administrations also embarked upon massive deficit financing that would have delighted even a contemporary Keynesian. In 1931 the Hoover Administration suffered a deficit of $462 million. While this amount may not appear sufficient to impress the deficit spenders of today, it nevertheless was sizable when seen in the light of 1931 receipts and outlays. The deficit exceeded receipts by 14.8 percent, which today would amount to some sixty billion. In 1932 the Hoover Administration spent $2.735 billion more than it collected in taxes, or 140 percent more than total receipts. Only in war years had outlays ever surpassed receipts by such proportions. During President Roosevelt's presidency federal spending exceeded revenues in every fiscal year. In fact, in 1933, 1934, and 1936, the deficits were greater than revenues. Yet, the American economy remained severely depressed. Even in 1937, the highwater mark of the Roosevelt New Deal, unemployment averaged twelve percent.

Keynesian Policies Breed and Aggravate Depressions

Most contemporary economists did not learn from the disasters of the Great Depression. They merely echo the explanations given by the most famous and influential economist of our century, John Maynard Keynes. Unemployment and depression are the result of inadequate effective demand. Therefore, monetary and fiscal policy must be employed to increase aggregate demand. The nominal amount of money must be increased, which causes interest rates to fall, investments to increase, and income to rise. But in case monetary policy should prove to be ineffective because individual hoarding may counteract an increase in the quantity of money, Keynes recommended direct government investment through government tax cutting and deficit spending.[1]

Keynesian doctrine makes the federal government responsible for full employment and demands more spending regardless of the state of the budget. The Full Employment Act of 1946, which legalized the sway of Keynesian thought in the United States, adopted the system of contracyclical compensatory finance as a basic policy. Since then all federal administrations from Truman to Carter have faithfully followed Lord Keynes's policy recommendations.

---

[1] John Maynard Keynes, *General Theory of Employment, Interest and Money, op. cit.*, p. 250; see also Alvin H. Hansen, *A Guide to Keynes, op. cit.*, pp. 21-22. For a more detailed analysis see Chapter 10.

It does not matter who resides in the White House and issues the spending orders. The consequences of contracyclical finance are always the same. If the monetary authorities expand credit in order to "stimulate," "bolster," or "revive" the national economy, they bring about distortions and maladjustments that in the end must be corrected by a painful depression. If the credit expansion is small, the depression will be relatively short and mild. If the expansion is prolonged and massive, the inevitable depression must be long and severe.

Long before Lord Keynes appeared on the scene with his lack-of-spending theory, Ludwig von Mises had explained the boom-and-bust sequence as follows: The creation of credit by monetary authorities causes interest rates in the loan market to fall below the natural rate of interest. This natural rate, or unhampered market rate, reflects the people's choices as to spending and saving, and is responsible for the relative proportions of production for the present and the future, that is, of consumers' goods and producers' goods. A rising rate of saving, for instance, causes producers' goods industries to expand as more economic resources become available for expansion and modernization. If, without such new savings, monetary authorities arbitrarily expand credit, interest rates tend to fall, which then misleads business men to invest more funds in the capital goods industries. Thus misled by artificially lower interest rates, they embark upon countless expansion projects that are unsupported by genuine savings. They engage in business activity that causes maladjustments and distortions.

Because of the lack of real savings, the investment boom is bound to run aground. The boom causes prices to rise, especially in the feverish capital goods industries. However, the prices of land, labor, and capital are business costs. When they soar, business profit margins begin to falter. In short, when business costs rise faster than revenue, the trouble begins. A recession develops in the capital goods industries. Businessmen are forced to delay or postpone their expansion projects, which in the light of the new price and cost structure no longer look very promising. During the recession a new readjustment takes place: The malinvestments are abandoned and capital once again seeks employment according to the true state of consumer spending and saving. The long-neglected consumers' goods industries become attractive again while the capital goods industries are forced to contract, painfully releasing capital and labor.[2]

This Austrian theory has explained the economic booms and busts

---

[2] Compare *The Theory of Money and Credit, op. cit.*, also his *Human Action* (Third edition, Chicago: Henry Regnery Company, 1966).

ever since 1912 when the first German edition of *The Theory of Money and Credit* appeared in print. It continues to provide the only satisfactory explanation of the rapid succession of booms and recessions that continue to plague the "mixed" economies of our time. The Keynesian explanation, on the other hand, despite its great popularity with academicians and politicians, not only fails to explain the trade cycle phenomenon, but also is responsible for monetary policies that generate the cycle.

In 1936 Professor Jacob Viner reviewed Keynes's *General Theory,* which had just appeared in print. In this review Professor Viner made a prediction that explains in a nutshell the dilemma of our time:

> Keynes's reasoning points obviously to the superiority of inflationary remedies for unemployment over money-wage reductions. In a world organized in accordance with Keynes's specifications there would be a constant race between the printing press and the business agents of the trade unions, with the problem of unemployment largely solved if the printing press could maintain a constant lead and if only volume of employment, irrespective of quality, is considered important.[3]

The credit expansion misleads businessmen into costly errors of expansion and modernization for which there is no consumer demand. The fiscal deficits that are to stimulate economic recovery and full employment bolster some industries while depressing others. If the housing industry becomes the recipient of federal largess it will prosper and expand so long as federal support is forthcoming. But when a few years later the injection of government funds is halted because other industries suffer from stagnation and now are clamoring for their share of the federal favors, the housing industry must fall into depression and unemployment. The same will be true if the federal subsidies cease to grow, but are stabilized at certain levels to which the industry is quick to adjust. In short, each and every injection of government funds artificially and temporarily bolsters the recipient industries, and makes them dependent on ever larger stimulating injections. As the government funds are obviously limited, and policies may necessitate a rotation of favors, a depression soon follows the stimulating injection.

Keynesian politicians rarely inquire into the source of funds that finance the deficits. They are prone to ignore the basic source of government revenue, taxation, which forcibly transfers funds from taxpayers to government. To stimulate a sagging economy Keynesians do not propose to raise the tax burdens in order to facilitate

---

[3] *Quarterly Journal of Economics,* LI (1936-1937), p. 149.

Age of Inflation

larger government outlays. They are fully aware that a budgetary
deficit covered by higher taxes would aggravate rather than alleviate
the economic situation. Also, Keynesians rarely propose to tap the
capital markets to finance the deficits. The federal demand for funds,
in competition with the demands of business, would drive interest
rates to such lofty levels that business would be forced to withdraw
and contract. A deficit thus financed would depress rather than stimulate economic activity.

To finance budgetary deficits the federal government may avail
itself of three sources of funds, two of which are depressive immediately and one a few years later. Keynesian politicians have learned to
depend on only one source: the expansion of money and credit as
conducted and managed by the central bank. This method of deficit
financing is depressive in the long run, for it promotes maladjustments that later need to be corrected by readjustments. These readjustments can be postponed for a while through ever larger injections
of newly created funds. Just as the drug addict injects more drugs
into his suffering body in order to prevent or merely postpone the
painful withdrawal symptoms, so the economists and politicians can
postpone the depression through ever larger injections of inflation.
But in the end, both the drug addict and the Keynesian economy
must face the agony of withdrawal lest they perish in a final spasm of
addiction.

We know of no more devastating critique of Keynesian policies
than that of Henry Hazlitt, the indefatigable champion of market
economics.

> Keynes's system was actually a reversion to the naive and
> discredited theories of the mercantilists and under-consumption
> theorists, from Mandeville and Malthus to Hobson. It was also a
> reversion to all the inflationist theories of the currency cranks,
> from John Law to Silvio Gesell.
> Keynes's proposals for 'the euthanasia of the rentier, of the
> functionless investor,' were proposals to rob the productive and
> expropriate their savings.
> Keynes's plan for 'the socialization of investment' would in-
> evitably entail socialism and state planning. Seriously carried
> out, it would remove any significant field for the exercise of
> private initiative and responsibility. Keynes, in brief, recom-
> mended *de facto* socialism under the guise of 'reforming' and
> 'preserving' capitalism.[4]

---

[4] Henry Hazlitt, *The Failure of the "New Economics"* (Princeton, New Jersey: D. Van
Nostrand, 1959), pp. 434, 435.

132

What has made the Keynesian system so influential and powerful the world over? We are living in an age of socialism which welcomes any and all arguments in its defense and on its behalf. At the most opportune time and in an ideal location Professor Keynes rebuilt the tools of deficit spending and currency depreciation, which governments had been using feverishly throughout the Great Depression. He blessed their tools, and they in turn knighted him and made him the most renowned economist of our time.

Automatic Stabilizers are Illusory

The followers of Keynes are not the only economists who are convinced that a depression can never happen again. Milton Friedman, the vocal dean of the Chicago School, while rejecting the contracyclical recipes of the New Economics, denies the possibility of economic depressions on other grounds. "There have been fundamental changes in institutions and attitudes in the United States since the Great Depression," Professor Friedman reassures us.[5] They are rendering a major depression in the United States "almost inconceivable."

Establishment of the Federal Deposit Insurance Corporation in 1933 was, according to Friedman, a basic change in American banking that made bank failures "almost a thing of the past." By converting all deposit liabilities of private banks into a federal liability, the Federal Deposit Insurance Corporation eliminated the basic cause for runs on banks, which was the depositors' attempt to convert their claims into federal currency. Since both deposits and currency are now federal liabilities, an important cause for bank runs, credit contractions, and economic depressions has thus been removed.

The second change in banking structure that assures economic stability, according to Professor Friedman, has been the increased importance of government obligations. The phenomenal growth in government debt has made government liabilities an important part of bank assets, which afford greater stability to the stock of money and credit. Finally, Professor Friedman rejoices about the severing of all links between gold and the internal supply of money. "The dethroning of gold reduces the sensitivity of the stock of money to changes in external conditions." Removal of gold from public circulation has made us independent at last from the vagaries of foreign influence, which will avoid monetary contraction and thus "an es-

---

[5]"Why the American Economy Is Depression-Proof," *Dollars and Deficits*, (Englewood Cliffs, New Jersey: Prentice-Hall, Inc. 1968), p. 74.

sential conditioning factor for the occurrence of a major depression."[6]

We do not share Professor Friedman's basic assumption that a depression can be avoided no matter how great the maladjustments caused by a previous inflation if only monetary contractions can be avoided. Once the harm is done and the boom has run its course the readjustment must necessarily be painful. The depression is an unavoidable phase of the trade cycle once it has commenced. For the central bank to embark upon credit expansion that is to prevent the liquidation of malinvestment can only delay the recovery and thus prolong the depression.

The Federal Deposit Insurance Corporation, which, in effect, makes every bank deposit a government liability, is designed to prevent the needed liquidation. Of course, it can do this successfully and thus delay the readjustment if newly created funds are used for the rescue action. Where would the government obtain the funds necessary to prevent massive liquidation of bank credit? From its central bank, of course. The stabilizing power of the Federal Deposit Insurance Corporation, in the final analysis, is nothing but the government power to create and emit new money. Therefore, we must here repeat our answer to the Keynesian contracyclical spenders: One more application of the very cause of cyclical upheaval cannot possibly prevent the consequences of earlier applications.

The increased importance of government obligations as bank assets, which imparts such great confidence to Professor Friedman, fills us with anxiety. It is indicative not only of the changing role of American banking from mediators of credit to fiscal agents of the federal treasury, but also of the great reliance on the inflationary powers of government. Where would government obligations be without the inflationary powers to support them? Every budgetary deficit would send United States Treasury obligations to greater discounts if it were not for the open-market purchases by the Federal Reserve System. But this very support through monetary expansion, while it may succeed in the short run, tends to be self-defeating in the long run, for it raises interest rates and thus reduces the market prices of fixed income obligations. This is why government securities in bank portfolios have been very poor investments ever since World War II, and banks endeavor to avoid them whenever possible. In fact, long-term United States Treasury obligations have, at times when interest rates rose significantly, inflicted crushing losses on American banks, which dubious accounting practices endeavor to hide. The banking losses then provide an important motive for early resumption of credit expansion.

---

[6] *Ibid.*, pp. 82-83.

The American Economy Is Not Depression-Proof

What Professor Friedman calls the "dethroning" of gold is to us the "default" of paper. After all, it was the creation of massive quantities of money substitutes that caused central banks to default on their obligation to redeem their currencies in gold. But this default did not bring stability and prosperity. On the contrary, it opened the gates for massive inflation and great instability. The *fiat* standard is more unstable than the gold exchange standard, which afforded less stability than the gold bullion standard, which in turn was less stable than the classical gold coin standard. The default in gold payments did stop the runs on banks because no one in possession of his senses would want to run for paper money, the supply of which is potentially unlimited. But the *fiat* standard does not make us independent of the vagaries of foreign influence. It has made the international money market more vulnerable than ever before. The United States dollar is stumbling from crisis to crisis, with grave dangers to international trade and cooperation and ultimately also to the stability of the American economy itself.

But it is not only the new monetary structure that affords Professor Friedman so much confidence in the lasting stability of the American economy. There is also a fiscal structure. "There can be no disagreement," Friedman asserts, "that the fiscal structure is now an exceedingly important and powerful 'built-in stabilizer'." [7] Government expenditures, both national and local, now amount to more than one-quarter of the national income. Although the relative growth of government casts dark shadows over political freedom, the change in the character of both expenditures and receipts has stabilizing effects on the business cycle, Friedman believes. A broad program of social security, unemployment insurance, and a farm program that supports product prices, all tend to increase government expenditures in depression and to reduce them in prosperity. The same contracyclical effects are derived from personal and corporate income taxation, which in boom or recession automatically creates budget surpluses or deficits and thereby offsets from thirty to forty percent of any national income change.

Finally, there has been an important change in American psychological climate, Professor Friedman reassures us. Before the Great Depression we were more afraid of inflation than of deflation; we wanted "hard money" at all costs. But the Great Depression has changed all that. That is why today, after decades of rising prices and monetary depreciation, the public is still seized by a real fear of depression. Swinging from one extreme to the other, the American people now readily suffer inflation in order to avoid depression. But

---

[7] *Ibid.*, p. 86.

they may not realize that the ultimate destination of inflation is destruction of the currency.[8]

We certainly agree with Professor Friedman that the ultimate goal of our built-in stabilizers is monetary destruction. But we do not share his swinging theory. The American public has approved of inflation and credit expansion ever since the Coolidge Administration; it clung to easy money throughout the 1930's, endorsed rampant wartime inflation during the 1940's, approved of contracyclical policies during the 1950's, applauded the accelerator policies of the 1960's, and relies on massive deficit spending at the present. The fever of inflation that has infected American economic thought is rising steadily and dangerously.

The doctrine of the built-in stabilizers reminds us of the professor who took up farming in his spare time. Before leaving for the cattle market in town, he loaded his truck with an exceptionally heavy load of every pound of beef he could squeeze on the truck. When his neighbor inquired about the reason for the heavy load our farmer retorted with an air of great learning: "On the muddy road to town the old clunker needs stability. The heavier the load the greater the stability!" Of course, a few miles down the road he got stuck in the mud. A tow truck finally pulled him out, after he was persuaded to lighten the load. The same is true with economic activity and employment. A heavy load of government expenses increases the danger of stagnation and depression. As the Keynesian contracyclical policies fail to impart stability to the American economy, so do the automatic stabilizers.

Floating Exchange Rates are Disruptive

The stage is now set for a sharp contraction of foreign trade and an international depression. The world monetary order is in disarray, and the chaos is inflicting incalculable harm on foreign trade and capital markets. An important cause of the difficulties is in the world *fiat* standard with its concomitant system of floating exchange rates.

The same ideological forces that bitterly oppose the gold standard also aim their vocal criticism at the stability of exchange rates. As the gold standard is decried as a barbarous relic of the past that inflicted untold hardship on mankind, so are stable exchange rates denounced for restricting trade and commerce and restraining economic development. In a strange twist of reasoning, some advocates of flexibility fancy themselves not only as bold reformers but also as the

---

[8] *Ibid.*, p. 90.

true champions of free market forces, which they invoke to determine exchange rates. Those economists who venture to defend stability are depicted as defending the interests of central bankers, bureaucrats, and currency controllers.

Unfortunately, the economic world is governed more by appearances than by realities, and most economic writings aim to make things appear what they are not. The criticism of the gold standard and exchange rate stability does not spring from the philosophy of individual freedom no matter how it is made to appear, but from the armory of interventionism. The gold standard as it gradually emerged in many parts of the world was *not* established by any conscious or deliberate act of the government; it evolved from the failure of the bimetallic standard. Moreover, where people are free to choose between paper money and gold currency they naturally turn to gold. The gold standard is a social institution that springs from inexorable economic law. It needs neither rules nor regulations, no legislation or government control, merely the individual freedom to own and trade gold.

When gold is the common medium of exchange, all money substitutes such as bank notes and demand deposits are redeemable in gold according to the terms of the issue contract. As the exchange rates between various gold coins are determined by their relative weights of gold, so are the rates of the substitutes. A British bank note that is redeemable in a coin weighing one ounce of gold equals an American bank note redeemable in the same quantity of gold. Their exchange rates are rigidly fixed by the relative weights of gold they represent. The economist who in this case argues for floating exchange rates acts like the bad debtor who, when called upon to repay his $1000 loan, pleads with his banker to "float" his promissory note to $900 or $800. He would like to default on his contractual obligation.

The question of exchange rate flexibility arises only when default is contemplated under the gold standard, or when the gold standard has given way to irredeemable government paper, commonly called the *fiat* standard. The advocates of flexibility usually champion a world-wide *fiat* standard, and many defenders of stability favor the gold standard. The debate usually concerns the Bretton Woods agreement. Both sides are rather unhappy about its exchange rate provisions. The former level their criticism at its alleged rigidities, while the latter find fault with its departure from stability. They point out that even the Bretton Woods system, which was established immediately after the Second World War, already departed substantially from the principles of the orthodox gold standard. It provided for a maximum fluctuation of currencies around their gold parities of two percent — one percent on each side of the parity. It authorized member governments to change their currency parities by ten per cent in either direction without prior authorization by the International Monetary Fund. Larger changes were authorized in case of "fundamental disequilibrium." In fact, the International Monetary Fund sanctioned more than two hundred devaluations until the demise of the system on August 15, 1971. The International Monetary Fund also promoted or at least facilitated inflationary practices through substantial financial aid, such as I.M.F. drawing rights and Special Drawing Rights, central bank loans, and reciprocal swap facilities. Without such assistance the countries with the most inflation would have suffered the consequences of their currency debasements much earlier and would have had to retrench much sooner.

The opponents of stability, while fancying themselves as courageous innovators, actually champion one of the oldest tyrannies known to man: the ancient and discredited system of flexible exchanges. Until the nineteenth century even metallic parities, which were normally determined by the relative weights of precious metals, were often uncertain due to incessant changes in the relative metal contents of the various coins. Consequently the notes that were redeemable in such coins fluctuated according to their chances of being convertible into certain quantities of precious metal. Even during the nineteenth century and throughout most of the twentieth, fixed parities were maintained by only a few advanced countries, while flexible exchanges were popular in many parts of the world, especially in the majority of less advanced countries. The history of Latin American currencies, for instance, is a long record of flexible exchange rates. Even the United States dollar was mostly floating during the first four decades of its existence, and after a brief period of stability during the 1840's and 1850's relapsed again into floating during and after the Civil War. It floated again from 1933 to 1934 when it was stabilized after a forty percent devaluation.

In almost every case the floating was accompanied by severe depreciation and followed by devaluation. Only in a few cases where currencies were floated from positions of strength did the flexible system work temporarily without dire consequences. The floating Canadian dollar between 1951 and 1962 and again since June 1970, and the West German mark in 1969 and again in 1971, faced *buying* pressures against which the monetary authorities could intervene easily and systematically through currency and credit expansion. Where floating exchanges were chosen from positions of weakness, a self-aggravating movement toward severe depreciation usually resulted. To halt this process and to save the currency from extreme depreciation, governments had to resort to unpopular measures of retrenchment. But the very justification of currency flexibility rests on the contention that flexibility would make retrenchment for the sake of defending exchange rates unnecessary.[9]

To retrench, that is, to balance government budgets through spending reductions in expensive social and economic programs and to reduce the rates of currency and credit expansion, is deemed to be undesirable because it interrupts economic growth. To achieve a desirable rate of growth from which both the private and public sectors can reap their benefits is a very popular objective. It must not be jeopardized by foreign influences and considerations, such as exchange rates and currency reserves.[10]

But we prefer retrenchment over non-stop boom and the stop-and-go system of runaway inflation followed by a serious depression. In fact, we would hope that all inflationary practices would be abandoned once and for all and thus all booms and busts be avoided. But in a world of welfare states and fiscal deficits such a hope is destined to be disappointed, which leads us to opt for the lesser evil, frequent retrenchments and readjustments. We do so not only for the sake of stable exchange rates of the national currency, but also to defend its domestic purchasing power and avoid disastrous booms and slumps. Whenever exchange rate stability precipitates the retrenchment it is eminently beneficial and desirable.

Some economists favor floating exchanges because they fear exchange controls and foreign trade controls which governments tend to resort to when defending given exchange rates. Floating exchange rates, they believe, discourage economic and monetary nationalism and promote freedom of trade and commerce. They fancy themselves as consistent champions of the market order, which they would like to invoke also in the case of exchange rates.[11]

Foreign exchange controls and trade restrictions are some of the most destructive instruments of economic nationalism. But we deny that they are the products of exchange rate stability. Foreign exchange controls, like any other economic controls, belong to the paraphernalia of economic statism. A completely regimented *fiat* currency is its most radical manifestation. It is rather naive to believe that a currency which is manipulated all the way from the printing presses to the national border will be left to pure market forces where its exchange rates are concerned. Since the exchange rate

[9]Paul Einzig, *The Case Against Floating Exchanges* (London: St. Martin's Press, 1970), p. 29 *et seq.*; see also Ragnar Nurkse, *International Currency Experience: Lessons of the Interwar Period* (Geneva: League of Nations Secretariat, 1944).

[10]Milton Friedman, *Dollars and Deficits, op. cit.,* p. 226 *et seq.*; cf. his *Essays in Positive Economics, op. cit.*

[11]J. Enoch Powell, *Freedom and Reality* (London: B.T. Batsford, 1969), p. 72 *et seq.*; see also his *Exchange Rates and Liquidity* (London: Institute of Economic Affairs, 1967).

affects not only the prices of all imported goods — and indirectly all other prices — but also economic activity and employment, governments feel called upon to assume exchange control. In short, the government that forces *fiat* money on its people must be expected to manipulate the foreign exchanges also. This is why floating exchange rates always tend to be "dirty" rates, rates that are rigged by numerous government controls, including foreign exchange controls.

But the most important and strongest theoretical argument advanced in favor of floating rates is yet another. It is the thesis of a trade equilibrium rate to which floating exchange rates are supposed to adapt themselves. There can be no import or export surpluses, according to this thesis, wherever the exchange rates are permitted to float toward the equilibrium rate. It is so simple — merely obeying demand and supply, floating exchange rates will settle at a level at which imports and exports do balance.[12]

The fact is that foreign trade is not the only factor that determines the demand for and supply of foreign exchange. Exchange rates are affected by the combined effects of transactions arising from several sources such as foreign trade, capital movements, speculative considerations, and even arbitrage. Their combined demand and supply create a tendency toward an *overall* rate that may differ substantially from the rate that emanates from trade only. In fact, it is a fair assumption that the forces generated by capital transactions, speculative transactions, and arbitrage transactions will not be neutral, *i.e.*, will not offset each other, and therefore will exert an important influence on the overall rate. Trade transactions may remain unbalanced for long periods of time while capital movements, speculation, and arbitrage affect the overall rate. Moreover, the great elasticity of these forces, which can be arranged and completed in a matter of minutes while foreign trade transactions may take weeks and months, makes them ideally suited for affecting the overall rate.

Imports and exports need not balance in order to equate the exchange market. A trade deficit may be offset by capital movements such as an increase in short-term indebtedness or long-term capital imports. Conversely, a trade surplus may be balanced by various forms of capital exports. For instance, for many years the United States enjoyed sizable trade surpluses that were more than offset by capital exports. In fact, a flight of capital may put exchange rates under pressure in spite of export surpluses, for adverse capital movements can be much stronger than foreign exchange movements resulting from trade surpluses. Capital movements may run counter

---

[12]Leland B. Yeager, *International Monetary Relations* (New York: Harper and Row, 1966), p. 54 *et seq.*

to or exaggerate a foreign trade imbalance in both the short and long runs. Over decades, capital movements proceed in certain directions, making some countries creditors and others debtors. The industrial countries of Europe and North America tend to export capital while, in spite of highly flexible exchanges and depreciation of their currencies, several Latin American countries continue to increase their international indebtedness.

Floating exchange rates do not automatically establish equilibria in foreign trade or even in long-term capital movements. For there is no tendency at all for long-term capital movements to balance even if exchange rates are free to take care of themselves. It is true that such movements may be affected by exchange rate considerations. A capital-exporting country with an overvalued currency, such as the United States in recent years, may accelerate its investments in capital-importing countries, especially if their currencies are undervalued and are expected to be revalued upwards. Except for such considerations, capital movements are basically independent of the position of exchanges. But they are greatly affected by such fundamental factors as safety of foreign investments from expropriation and confiscatory taxation, fear or hatred of foreigners, honesty and industry of native populations, political stability and government attitude, and last but not least, the availability and cost of investment capital, natural resources, and many other factors that affect the prospects of business profits. The same is true in all cases of disinvestment. Exchange rate adjustments may influence such decisions, but more fundamental considerations play a decisive role.

It is obvious that there can be no exchange rate equilibrium at which both investments and disinvestments are kept in equilibrium or where such capital movements would achieve a balance for trade surpluses or deficits. Capital movements may aggravate the trade imbalance as capital tends to leave the countries with social and political upheavals that are likely to jeopardize the safety of private investments. Even the mere expectation of such upheavals may trigger a flight of capital to safe harbors. Capital may flow counter to the trade imbalance in confidence of continuous safety and profitability in spite of some currency depreciation.

But even if we were to assume that the movements of capital would happen to balance at an exchange rate at which trade is "at equilibrium," speculative transactions could effect a different overall rate. Speculation, that is, foreign exchange transactions embarked upon in expectation of a profit through changes in exchange rates, may anticipate political troubles, harmful strikes, crop failure, or any other factor at home or abroad that may affect exchange rates. Speculative activity may conceivably be in balance through equal buying

141

and selling, or when most speculators take the same view, may generate pressures towards moving the exchange rates. In the vast majority of cases speculation moves floating exchange rates towards a new overall rate that differs from the equilibrium level for foreign trade and capital movements.

The advocates of floating exchanges are convinced that speculation helps to establish the foreign trade balance. But speculators have no way of knowing in advance what the foreign trade accounts are going to be. Available information that is released by government is rather unreliable, since it covers past trade which may not be indicative of future trade. With stable exchanges, speculators are apt to counteract each other. For instance, some may sell a currency in anticipation of a trade deficit while others may establish long positions in the belief that existing parities will be maintained. Only when a devaluation is believed to be unavoidable and imminent will all speculators act alike and thus add their weight to the devaluation pressures. With floating exchange rates, however, any event, no matter how small, could trigger strong speculative movements that would cause exchange rates to fluctuate widely. The prospects of bigger profits would attract ever more speculators. Whether they are right or wrong in their assessment of the situation, their activities would move toward overall rates that would leave imports and exports unbalanced.

But even if speculators' transactions as well as capital movements were not to divert exchange rates from their trade equilibrium levels, there would still be arbitrage that could have disturbing influences. Arbitrage normally does not change the demand and supply constellation, since it aims to gain from discrepancies between different markets (space arbitrage), or different forward rates for different maturities (time arbitrage), or from differences between spot and forward rates (interest arbitrage). Nevertheless, in volatile markets arbitrage may add its pressures on exchange rates.

Because all free exchange markets constitute one vast international market, large funds can be shifted easily from one center to another. Let us assume that the United States dollar is under pressure in London and that the Germans, as a result of a large flow of dollars into Frankfurt, decide to sell dollars for sterling in London on a large scale. Such an operation would result in a depreciation of the dollar and an appreciation of sterling, which would exaggerate the weakness of the dollar, adversely affect the important dollar-sterling rate, and generate unfavorable psychological effects on the freely floating United States dollar. Under fixed parities the impact of this German selling would remain rather limited due to the support points mechanism.

Time arbitrage may also affect the overall equilibrium. Although it does not affect the supply of or demand for foreign exchange, it may, for instance, put heavy pressure on short forward rates, which in turn may depress spot rates. Interest arbitrage may directly exert pressures on the spot rate while relieving the forward rates, always moving the exchanges toward an overall rate that is likely to differ from the trade equilibrium.

With the system of floating exchanges, adjustments would necessarily be erratic and self-aggravating because no one would know the position of the "equilibrium rate." Exchange rate movements would tend to be extreme, and the exchanges would have to be grossly overvalued or undervalued before positions would be covered and new operations be undertaken to reverse a given movement. After all, with the floating system, the central bank would neither intervene in the market nor change its monetary policies in order to stabilize the exchanges. As the causes that generate the exchange pressures would not change, the exchange movements would tend to go very far in anticipation of a continuation of the causes and surely exceed the trade equilibrium level. Furthermore, excessive depreciation through wide exchange movements would cause goods prices and wages to rise, which in turn would cause the overall rate to fall.

Excessive depreciation through wide exchange movements could be avoided through credit restraint, balanced budgets, and other restrictive measures, of course. But the main argument raised on behalf of floating exchanges is the very superfluity of unpopular restraint that is said to hamper economic expansion and prosperity. In reality, floating exchanges require extreme measures of restraint to prevent excessive depreciation and chaotic exchange conditions. Because such measures would be rather unpopular the depreciation would probably be allowed to continue and accelerate. Moreover, since prices are rather inelastic downwards and quick to adjust upwards, it is tempting to justify any depreciation of the exchange no matter how exaggerated it may first have been. Because business costs could not adjust downward, an occasional appreciation would soon cause a recession, which would call for more inflation and credit expansion. With the system of floating exchanges, depreciation would tend to be self-perpetuating and accelerating.[13]

But even if floating exchanges would have no such dire consequences they would probably cause foreign trade to decline and the world economy to slump. A worldwide depression would follow major exchange movements that paralyze foreign trade. It is quite

---

[13]Robert Triffin, *Our International Monetary System: Yesterday, Today, and Tomorrow* (New York: Random House, 1968), p. 72 *et seq.*

true that importers and exporters would normally safeguard their interests against fluctuations of exchange through forward covering facilities. But with floating exchanges such facilities would be very expensive, in fact, too expensive to justify many trade transactions, or would not be available at all. But the need for cover would be greater by far in order to cover incalculable exchange risks. When exchange rates fluctuate widely no foreign trader could feel secure with uncovered claims or liabilities. In fact, facing even mild exchange movements, he would seek to cover his commitments. The demand for covering facilities would therefore be very great and the costs very high. Moreover, this demand would be reinforced by the desire for hedging and speculative purposes, which would grow significantly in periods of wide exchange movements. The high costs of forward cover would probably be prohibitive for many transactions, which would cause foreign trade to contract. Especially in industries with low profit margins, such as raw materials, the high costs of forward exchange would cause importers to forego the transaction, which would have serious consequences on economic production.

On the other hand, the supply of forward exchange facilities would tend to shrink considerably with the system of floating exchanges. Commercial banks would greatly reduce their forward commitments in widely fluctuating currencies because of the risk of heavy losses through unforeseen exchange movements. They would have to ration their facilities, which would leave some transactions uncovered. Or they would insist on sizable deposits by customers, which again would raise exchange costs. Thus while the demand for forward exchange would probably multiply, the supply would be severely curtailed. Importers and exporters themselves would have to assume the risk of losses through unexpected movements of exchange rates.[14]

It is true that the many disadvantages of the system of floating exchanges are mitigated by the establishment of currency areas in which the parities remain relatively stable. Minor currencies become stable satellites of the major currencies that float, or some are kept stable in terms of gold while others float, or some floating currencies are kept stable in terms of each other through government intervention. But the very disadvantages of floating exchanges described above are felt also between currency areas. Exchange movements would tend to become self-aggravating and widely fluctuating, and depreciation would accelerate. Foreign trade among the areas would tend to contract because of the risk of exchange losses. Forward exchange facilities would either not be available for trade between

---

[14] Paul Einzig, *The Case Against Floating Exchanges, op. cit.* p. 110, *et seq.*

the areas or be offered at very high costs. Finally, the instability of exchanges between the currency areas would jeopardize the confidence and stability within the areas and bring about their gradual disintegration.

On August 15, 1971, the system of floating exchanges was universally adopted when President Nixon repudiated all obligations to pay gold. With over $50 billion in current liabilities and less than $10 billion of gold left in its vaults, the United States finally faced the day of reckoning for a decade of deficit spending and currency depreciation. In an atmosphere of utter international disarray the United States defaulted on its obligations. But to the American people the default was presented as a defiant move to spite speculators and obtain better treatment for American goods in foreign markets.

The Smithsonian Agreement of December 1971, which President Nixon called "the most important monetary agreement in the history of the world," attempted to salvage the old monetary order. But it failed after only thirteen months. In March 1973 the United States government again led the world to the system of floating exchanges. It thereby set the stage for a sharp contraction of foreign trade and a worldwide recession.

VI
The Quest for Monetary Stability

Economic life is a process of perpetual change. Man continually chooses between alternatives, attaching ever-changing values to economic goods. Therefore, the exchange ratios of his goods are forever adjusting. Nothing is fixed and therefore nothing can be measured. The economist searching for stability and measurement is like the music lover who would like to measure his preference for Beethoven's *Eroïca* over Verdi's *Aïda*.

Money is no yardstick of prices. It is subject to man's valuation and actions in the same way as are all other economic goods. Its subjective as well as objective exchange values continually fluctuate and in turn affect the exchange ratios of other goods at different times and to different extents. There is no true stability of money, whether it is *fiat* or commodity money. There is no fixed point or relationship in economic exchange.

Despite this inherent catallactic instability of economic value and purchasing power, the precious metals have served man well throughout the ages. Because of their natural qualities and their relative scarcity, both gold and silver have been dependable media of exchange. They are marketable goods that gradually gained universal

147

acceptance and employment in exchanges. They even could be used to serve as tools of economic calculation, inasmuch as their quantities changed very slowly over time. This kept changes in their purchasing power at rates that could be disregarded by business accounting and bookkeeping. In this sense we may speak of an accounting stability that permits acting man to compare the countless objects of his economic concern.

Throughout the long history of money a clamor for this stability always arose when governments engaged in coin debasements and paper money inflation. Certainly the Romans yearned for monetary stability when their emperors resorted to every conceivable device of monetary depreciation. Medieval man longed for stability when his prince clipped, reduced, or debased the coins and defrauded him through such devices. Throughout the seventeenth and eighteenth centuries the early Americans sought monetary stability when the colonial governments issued legal tender "bills of credit," regulated the exchange ratios between British and Spanish coins, and imposed wage and price controls. Americans were dreaming of monetary stability during the Revolution when the Continental Congress emitted vast quantities of Continental Dollars until they became utterly worthless.

Man's only hope for monetary stability is the abstention of government from monetary depreciation. This is the only permissible meaning of our search for stability, which is as old as inflation itself. In our century, it again has gained in intensity and urgency as governments the world over are waging devastating wars and engaging in massive redistribution of economic income and wealth. The savings and investments of millions of people are at stake. In the United States alone, the volume of long-term loan capital is estimated at more than three trillion dollars. Obviously, such a magnitude of credit lends economic, social, and political importance to the quest for monetary stability.

Our high rates of productivity, wages, and standards of living are built on an effective capital market. In the United States, some $40,000 has been invested per worker, which makes him highly productive and yields wage rates that are the highest in the world. More than one-half of this capital investment comes from lenders, such as bondholders, banks, and other institutional investors. Obviously, their direct stake in this marvelous apparatus of production depends on the stability of their dollar claims. They comprise what is commonly called "the middle classes" who do not own the facilities of production. They do not directly own the stores, factories, farms, and livestock, but merely provide the loan capital that helps to build and improve them.

The savers and investors are not alone in their great concern for

148

monetary stability. Anyone whose income depends on his labor productivity must be vitally interested in the efficient functioning of the capital market that supplies him with tools and equipment. The economic well-being of every manual laborer directly depends on capital investments just as that of office workers, business executives, physicians, dentists, and teachers does. In fact, everyone has a stake in monetary stability and economic productivity. Even government itself, which likes to issue ever more money in order to facilitate deficit spending, depends on the purchasing power of money. After all, money is the only economic good at the disposal of government, permitting it to acquire other goods and services and redistribute real income and wealth. When money ceases to function as a medium of exchange, government ceases to function in any form.

Accounting Stability

The hope for monetary stability, as we define it, is man's quest for government abstention from monetary depreciation. The only stable money, in the long run, is the money of the market: It is nonpolitical money. Real stability comes with the separation of political power from control of money.

Of course, we realize that the prospects for a dismantling of the monopolistic power which government now is wielding over money, or even for a total removal of government from the monetary scene, are rather slim. Public opinion, in its present ideological color, does not permit a reduction of government power. But it may change in the future as the government issues of *fiat* money continue to depreciate, breeding countless economic and social evils. Be that as it may, the monetary theorist does not allow himself to be intimidated by public opinion or the trend in policy. His thoughts and deliberations are free to seek truth and pursue his ideals, even the dismantling of government power over money.

To remove government from all monetary affairs is to deny all government prerogatives in monetary matters. Government must have no special rights and privileges in the market place for money. In particular, the following governmental powers to which our generation has grown accustomed must be rescinded:

1. *The legal tender laws* that dictate what legal money shall be. There is no need for government to specify the kinds of money in which contracts may be written, or for government in any way to limit the freedom of contract. Surely, no degree of convenience that may come from a single currency system can outweigh the dangers of a monopolistic system that permits government, through legal tender legislation, to force its depreciating money on its people. Legal tender

is the very device that prevents an easy escape by inflation victims into other monies and permits inflation to rage on until it becomes a fatal social disorder. It permits the massive transfer of income and wealth from hapless creditors to puzzled debtors, generating vast amounts of inflation losses and gains. In fact, legal tender legislation establishes the monopoly *par excellence* that permits the money monopolist to reap incalculable gains through the gradual depreciation of his product.

2. *The central banking system* that subjects financial institutions to a central authority and redirects their resources toward fiscal uses and economic policies. The central bank is the monetary arm of government that facilitates the financing of budgetary deficits through monetary expansion. It serves as a crutch to commercial banks, which it enables to expand credit to the limit of their reserves. When their reserves are exhausted it provides new excess reserves in ever larger quantities. In short, the central bank removes all checks on inflation and coordinates the inflation effort. It must be summarily abolished if the freedom of the money market is to be restored and monetary stability returned.

3. *The compulsory monopoly of the mint* that permits government to determine what coins shall be used in exchange. The rationale of the mint monopoly as given by governments throughout the ages is the convenience of a uniform coinage system. But no matter how popular this convenience may be, it affords government important sources of revenue: seigniorage, which is the monopolistic charge for minting coins, and debasement, which secretly or openly dilutes or reduces the weight of the coin. As the mint monopoly was the first step toward government control over money, its removal is essential for the restoration of monetary freedom.

Few economists, if any, are advocating a stabilization of money through such comprehensive reforms. In the ideological climate of today, any deliberation along such lines, while it may be sagacious economic theory, is out of step with political reality. Therefore, most economists limit their deliberations to the search for monetary stability as it existed a few decades ago. Their inquiries are encompassed by political or historical considerations and colored by the hope of being "practical" and "effective."

We need not here enter a discussion of who is more practical and effective: he who uncompromisingly seeks to draw his conclusions and reveal irrefutable truths, or he who permits his deliberations to be colored by that which is more popular. In fact, most economists seek to be realistic and, therefore, advocate a limited reform that would restore monetary stability of their national systems as they existed in the recent past. American economists who are hoping and working for such a stability would like to restore the quality and integrity of the United States dollar.

Balancing the Federal Budget

To stabilize the United States dollar, *i.e.*, to safeguard its present purchasing power, obviously requires the immediate cessation of the inflation process. The monetary authorities must cease and desist from expanding the quantity of money in any form. But before this expansion can be halted the federal government must learn to live within its means and abstain from making further demands on the central banking system.

To the federal government, inflation is a convenient device for raising revenue. It easily covers budget deficits which otherwise would deplete the loan market, raise interest rates, and depress the economy. It turns deficit spending, which normally causes economic depressions, into spending sprees that generate the popular, and yet so pernicious, economic booms. Inflation boosts government revenue as it raises everyone's tax rates and thus absorbs an increasing share of individual income. It repudiates government debt as it reduces the purchasing power of all debt. In this respect it is a silent tax on all creditors and money holders. With a federal debt of some $800 billion, an inflation rate of ten percent reduces the value of the debt by $80 billion, which is taken from the owners of the Treasury obligations and transferred to government as the debtor, for more spending in the future.

In today's atmosphere of government welfare and economic re-distribution, to balance the budget and thus refrain from its inflationary financing is no easy political task. An estimated 81.3 million Americans, or 38 percent of the total population, are now enjoying redistribution dollars from government (retirement and disability income, 28.6 million; survivor benefits, 8.9 million; supplemental income, 6.6 million; unemployment compensation, 6 million; active military duty and dependents, 3.5 million; civil servants and their dependents, 27.7 million). While the trend continues to favor ever more programs with more redistribution beneficiaries, it is difficult to envision a modification of the transfer process. And yet, the task is urgent; the great budgetary pressures exerted by the popular quest for economic transfer must be alleviated and the budget be balanced through cuts in spending. Without such a balance, the inflation will rage on.

We cannot expect many beneficiaries readily to vote for a reduction, much less a removal of their benefits. Under the influences of the prevailing social and economic ideology they are convinced that they are morally entitled to their favors. They noisily oppose any modification affecting their innate "rights" to other people's income and wealth. In fact, their redistributive aspirations often induce their political representatives in Congress to authorize and appropriate even more money than the President is requesting. Such programs as social security, medicare, anti-poverty, housing, aid to education, environmental improvement, and pay increases for civil servants are so popular that few politicians dare to oppose them.

The situation is not hopeless as long as only 38 percent of the population are transfer beneficiaries and 62 percent the primary victims. However, many victims do not realize that they are victimized by the redistribution process. With low personal incomes their tax liabilities may be insignificant. Without money in the bank or in a pension fund, the inflation may be of no concern to them. But they do not realize, unfortunately, that the price of every product or service they buy has been boosted greatly by the taxes imposed on the producer. It is the consumers who ultimately feel the effects of the corporate taxes and other levies on business. Consumers also suffer diminutions of income and wealth when inflation raises their income tax rates, and boosts goods prices faster than incomes.

Other victims may be unconcerned because they themselves derive some clearly visible benefits from the political transfer process while their losses are hidden in a maze of taxes and prices. The parents of children in government schools or universities are counting their transfer blessings that hopefully exceed the transfer losses. This is why millions of middle class victims continue to favor the growing role of government as a transfer agency. They mistakenly conclude from the visible benefits they receive that their benefits exceed the losses, and therefore are led to approve of the basic principles and objectives of the whole transfer system.

Facing the Depression

Any stabilization program must make preparations for the inevitable depression. After all, the present system embodies at least two powerful depressive forces which a monetary stabilization would unleash. This is why the acid test of every stabilization attempt is the depression that soon appears in its trail.

A powerful depressive force is the very burden of government. Without the monetary expansion that helps to finance the transfer programs, the high costs of government on all its levels would soon depress economic activity. A sixty-five billion dollar deficit like that suffered in fiscal year 1976 would simply crush the capital market and precipitate a devastating depression. But even if the government budgets were balanced, the combined load of federal, state, and local governments, which is estimated to exceed forty percent of national income, could not be carried by the "private sector." As a result of monetary stabilization, there would be no longer any inflation victims helping to finance government spending and public debt; government would have to rely exclusively on taxpayers and lenders. But this massive shift of burden from money holders and inflation victims to the the taxpayers and lenders would have the same depressive effects as a new deficit that consumes loan capital and invites additional taxation. This is why any attempt at monetary stabilization must be accompanied by drastic reductions in government spending.

If our money were stable, business would soon be threatened by the scissor effects of stable prices and rising costs. When business taxes are raised, business must curtail its operations. When powerful labor unions raise business costs through higher wages or lower labor productivity while goods prices are stable, business may suffer economic stagnation and losses. Therefore, any attempt at monetary stabilization must be accompanied by a reduction in business taxes, which in turn must be *preceded* by a reduction in government spending. Without this spending cut a mere reduction in taxation that leads to budget deficits and a shift of the costs of government to the loan market would bring no relief to business.

Another powerful depressive force at the time of monetary stabilization is the economic distortion and maladjustment which previous inflation and credit expansion are leaving behind. After many years of inflation the economy is so badly disarranged that a return to normalcy would be marred by painful withdrawal symptoms. When the monetary authorities expand the quantity of money and credit, they cause interest rates to fall at first. Business is then tempted to embark upon new expansion and modernization projects, taking advantage of the lower interest costs. But the feverish activity that follows is falsely induced by newly created money and credit, unsupported by genuine savings. The feverish bidding for land, labor, and capital goods raises their prices. That is, business costs soar and now render many a project unprofitable. Many may have to be abandoned or written down as business failures — unless new money and credit are made available to support the malinvestments. During many years of inflation countless economic undertakings were spawned by easy money considerations and sustained by ever more inflation. This is why any attempt at monetary stabilization would not only reveal the shocking extent of disarrangement and maladjustment, but also would need to prepare for and cope with the depression.

In his course of action the monetary reformer faces the choice between two possibilities. He may rely completely on the flexibility

153

and ingenuity of business to achieve new profitability through cost-cutting readjustment. He may do so with confidence in the individual enterprise system and in the knowledge that throughout the United States economic history, prior to the radical interventionism of the Great Depression, American business always rebounded quickly from occasional stagnations and depressions. Or the reformer may want to give business recovery a boost through tax reductions. Of course, such a reduction must again be accompanied by cuts in government spending lest its burden merely be shifted to the loan market. In any case, during the trying weeks and months of the stabilization crisis, it is absolutely essential for the success of any stabilization program to resist arduously and successfully any temptation and public pressure to return to deficit spending and easy money.

Restoring the Labor Market

The inevitable stabilization depression must be expected to be especially painful because the United States labor market, after more than fifty years of government intervention, has lost its viability and flexibility to cope with necessary labor adjustments. Even without the special strains of a stabilization depression, the United States unemployment rate presently (1978) stands at 7.8 percent. A policy of monetary stabilization that would deny government the right to launch new deficit spending and easy money policies would soon encounter intolerable multiples of this unemployment rate — unless the labor market is restored to cope with the expected increase in unemployment. Without a labor market vitalization any attempt at monetary stabilization is bound to run aground on unbearable rates of unemployment.

To vitalize the labor market it would be necessary to rescind the government intervention of half a century. According to the late Roscoe Pound, one of the most eminent legal philosophers of our time, the labor leaders and labor unions are enjoying legal privileges and immunities which only kings and princes enjoyed during the middle ages. In the 1930's the United States Congress granted labor unions and their members the legal right:

> . . . to commit wrongs to person and property, to interfere with the use of highways, to break contracts, to deprive individuals of the means of earning a livelihood, to control the activities of the individual workers and their local organizations by national organizations centrally and arbitrarily administered beyond the reach of state laws — things which no one else can do with impunity.[1]

---

[1]Roscoe Pound, *Legal Immunities of Labor Unions* (Washington, D.C.: American Enterprise Association, 1957), p. 21.

Two statutes, the Norris-LaGuardia Act of 1932 and the Wagner Act of 1935, radically changed the nature of labor relations. The Norris-LaGuardia Act drastically limited the jurisdiction of the federal courts in labor disputes and especially prohibited the courts from enjoining coercive labor union activities. Before the Act, the federal courts had been enjoining violent, intimidatory, coercive activities of the unions, although peaceful strikes were sanctioned. The Norris-LaGuardia Act made practically all union conduct unenjoinable by the courts.

The National Labor Relations Act (Wagner Act) gave one-sided emphasis upon "unfair practices" by employers and eliminated all possibilities of direct access to the federal courts. It made it an "unfair practice" for an employer to interfere with, restrain, or coerce employees in the exercise of their rights to form a union organization. It forbade employers to interfere with the formation and administration of any labor organization. Above all, the Wagner Act took all labor cases out of the courts of law and transferred them to the new National Labor Relations Board. This Board is a quasi-judicial administrative tribunal whose members are appointed by the President. They have often been accused of corrupting the law that is already biased in favor of the unions.

Federal labor laws have been setting minimum wage rates ever since 1933. The present rate is $2.90 an hour, to which we must add the legal fringe benefits amounting to approximately twenty-five to thirty-five percent, so that the minimium costs of employment of every American worker, even the least productive, may exceed $4.00 per hour. It is estimated that at least three million idle Americans owe their unemployment to this labor law. Teenagers and uneducated, unskilled minority workers are its primary victims. In a stabilization crisis the minimum wage law may deny employment to several additional millions.

The Davis-Bacon Act as amended in 1961 authorizes the Secretary of Labor to set minimum wages in construction that is financed, subsidized, insured, or underwritten by federal agencies. The Secretary usually sets a minimum that coincides with the going labor union pay scale. In most trades the pay for construction apprentices, for instance, stands at $7.50 per hour, which readily explains why there are no young people at work on construction sites.

The system of unemployment compensation in its present form is a powerful force for unemployment. It provides for compensation up to $125 per week for 65 weeks, in addition to some family allowances. It is supplemented by a generous food stamp program, and, in many cases, by various employer and union benefits. Altogether, the system paralyzes the market for unskilled labor through offering benefits for unemployment that may approach or even equal the pay for actual work performed. It leaves a tiny margin of financial incentive which for millions of workers does not offset the disutility of labor. In short, to many people a week's leisure may be worth more than the small income increment that may be earned from a week's work.

All such handicaps to productivity need to be removed, or at least reduced, when the national currency is stabilized. It is very simple to halt inflation by ordering the central bank to cease and desist from any further money creation. But it is extremely painful, after many years of government intervention, to suffer the withdrawal symptoms. They point up not only the economic difficulties of any stabilization policy, but also its ideological and educational complications. In fact, they raise the ultimate reform question: Are the people prepared to suffer the withdrawal pains that will be all the more excruciating the more they obstruct and restrict the labor market? In the pains of a stabilization crisis, will they succumb, once again, to the temptations of easy money and deficit spending? Or will they see it through, all the way, all the way to stable money?

The optimists in our midst are convinced that the American people will have the moral strength and economic wisdom to effect a complete turnabout when the ultimate destination of the present road comes in sight. They are hoping and praying for a rebirth of America in freedom and integrity. The pessimists, however, point to the transfer system and its great popularity and speak of a point of no return. They despair about man and his ability to learn from such a complex experience as the decline of his economic and social order.

Make Peace with Gold

Whoever ventures to speak kindly of gold or the gold standard places his good name and professional reputation in great jeopardy. The number of advocates of gold as money has dwindled to a tiny remnant whose voice is easily lost in the noise of popular monetary discussion. Argument with "gold philes" usually proceeds by ridicule and contempt rather than analysis. According to one monetarist, the typical academic supporter of the gold standard has not gone much "beyond sloganizing." Only the advocates of *fiat* money are engaged in serious scientific discussion.

While the thought of gold as money is summarily rejected as an antiquated collection of slogans, the world of economic reality can not escape from gold and its many ramifications. It seems that all the denunciations of gold merely reinforce its position in the aspirations of men and its role in the money markets of the world. In fact, there seems to be a correlation between the intensity of the official attacks on gold and the severity of monetary crises.

The schism that divides the friends of gold from their adversaries is not only utilitarian but also philosophical. The case for gold is solidly built on some basic considerations of political philosophy to which the advocates of *fiat* money quickly object. "Money is not an invention of the state," wrote Menger. "It is not the product of a legislative act. Even the sanction of political authority is not necessary for its existence."[2] Money is the product of man's division of labor and exchange economy. Wherever enterprising men sought to exchange their goods and services for more marketable goods that facilitated further exchanges, the precious metals emerged as the most marketable goods and thus the money of most people. Gold and silver were valuable because they served man's needs. In contrast to other useful commodities they could be easily divided, transported at low cost, and stored in relative safety. For some 2500 years small pieces of gold and silver, called coins, constituted universal money. They survived for two millennia in spite of countless attempts by hosts of governments to manipulate them or replace them with their own media. This awareness of the very nature of money and the natural characteristics of precious metals in the service of economic exchange leads us to believe that gold and silver coins probably will survive the next two millennia. And the gold standard, in one form or another, will prevail long after the present rash of national *fiats* is forgotten or remembered only in currency museums.

We are fully aware that at the present gold is no longer the world's money. Shackled by countless restrictions and prohibitions it is buried in the vaults of several central banks or hidden in countless private hoards. Until recently it still served as the governments' money for payments to one another. But even this limited role of gold came to an end in 1968 when the United States and Great Britain, by far the biggest debtor countries, no longer could meet their international obligations. Introduction of the two-tier system, which repudiated all gold obligations to private note holders and actually halted gold payments among governments themselves, signaled the end of gold as world money. It was formally disclaimed in March 1973 when the United States led the world to a universal *fiat* system.

We are not contending that the gold standard affords universal monetary stability, and that gold coins are endowed with unchanging purchasing power. In a changing world of human action no money can be neutral or stable. Even a one hundred percent hard-money

---

[2]Carl Menger, *Principles of Economics* (Glencoe, Illinois: The Free Press, 1950), p. 257.

gold standard, in which the currency of each country would consist exclusively of gold, cannot afford stability of purchasing power to its gold coins. Just as the price of an economic good is ultimately determined by the subjective valuation of buyers and sellers, so is the purchasing power of money. Individual valuation of money is subject to the same considerations of demand and supply as that of all other goods and services. People expend labor or forego the enjoyment of other economic goods in order to acquire money. At times they bid for money, at other times they offer money, and all this bidding and offering ultimately determines the purchasing power of money in the same way as it determines the mutual exchange ratios of other goods. All plans to make money stable are contradictory to human nature and dangerous to individual freedom, for they would call on government to enforce the impossible. The quest for "stable money," therefore, is forever futile unless we mean thereby a quest for money that is free from the political processes of public treasuries and central banks. All we can ever hope for is monetary freedom that embodies the freedom of contract and choice of money. In freedom, we are confident the American people once again would prefer gold and silver coins over depreciating political *fiat*.

Our choice of the monetary system is of crucial importance. Do we want a system in which government creates and manages money through the political process? Or do we prefer acting people to make the choice? If we rely on government we must be prepared to live with government *fiat*, which is ideally suited to serve political ends. It can be expanded or contracted at will, always accommodating the policy of the moment. Above all, it can be inflated at will to supplement government revenue.

On the other hand, if we allow free people to make the selection, they may choose a great variety of marketable goods as their media of exchange. In the past, in a selective process that took several thousand years, they chose the precious metals, gold and silver, as their money. They may choose them again if given the freedom of choice. Government need not establish the gold standard by any conscious or deliberate act. In fact, the gold standard needs neither rules nor regulations, no legislation or government control, merely the individual freedom to own and use gold. Of course, this freedom of gold ownership embodies the freedom not only to buy and sell gold for use in industrial production, but also to employ it in exchange.

The gold coin standard means sound money; it makes the value of money independent of government. It cannot achieve the unattainable ideal of an absolutely stable currency, to be sure. But it protects the monetary system from the influence of governments, as the quantity of gold in existence is utterly independent of the wishes and manipulations of government officials, politicians, parties, and pressure groups. There are no "rules of the game," no arbitrary rules which people must learn to observe. It is a social institution that is controlled by inexorable economic law.

The issuers of money substitutes, whether private or public, keep their currencies at par with gold through unconditional redemption. The issuing bank buys any amount of gold against its currency or deposits at the parity rate, and sells indiscriminately and on demand any amount of gold against its notes or deposits. It thereby renders no national service, nor "defends" or "protects" its currency. It merely fulfills the contract it made when it issued the money substitutes.

Under the gold coin standard inflationary policies are not rendered impossible, but rather made difficult. Redemption demands and the threat of drains of their gold reserves would restrain the issuers of money substitutes from inflationary expansion, for any such expansion would alarm the owners of substitutes and cause them to demand redemption in gold coin, which would spell ruin to the issuer. As the gold standard makes inflationary policies rather difficult, it also avoids the wide fluctuations of economic activity known as the business cycle. It forces the issuers of money substitutes not to exceed very narrow limits, and thus efficiently checks credit expansion.

The international gold standard evolved without intergovernmental treaties and institutions. No one had to make the gold standard work as an international system. When the leading nations of the world had adopted gold as their currency the world had an international money. It is true, the coins bore different names and had different weights. But this hardly mattered as long as they consisted of gold and could be exchanged freely. After all, an ounce of gold is an ounce of gold whether it consists of eagles or sovereigns.

The gold standard united the world as international payments ceased to be a problem. It facilitated international trade and finance, and thereby promoted a worldwide division of labor. Countries specialized in those internationally traded commodities in which they enjoyed the greatest comparative advantage. But above all, the gold standard encouraged exportation of capital from the industrial countries to the backward areas. Without the fears of devaluation losses or transfer restrictions, European capital eagerly sought profitable employment opportunities on all continents. It developed commerce and industry and thus improved the working and living conditions all over the globe.

The history of the gold standard is a voice forever sounding the principles of free and honest money. The history of *fiat* money is little more than a register of monetary follies and inflations. Our

Age of Inflation

present age merely affords another entry in this dismal register. We may hope for an early return to monetary freedom and sound money, but realization is hidden in the dark clouds of the future. Sound money is the most prominent concomitant of economic freedom and morality; *fiat* money is an inevitable symptom of their absence.

Professor William Graham Sumner, the great Yale economist of the pre-Federal Reserve era, put it this way:

> Scheme after scheme has been proposed and tried for realizing the gain which it was believed that cheap money could produce for the public; that is, for those who buy and use currency. This gain has been purchased as the alchemists pursued the philosopher's stone, by trial and failure. Whether there be any such gain or not, our attempts to win it have all failed, and they have cost us, in each generation, more than a purely specie currency would have cost, if each generation had had to buy it anew. . . . The revulsions to which the system was subject overwhelmed us in every decade. The notions on which the system was based are proved to have been delusions, disastrous to everybody concerned, including those who tried to profit by them.[3]

Our generation is pursuing the alchemists' money with greater fervor than ever before. For the first time in the history of the world, inflation is engulfing the entire globe. The only difference between the various countries is the rate of inflation at which governments depreciate their currencies. Some are inflating at single-digit rates, which makes their currencies relatively "strong." Others are inflating at double- and triple-digit rates, which makes for "weaker" currencies. And all are making international payments in stronger currencies, especially United States dollars, which are depreciating at ever faster rates. Like a herd of stampeding cattle approaching a gully, the world is rushing toward monetary chaos.

Many attempts at salvaging the *fiat* order will be made in the coming years. Temporary compromises may be worked out between various inflators. But foreign trade and international investment are bound to suffer severely from the monetary depreciation that inflicts losses on creditors and grants gains to debtors. Because the United States dollar is the most popular international currency, the dollar inflation is bestowing huge gains on the United States, while it inflicts staggering losses on countries with large dollar holdings. For more than two decades the United States flooded the world with dollars through its balance-of-payments deficits. It was exporting its depreciating currency while it was importing foreign goods and services or

---

[3] William Graham Sumner, "History of Banking in the U.S.," *The Journal of Commerce and Commercial Bulletin*, 1896, p. 472.

buying foreign assets and facilities. For the most prosperous country on earth to conduct, advocate, and defend such monetary policies — making it the biggest debtor country on earth — is to greatly weaken the United States position of leadership in the world.

The precariousness of the international monetary order raises the spectre of an international catastrophe similar to the money panic of 1931 and the subsequent disintegration of the world economy. The Eurodollar market with its $200 to $300 billion of short-term American obligations is extremely vulnerable to sudden breaks and runs that may turn into a world-wide dollar panic. After all, how long can the foreign dollar holders be expected to hold on to their falling dollars? What measure of financial loss can foreign individuals and institutions be expected to withstand? Growing losses provide the material of which panics are made when debtors are forced to draw on all their resources, including their dollars, via the exchange markets. The United States dollar could fall to unbearable levels that in turn would greatly disrupt foreign trade relations. In defense against United States dollars and goods, national barriers would be erected the world over, triggering a trade war and precipitating protectionism and finally isolationism. Such a development would spell depression the world over.[4]

This is why a consolidation of United States foreign liabilities is a paramount prerequisite for any attempt at stabilization. Some $100 billion of foreign dollar balances must be funded in long-term interest-bearing obligations before the monetary situation can stabilize. In short, the United States is in dire need of long-term loans from its creditor countries in order to consolidate the threatening debt.

We are confident that the United States could secure such loans at an international conference at which the case is honestly presented. After all, European countries look on the United States as the leading financial, economic, and military power of the West upon whose strength and power they must rely. No one but a confirmed totalitarian collectivist or a naive fool can possibly be interested in financial disaster and economic disintegration that may bring destruction to the Western order and triumph to world Communism. But it is essential that the United States seek such help from its creditors before it is too late. Of course, in order to secure the longterm assistance it would have to return to dollar convertibility into gold.

A "tough position" by the United States government can only invite disaster. To throw the responsibility on its creditors, to demand that countries with surpluses in their international payments con-

---

[4] Compare "An Interview with Jacques Rueff," *Barron's*, September 20, 1971, pp. 3, 8, 12.

tinuously adjust their currencies upward against the dollar, is to negate all hope for world monetary reform. Countries with strong currencies cannot and will not raise the value of their currencies to the extent considered desirable by the United States. But even if they would, and the United States is permitted to earn balance-of-payment surpluses of some $10 to $12 billion a year at the price of stagnation and unemployment in creditor countries, the new surpluses of one billion dollars per month would be utterly insufficient to meet current United States obligations of more than $200 billion.

It is too late for such palliatives as revaluation of strong currencies or devaluation of the dollar by ten percent without consolidation of the United States debt. How can a ten percent dollar devaluation meet United States obligations of more than $200 billion? A devaluation tends to make American producers more competitive in world markets, to be sure, and it might possibly check the growth of German, Swiss, Japanese dollar balances. But it does not solve the pressing currency crises. Even a fifty percent dollar devaluation, which would reduce the international value of the United States dollar by one-half and cut the United Stats debt in half, could not be expected to save the situation. It would merely trigger a round of worldwide currency devaluations equal or similar to the United States dollar rate.

In conjunction with a prompt consolidation of current United States debt such a devaluation would be in order, for it would provide creditor countries with "devaluation profits" on their gold holdings that would induce them to grant the needed consolidation loans. If the United States were to devalue its dollar to the market rate of exchange with gold, let us say, to 1/200 of an ounce of gold, and resume gold payments at that rate, international payments could be resumed in gold and freely convertible dollars. Other free-world countries would follow suit immediately, which once again would give the world one dependable international currency — gold.

Because gold is the only international money that has survived the crises unscathed, it must be permitted to take the place of the defunct United States dollar. It affords stability and discipline which no *fiat* currency can provide. After all, managed currencies are the products of political manipulations by parties and pressure groups, and all are destined to be destroyed gradually by weak administrations yielding to popular pressures for government largess and economic redistribution. No such currency can serve for long as the international reserve currency to which all others can repair. The United States dollar is no exception.

The Bretton Woods standard is dead, and any attempt at its revival is bound to be disappointing. It died from its very own characteristic:

the extreme flexibility that permitted its exchange component, *i.e.*, United States dollars, to flood the world. Its design was not American. At first, other countries were eager to hold dollars rather than gold in order to earn interest on their reserves. But when some ten years ago the United States government finally recognized that the gold exchange standard enabled it to export some of its inflation and painlessly finance growing balance-of-payments deficits with its own money, it resisted all efforts at reform. In fact, it did everything in its power to prolong the system through such dubious devices as foreign currency loans, swap arrangements, the two-tier system, Special Drawing Rights, *etc.* It defended the system and reaped its benefits until the world would take no more. This is why the gold bullion standard that preceded the Bretton Woods standard must be the immediate objective of any monetary reform. National currencies must again be convertible and redeemable in gold, and international balances must again be settled in gold.

It is natural that American monetary authorities should defend the bankrupt order that is rendering their inflation and balance-of-payments deficits so painless. They would like to maintain the *fiat* order that forces creditor countries with "stronger" currencies to accelerate their inflations in order to keep in step with the United States dollar. On this road there are many more monetary crises to come.

There is an alternate road that leads to monetary stability and economic cooperation. It is short and direct, and yet so narrow that it would take great political courage to traverse. First, on this road the United States government would immediately cease and desist from any further currency creation and credit expansion. It would bring its own financial house into order by refraining from any further deficit spending and by balancing its budgets through reductions in spending. Second, it would seek to consolidate some $100 billion of short-term United States obligations to foreign governments and central banks with long-term loans. The debt would have to be amortized over ten years or more and carry interest at the Eurodollar market rate. Third, it is high time to make peace with gold. The freedom of all Americans to make payments in gold must be restored immediately. Everyone must be free to buy and sell, to lend and borrow, to import and to export any quantity of gold and to use it in all his economic exchanges.

Finally, in order to give substance and enduring value to the United States dollar, it must be made freely convertible into gold. The market exchange ratio between the two must be made the legal parity at which unconditional convertibility must be assured. In short, this road leads us back to the gold standard, a social institution that is controlled by inexorable economic law.

Build on Gold

Most contemporary proposals for United States dollar stabilization merely aim at changing monetary management. The outsiders are criticizing the insiders for deficient and improper management of government money. Observing some undesirable consequences of insider policies, the outsiders eagerly proffer advice and assistance in correcting the shortcomings, or better yet, they clamor to assume control and apply their own remedies. The insiders at the helm of the monetary planning boards are noisily defending their actions with ever-changing doctrines and theories to explain the symptoms and consequences of their own policies. Their position of defense is rather difficult, for the United States dollar continues to depreciate and the American economy continues to suffer from deep recessions and feverish inflations. Both the insiders and outsiders fully agree on the desirability of money management and reform. In this sense, both are "*fiat* reformers."

The "Gold School" of monetary thought seeks to reduce and ultimately abolish the role of government in monetary exchanges. Its various adherents do not fully agree on the ways and methods of currency reform, but they basically agree on the shortcomings of political legal tender money and the preferability of commodity money, especially gold. No reasonable economist would want to revolutionize economic life through a radical monetary reform. He does not want to make gold the only money, forbidding government issue of any kind and suppressing banknotes and demand deposits used as media of exchange. Such a reform would require radical government intervention and greatly reduce the quantity of money. Prices and wages would have to be drastically cut, which no modern society could withstand in an orderly fashion.

The answer to the question of currency reform can be found in three thousand years of experience with the gold standard. How did it emerge in the past? It arose from three different situations: unadulterated monetary freedom, failure of the bimetallic standard, and government substitution of gold for other monies. The last avenue was chosen by a few nations, such as Germany, which endeavored to imitate the financial success and progress of the gold standard nations. When the industrialized countries, such as England and France, prospered with the gold standard, others adopted it through quick substitution. Their approach was that of latecomers who for good reasons imitated the successful leader. It is obvious that in our age of *fiat* money this avenue to the gold standard is closed for lack of a leader. It is rather unrealistic to expect the United States govern-

ment to provide this leadership. It would have to renounce its inflationary ways and, at heavy expense, substitute gold coins for Federal
Reserve Notes.

Most Western nations arrived at the gold standard via the failure
of the bimetallic standard. The legal standard of the United States
from 1792 to 1873 was bimetallic. Both gold and silver served as
money. Similarly, a double standard in which both gold and *fiat*
money are legal money could be used to re-establish the gold standard. But it requires the cooperation of government, which an administration indulging in deficit spending is unlikely to provide. The
administration would have to abandon any further inflation and
prevent any further expansion of money substitutes. At the same
time all restrictions on gold contracts and clauses would have to be
repealed, which would permit gold to function as money.

A double standard would probably result in an inflow of considerable quantities of foreign gold as some Americans would want to
own some gold and make contracts stipulating payment of gold. The
exchange ratio between gold and government money at first would
be determined by the demand for and supply of both kinds of money.
Let us assume it to be $200 per ounce of gold. If the government now
establishes a legal parity of the dollar to gold at any ratio *other* than
200 to 1 it brings into operation Gresham's Law. That is, artificially
overvalued money tends to drive artificially undervalued money out
of circulation. Let us say that the government sets a ratio of 210 to 1,
or even 220 to 1. It obviously overvalues gold and thereby creates the
gold standard. Gold gradually replaces government money in the
people's cash holdings. This road to the gold standard is rather
circuitous. Nevertheless, as it makes few demands on government it
has been the most travelled road during the last two hundred years.
The United States government used it in 1834.

Ludwig von Mises, the late dean of monetary theory, would establish the gold standard without this circuitousness. He would, once
the exchange ratio between gold and government money has been
found in the free market, adopt this ratio as the new legal parity of
the United States dollar and secure its unconditional convertibility at
this parity. Finally, transition from this gold-bullion standard to the
gold-coin standard would be achieved by the United States Treasury
exchanging all five, ten, and perhaps also twenty dollar bills for
newly minted gold coins.[5] This proposal for reform is most comprehensive and complete, for it envisions creation of a classical gold-coin
standard by a single law. Of course, it assumes a state of economic
and political enlightenment that surpasses by far the present state

---

[5] *The Theory of Money and Credit, op. cit.,* p. 448 *et seq.*

of economic and political thought.

Restoration of the gold standard may be a long and arduous task. Since it was lost in a gradual erosion of monetary freedom, we may have to retrieve it slowly and painstakingly on the road back to freedom, which gives it birth and meaning through inexorable economic law. This is why we seek no reform law, no restoration law, no conversion or parity, no government cooperation, merely freedom. That road is short and direct. Depending on the resistance offered by popular ignorance and prejudice, by government greed and lust for power, it may take us many years to traverse. For the weary traveller it has several intermediary stops that provide convenient targets for supreme effort.

The first objective must be the freedom to trade and hold gold. Everyone must be free to buy and to sell, to lend and to borrow, to import and to export any quantity of gold, to hold it at home or abroad, whether minted or unminted. There must be no government interference with the gold markets, no regulation or control, no taxation or dictation that would sabotage the gold markets. Dozens of nations in all continents actually enjoy this rudimentary freedom. Americans lost it "temporarily" in 1933 when the Roosevelt Administration seized all private gold holdings, and regained it, one hopes permanently, on January 1, 1975.

The next objective must be the individual freedom to use gold in all economic exchanges. The people must be free to use gold when they buy goods and services, without the interaction of government money. That is to say, the legal tender law, which decrees that government money must be accepted in payment of all debt, public and private, must exempt "gold contracts" and "gold clauses" that specifically call for payment of certain measures of gold. In short, the ordinary law of contract must be permitted to function.[6]

At this point we shall have arrived at the "parallel standard." It would not in the least curtail government operations or impede government finance. The Federal Reserve System could continue its operations, its inflation and credit expansion, and the United States Treasury would receive taxes and make payments in Federal Reserve money. All contracts stated in United States dollars would have to be met in United States dollars; but contracts in ounces and grains of gold would have to be met in gold. Government money and gold

---

[6]On October 28, 1977, President Carter signed a bill (H.R. 5675 and S. 79) that restored the freedom to enter gold contracts. But financial institutions continue to be captives of government regulatory authorities who disapprove of gold clauses and contracts. The Internal Revenue Service continues to extract income and capital gains taxes from gold owners whenever they show *fiat* dollar gains. Under those conditions the freedom to enter gold contracts is rather spurious.

would be circulating side by side. The relative supplies of and demands for the two monies would determine their exchange ratio, which would continually fluctuate in response to demand and supply.

The third objective on the road to the gold standard would be the individual freedom to mint coins. The first coins were minted by private individuals and goldsmiths. Private coins have circulated throughout history, in California as late as the 1860's. Because these coins would not be endowed with "legal tender," no one would be obliged to accept them in payment of a debt. He who would deem them too much trouble to weigh or test, or would distrust the minter's stamp and guarantee, would be free to use Federal Reserve Notes. After all, only Federal Reserve money would be legal tender except where gold payment was contractually required.

The fourth and final phase is not really vital for the restoration of the gold standard. An enlightened government may at this time decide to make its own money freely convertible into gold. It may adopt the going exchange ratio between the two as the legal parity and then secure unconditional convertibility of its money into gold. This phase, which does not materially enhance our monetary freedom, would merely legalize the gold standard that would gradually emerge on the road to freedom.

Under present ideological conditions no one could possibly conduct a successful currency reform. To save the United States dollar would require a complete reversal of present economic and monetary policies of the United States government. It would not suffice merely to stabilize the currency through credit restrictions and the reduction of spending sufficient to result in balanced budgets. For such a solution would immediately throw the American economy, which has more than six million unemployed even during boom times, into severe depression and unemployment. No political party would dare to recommend, much less administer, this medicine for monetary stabilization. Therefore, the currency reform necessitates a simultaneous economic reform that reduces the unbearable burden of government intervention. Business taxes, which are among the highest in the free world, would have to be lowered considerably, and the markets freed from bureaucratic intervention. At the same time, the numerous legal immunities and privileges of the labor unions would have to be abolished in order to restore a flexible labor market. Only a free labor market can absorb the labor that undoubtedly would be set free by the currency stabilization. Whether an administration that is capable of such a radical reversal of present-day policies can soon be found is a political question, the answer to which must be sought in the realm of political understanding.

Without this radical reform, which is tantamount to a full retreat from the New Deal, the Fair Deal, the New Frontier, the Great Society, and the New Republicanism, further deterioration of the United States dollar is inevitable. With this monetary deterioration must come a decline in world trade and commerce, in peaceful cooperation and division of labor. In fact, the disastrous consequences of our monetary policies can only be surmised. We may finally experience what many other nations have encountered during this century, a rapid depreciation of the currency with all its economic, social, and political calamities. Whether, under the intense strains of such a currency disorder, we have the moral strength and economic wisdom to choose the ways of freedom, that is the crucial money question.

A Point of Cure

Government affects individual incomes by virtually every decision it makes. Agricultural programs, veterans' benefits, health, labor, and welfare expenditures, housing and community development, federal expenditures on education, social insurance, medicare and medicaid programs, and last but not least, numerous regulations and controls affect the economic conditions of every citizen. In fact, modern government has become a universal transfer agency that utilizes the political process for distributing vast measures of economic income and wealth. It preys on millions of victims in order to allocate valuable goods and services to its beneficiaries. With the latter, transfer programs are so popular that few public officials and politicians dare oppose them.

The motive powers that drive the transfer order are as varied as human purposes themselves. The true motives are often concealed, and a hollow pretext is pompously placed in the front for show. Yet man is more accountable for his motives than for anything else. A good motive may exculpate a poor action, but a bad motive vitiates even the finest action. Conscience is merely our own judgment of the right and wrong of our action, and therefore can never be a safe guide unless it is enlightened by a thorough understanding of the implications and consequences of our actions. Without an enlightened conscience we may do evil thoroughly and heartily.

An important spring of action for the transfer society is the desire by most people to get even in the redistribution struggle. "I have been victimized in the past by taxation, inflation, regulation, or other devices," so the argument goes, "therefore I am entitled to partake of this particular benefit." Or the time sequence may be reversed: "I'll be victimized later in life," pleads the college student, "and therefore I want state aid and subsidies now."

This argument is probably the most powerful pacifier of conscience.

It dulls our perception and discernment of what is evil and makes us slow to shun it. After all, we are merely getting back "what is rightfully our own." With a curious twist of specious deduction, the friends of individual liberty and private property defend the modern welfare state, which continually seizes and redistributes private property by force. "Man is entitled to the fruits of his labor," they argue. "We are merely getting back that which is rightfully and morally our own." They borrow the arguments for the private property order to sustain the political transfer order.

Surely getting back that which is rightfully and morally our own is a principle that is rooted in our inalienable right to our lives. It is a property right that springs from our human rights and from the right to life itself. It is the right to restoration of the fruits of our efforts and labors of which we are deprived by deceit, force, or any other immoral practice. It is a specific right to recovery or compensation from those who are wronging us or have injured us in the past. This right to restoration does not beget the right to commit the very immoral act from which we seek restoration, to imitate others in acting immorally, or to seek revenge against the trespassers or innocent bystanders. But this is precisely what the "get even" advisers urge us to do.

In an unfortunate automobile accident we may be hurt or injured, or our vehicle may be damaged, because of the negligence of another driver. This gives us the right to demand restoration and compensation from the other party. But it does not give us the right to seize another car parked in the neighborhood, or to return to the road and injure another driver. Our home may be burglarized and we may suffer deplorable losses in personal wealth and memorabilia. This does not bestow upon us the right to do likewise to others. But the "get even" advocates are drawing this very conclusion. He who is desirous of "getting even" in the politics of redistribution longs to join the army of beneficiaries who are presently preying on their victims. They would like to get their "money back" from whomever they can find and victimize now. Like the victim of a burglary who becomes a burglar himself, they are searching for other victims. But in contrast to the new burglar who may be aware of the immorality of his actions, the "get even" advocate openly defends his motives while he is pursuing his political theft.

We cannot get even with those individuals who deprived us of our property in the past. They may have long departed this life or may have fallen among the victims themselves. We cannot get even with them by enlisting in the standing army of redistributors. We merely perpetuate the evil by joining their forces. So we must stand immune to the temptations of evil, regardless of what others are doing to us.

The redistribution must stop with us.

The Redistributive State has victimized many millions of people through confiscatory taxation, inflation, and regulation. Government, acting as the political agency for the coercive transfer of property, seized income and wealth from the more productive members and then redistributed the spoils to its beneficiaries. Although many millions of victims and beneficiaries were involved, which often obscures the morality of the issue, the forced transfer took place between certain individuals. The beneficiaries who used political force to obtain the benefits cannot easily be recognized in the mass process of transfer. But even if we could identify them, and establish a personal right to restoration, our property has been consumed long ago. A vast army of beneficiaries, together with their legions of government officials and civil servants, consumed or otherwise squandered our substance. There is nothing to retrieve from the beneficiaries who probably are poorer than ever before, having grown weak and dependent on the transfer process.

When seen in this light, the "get even" argument is nothing more than a declaration of intention to join the redistribution forces. It may be born from the primitive urge for revenge against government, state, or society. But it is individuals who form a government, make a state, and constitute a society. By taking revenge against some of them for the injuries suffered at the hands of others, one is merely reinforcing the evil.

Revenge is a common passion that enslaves man's mind and clouds his vision. To the savage it is a noble aspiration that makes him even with his enemies. In a civilized society that is seeking peace and harmony, it is a destructive force which law seeks to suppress. But when the law itself becomes an instrument of transfer, the primitive urge for revenge may burst forth as a demand for more redistribution. It becomes a primary force that gives rise to new demands or, at least, reinforces the popular demands for economic transfer. The common passion for revenge, no matter how well concealed, undoubtedly is an important motive power of social policy that leads a free society to its own destruction.

No wealth in the world and no political distribution of this wealth can purchase the peace and harmony so essential to human existence. Peace and harmony can be found only in moral elevation that reaches into every aspect of human life. A free society is the offspring of morality that guides the actions and policies of its members. To effect a rebirth of such a society is to revive the moral principles that gave it birth in the beginning. It is individual rebirth and rededication to the eternal principles of morality that are the power and the might. The example of great individuals is useful to lead us on the way, for nothing is more conducive to morality than the power of a great example.

To spearhead a rebirth of our free society, let us rededicate ourselves to a new covenant of redemption, which is a simple restatement of public morality. In the setting of our age of economic redistribution and social conflict it may be stated as follows:

No matter how the transfer state may victimize me, I shall seek no transfer payments, nor accept any.

I shall seek no government grants, loans, or other redistributive favors, nor accept any.

I shall seek no government orders on behalf of redistribution, nor accept any.

I shall seek no employment in the government apparatus of redistribution, nor accept any.

I shall seek no favors from the regulatory agencies of government, nor accept any.

I shall seek no protection from tariff barriers or any other institutional restrictions on trade and commerce.

I shall seek no services from, nor lend support to, institutions that are creatures of redistribution.

I shall seek no support from, nor give support to, associations that advocate or practice coercion and restraint.

We do not know whether our great republic will survive this century. If it can be saved, great men of conviction must lead the way — men who with religious fervor and unbounded courage resist all transfer temptations. The heroes of liberty are no less remarkable for what they suffer than for what they achieve.

To reverse the trend and reduce the role of government in our lives, and thus alleviate the government deficit and inflation pressures, is a giant educational task. The social and economic ideas that gave birth to the transfer system must be discredited and replaced with the old values of individual independence and self-reliance. The social philosophy of individual freedom and unhampered private property must again be our guiding light.

VII
Inflation and Liberty

In the second half of the twentieth century the most vexing economic problem — the most intractable, unresolved, and foreboding problem — is that of inflation. It causes grievous distress to most countries of the world, and ravages societies, rich and poor, on both sides of the Iron Curtain. It is hardly surprising, therefore, that it has given occasion to countless books and articles, speeches, lectures, and broadcasts. Yet it is one of the great paradoxes of the age that it roars on with accelerating force, devouring not only economic income, wealth, and security, but also tearing down, one by one, the economic, social, and political pillars of free societies.

There is a broad measure of agreement among economists that "excessive" inflation brings about a collapse of the monetary system, that it consumes business capital, destroys the exchange order with its productive division of labor, and finally reduces economic life to primitive barter. Many even admit that too rapid a rate of inflation perpetrates a grievous fraud upon all savers, particularly the retired and pensioners, and that it impoverishes the middle classes. But their agreement is like that of alcoholics who generally admit that on occasion they have imbibed too much. Like most alcoholics who discount the danger of growing addiction and cumulative effects on their physical and mental well-being, most economists demand small doses of monetary injections, which are said to refresh and stimulate the economic body. They speak of "flexibility" and "adjustability" of the money stock, and favor, for one reason or another, its continuous expansion by monetary authorities.

In the Western democracies the popularity of the leading political parties vying for governmental power rests on their commitment to the welfare state, that is, economic redistribution and transfer by political force. They welcome the monetary theories of these economists, who in turn gladly accept the honors and favors of the transfer governments. The theories show the way for governments to engage in a new dimension of economic transfer that not only endows them with unprecedented economic power, which in turn gives rise to political power, but also weakens the political opposition pleading for limitations of government power and preservation of the private property order. The alliance between the economic profession and the politics of redistribution is sealing the fate of national currencies.

Monetary disorder is a mortal enemy of the private property order, and a serious threat to economic well-being and individual liberty. Its evil effects are felt in various ways:

1. It profoundly modifies the social order and breeds economic and political radicalism among its countless victims. It destroys the savings of the middle classes and reduces the real earnings of wage earners, who learn to distrust the price system. Realizing the inequity of distribution, most victims put their faith in strike action or government intervention.

2. Inflation causes maladjustments of production to consumer demand as prices adjust to inflation with unequal flexibility. Production that is deemed "essential" and therefore controllable by public authorities is hampered and restricted, while non-essential production tends to expand.

3. Governments are eager to apply coercion to mitigate the unpopular effects of their own inflation. With growing popular support they resort to such comprehensive measures as price, wage, and rent controls. They substitute public expenditure for shrinking private investment. They formulate "development plans" and create new bureaucracies for their implementation.

4. In its early stage of development the transfer policy was limited to a few cases of individual assistance. State aid was intended to alleviate the plight of the needy who were unable to care for themselves. But inflation continuously enlarges the circle of the needy and therefore the scope of government functions. It is a self-per-

petuating force that calls for more redistribution, which in turn invites more inflation. Wilhelm Röpke, the eminent German economist and primary architect of Germany's miracle of revival after World War II, likened the process to that of "a revenue-pumping station, working day and night, with its tubes, valves, suction and pressure streams."[1] Its pumps deliver a steady stream of benefits derived from two classes of victims, the more productive taxpayers and the inflation victims.

5. As politics encroaches ever more widely on economic and social life, the sphere of individual freedom and independence is constrained accordingly. Simultaneously, the sphere of international cooperation and integration is compressed by growing economic nationalism. All welfare state institutions are national in scope and domain: public assistance and relief, social security and unemployment benefits, tariff protection and quota restriction, government orders and subsidies. By their very nature social services are nationalized services that are designed to benefit residents only. The benefits are conferred by national governments on their constituents, which tends to confine the beneficiaries within their national boundaries. The victims of the redistribution process, on the other hand, may want to escape to friendlier shores, which government seeks to prevent through public law and compulsion.

6. In desperation about the Western drift toward economic catastrophe, many writers are longing for a strong political leader who will bring salvation. "Mankind is seeking — and waiting for — a leader," writes Jacques Rueff, the distinguished French economist, "who will display the courage and intelligence required to rescue us. If such a leader does not exist, or if political circumstances prevent him from emerging, man's destruction is as inevitable as that of a man falling from the roof of a skyscraper."[2]

The Illusion of Controls

One of the most popular "remedies" for the undesired effects of inflation is price controls. Sooner or later the advocates of price controls may realize that such controls constitute the very antithesis of economic freedom. Either the people are free to conduct their economic affairs as they see fit, or they are denied this freedom by regulations and controls. Price and wage controls are people controls. Surely no serious student of economics would hope to fight inflation effectively with price and wage controls. The relationship between the two phenomena is about like that between a band-aid and a

---

[1] Wilhelm Röpke, *Welfare, Freedom and Inflation* (London: Pall Mall Press Ltd., 1957), pp. 38-39.

[2] Jacques Rueff,, *op. cit.*, p. xiii.

malignant tumor of the brain. Inflation is the cancerous multiplication of money by our monetary authorities in order to cover federal deficits or create new credits for the benefit of business. Governmental price and wage controls limit the people's freedom to make economic exchanges in accordance with their choices and preferences, but they do not in the least affect the ability of the authorities to multiply and depreciate the money.

Price and wage controls tend to raise business costs. As the ultimate decisions are made in Washington, business becomes more bureaucratic. It needs to seek permission for price and wage changes, file detailed reports, and face government controllers and auditors. Business decisions are inevitably delayed as government agents ponder about their final approval. Wherever the controls cause shortages or merely slow deliveries, business becomes less efficient, which raises production costs. Moreover, labor tends to become less productive as a result of material shortages. Workers feel cheated and betrayed by the controls as wage contracts are superseded by wage decrees and reinterpreted by control officials. The controls breed dissatisfaction and conflict.

But in spite of all labor complaints, the price controls must be expected to be more severe than the wage controls. After all, the controllers, who are politicians or their appointees, cannot afford to antagonize millions of workers on whose votes their chances for re-election depend. On the other hand, a tough stand toward business may be rather popular and therefore rewarding politically. Especially if the controllers are Republicans, who are suspect anyway of being pro-business, they cannot afford to be lenient, but must be expected to be very strict in controlling prices. Stable prices and rising costs make production unprofitable and thus precipitate economic stagnation and depression.

Price controls lead to all-round controls. When the economy begins to reveal the disruptions and distortions — the shortages and stagnations — engendered by the controls, the government is unlikely to plead guilty of having inflicted such evils on its people. It has never done so in the past, and future administrations cannot be expected to act differently. Instead, they will find new culprits to blame and new tasks to perform in order to alleviate the evils of prior intervention. When economic output is lagging, government will resort to more financial stimuli, such as easy money and deficit spending. When unemployment rises it will embark upon more public works and full-employment measures. When shortages make their appearance it will introduce rationing, allocations, and priorities. When people begin to ignore the price controls and seek relief on black markets it will prosecute them with growing severity. In all phases of economic life the government will assume command.

Such an ominous trend may be of little concern to a society that has lost its genuine love and deep regard for individual freedom. A nation eager to be led cannot be frightened by the prospect of a command order. But it may hesitate to pursue the road to all-round controls if the awesome price is known that must be paid for such an order.

We are enjoying the highest standard of living on earth. With an average income of more than $6,000 per person per year, we excel all others by wide margins. Even our "underprivileged" black minority, with an average per capita income of more than $4500 per year, lives better by far than the vast majority of Europeans, not to mention the Africans, Asians, or South Americans. Any disruption of our economic system can have but one effect on our level of living: to reduce it substantially.

Indeed, to disrupt or depress a highly developed division-of-labor and exchange economy, such as ours, must have dire consequences. You can reduce the speed of a donkey cart without much loss of distance traveled, but if you slow the forward thrust of a jet plane you'll lose many miles in a matter of minutes. When the American economy slows down and our standard of living falls substantially, the psychological and sociological effects could be disastrous. In the demoralizing atmosphere of the transfer state, millions of Americans have grown accustomed to free government services and benefits. They are demanding the maximum of welfare from the community, giving little or nothing in return. Labor unions are making insatiable wage demands for a minimum of productivity. How will the American people take to depression and deterioration with shrinking wages and benefits?

The reaction may be militant and violent. Guided by doctrines of conflict and convinced of their inalienable rights to government care and egalitarian redistribution, they may insist on their rights. After all, our transfer politicians, parties, and intellectuals have for forty years convinced them of the social justice of their claims. Are these now to be abrogated in the face of economic adversity? Moreover, their collective organizations wield the necessary political power to extract their due share from the body politic. But if this body should fail to yield the expected benefits, will the millions of beneficiaries peacefully suffer the welfare cuts? Will the labor unions peacefully consent to wage cuts? If they do not, our redistributive society may be torn asunder by civil conflict and strife. Business establishments may be looted, our cities burned, and law and order may give way to violent disorder. Since the first redistributive measure, several decades ago, this has been the ultimate destination of the Redistributive State.

Finally, economic and social deterioration of such major magnitude strengthens the call for law and order. When society can no longer cooperate voluntarily and peacefully, the raw power of the State will be used to enforce some measure of cooperation. Vast emergency power will be thrust on the President, who will be expected to restore civil order. For this grim task the most ruthless politician is likely to rise to the top, surrounded by the most ruthless advisors and lieutenants. They will eagerly crush all dissent and bring peace to the society so bent on strife and self-destruction. They'll bring the peace that is totally inimical to individual enterprise and personal freedom.

This scenario of things to come is merely one of many engendered by thought and reflection. There are others that come to mind, and many more which we cannot comprehend. We are forever blind to the future, but always living for it. Let us, therefore, make the best use of the present, with courage and dedication, and fulfill our parts. Henry Wadsworth Longfellow's words, written one hundred years ago, ring forever true:

> *Look not mournfully into the Past.*
> *It comes not back again.*
> *Wisely improve the Present.*
> *It is thine.*
> *Go forth to meet the shadowy Future,*
> *without fear, and with a manly heart.*

Even in evil we can discern the rays of light and hope, for man may gradually come to see, in suffering and misery, the error of his ways. We know of no greater economic folly than the combina-tion of inflation and price controls, in which many Americans have placed their ultimate trust. And yet, we are ever hopeful that, in the end, reason and virtue will prevail over error and evil.

Terms

acatallactic From catallactics, n.; catallactic, adj. Catallactics is the theory of the market economy, that is, of exchanges and prices. Lack of this theory is called *acatallactic*.

acceleration principle In Keynesian theory, the principle that changes in demand for finished goods and services tend to give rise to much greater changes in the demand for producers' or capital goods.

a priori Self-evident, known by reason alone without any appeal to experience or sensory perceptions.

arbitrage The simultaneous or nearly simultaneous purchase and sale of a good — money in particular — in order to profit from price discrepancies in different markets. See also **interest arbitrage, time arbi-trage, space arbitrage.** The effect of arbitrage is to eliminate price differ-ences.

balance of payments A statement of international transactions which give rise to money payments between countries, covering: (1) current accounts including trade and services, (2) capital accounts including short-term and long-term items, (3) unilateral transfers by gifts of governments and individuals.

balance of trade A statement of the value of merchandise exports and imports. In mercantilistic terminology, a "favorable" balance refers to a net export surplus, an "unfavorable" balance to a net import surplus.

bimetallic standard A monetary system in which gold and silver coins are used as standard money.

black market A generic term describing economic transactions in violation of price controls and ration regulations.

Bretton Woods Agreement Agreement reached by an international conference at Bretton Woods, New Hampshire, in 1944, for the establishment of an *International Bank for Reconstruction and Development* and an *International Monetary Fund*. The American position at the conference was prepared by Harry Dexter White. The British proposal was in large part the work of John Maynard Keynes.

British Currency School A nineteenth century school of thought which advocated that all future changes in the nation's quantity of money should correspond precisely with changes in the nation's holdings of monetary gold. It opposed any discretionary increases or decreases in the quantity of money by central or commercial bankers.

business cycle Significant changes which take place in business conditions over a period of time. A feverishly booming prosperity ends in an acute crisis or panic, which is followed by stagnation and unemployment popularly called a recession or depression.

capital A concept of economic calculation which, in the market system, expresses in monetary terms the capital goods and savings belonging to a natural or legal person.

capital goods Produced factors of production, such as tools, buildings, transportation facilities, *etc.* that make human labor more productive.

catallactics The theory of the market economy, which is an important part of the general theory of human action called praxeology.

central bank A dominant bank of a country with official or semi-official status in the government of the country. It issues the national currency, discounts notes and promissory notes, conducts open-market operations, and holds reserves for other banks. The first central bank was the Bank of England, which was changed from a private bank to a central bank by the granting of unique legal privileges.

Chicago School The Chicago School is a loosely defined group of economists historically associated with the University of Chicago whose fundamental characteristic is its empirical epistemology. Its foremost contemporary representative is Dr. Milton Friedman.

clearing house An agency established by banks or brokers to reduce the labor of paying and receiving funds due one another. Each member's *net* credit or debit to another member is settled by transfers of *net* balances to or from established accounts.

command system Also called *command order.* The politico-economic system in which government commands replace decisions freely made by individuals.

commercial bank A bank which accepts deposits subject to withdrawal on demand.

commodity bill doctrine The doctrine that promissory notes, drafts, and similar documents representing loans secured by commodities provide an elastic credit system.

commodity money A commodity, such as gold or silver, which is used as money.

common law The body of unwritten law developed primarily in England by judicial decisions based upon Scripture and custom, constituting the historical basis of the English and United States legal system.

constitutional law The body of law that developed from commentaries upon and judicial decisions made pursuant to the United States Constitution. Unlike common law, constitutional law is written, though not codified.

consumers' good A good used directly in satisfying a human want.

contract law The division of law that concerns the interpretation, application, and enforcement of contracts among contracting persons.

contracyclical policies Interventionist policies that are intended to counteract the undesired but inevitable effects of previous credit expansion.

crawling peg A price imposed by a government or central bank that is changed frequently by small amounts.

demand deposit A bank deposit that is withdrawable on less than thirty days' notice.

depression The period of a business cycle when production is lowest and unemployment highest.

devaluation Reduction of the gold or silver content in the monetary unit or, where one currency is quoted in the currency of another country, reduction of the number of foreign units exchangeable for one domestic unit.

discount A reduction of the principal amount, or the face value or list price.

disutility of labor The discomfort, inconvenience, fatigue, or pain inherent in human effort. All labor, mental or physical, is character ized by disutility.

epistemology The theory of human knowledge. It is concerned primarily with the origin, structure, methods, and validity of knowledge.

equilibrium A state of rest or inaction in which all opposing forces and influences are exactly equal and in balance. In economics, it is a concept used for analytical purposes, but it is never observed in any actual economic system.

European Economic Community The official name for the Common Market, which is an economic union established in 1958, originally including Belgium, France, Italy, Luxembourg, the Netherlands, and West Germany.

exchange rate The ratio at which units of two currencies are exchanged.

factors of production Economists usually distinguish three factors of production — land, labor, and capital. "Land" includes all the natural elements, including water; "labor" is both physical and mental;

and "capital" is that personal wealth that has been produced by the intelligent application of labor to land and will be used to produce more goods.

fiat money A coin or piece of paper of insignificant commodity value that government has declared to be money and to which it has given "legal tender" quality.

fiduciary money Money-substitutes, such as bank or treasury notes and demand deposits, that exceed the cash reserves immediately available for their conversion into proper money.

fine tuning A term in the jargon of some economists who believe that economic activity can be carefully and precisely governed by government manipulation. It presupposes a mechanical relationship between the quantity of money and its effects on prices and markets, and ignores the subjective valuations made by millions of individuals.

fiscalist An economist who believes that the fiscal (budgetary) policies of government are more important than its monetary policies in regulating economic activity.

gold standard That monetary system in which gold is money. All types of money substitutes are freely convertible into gold at a specified rate.

Gresham's Law Popularly stated, "Bad money drives out good money." Attributed to Sir Thomas Gresham (1519-1579), the law states that a legally overvalued currency will be used for exchange and an undervalued currency will be hoarded. It is a special application of the knowledge of price and government interference with price.

holism, n. A concept of epistemology according to which economic knowledge can be gained from totals or aggregates rather than the actions of individuals. **holistic, adj.**

hyperinflation A severe or large increase in the money supply; in this book, hyperinflation is also used colloquially to mean a rise in the cost of living at a rate greater than one hundred percent per year.

inflation A popular nonscientific term that connotes a large increase in the supply of money and credit which results in lower purchasing power of the monetary unit. Such an increase results in higher prices for goods and services. Colloquially, inflation means generally rising prices.

flexible exchange rate A monetary system with a monetary unit whose rate of exchange is subject to instant change by order of a government agency or because of fluctuations in the international money markets.

floating exchange rates Synonym for flexible exchange rates.

forward cover or **foreign exchange future** The purchase or sale of a foreign exchange futures contract in order to meet a payment due at a future date in a foreign currency. It avoids exposure to exchange rate fluctuations.

frictional employment Temporary unemployment due to changes in the demand for or supply of specialized labor.

gold bullion standard The monetary system in which gold bullion, as distinguished from gold coins, is the standard medium of exchange.

gold coin standard The monetary system in which gold coins, as distinguished from gold bullion, are the standard medium of exchange.

gold exchange standard A monetary system in which both gold and the currency of some gold standard country constitute the standard media of exchange or reserve currency.

institutional unemployment As distinguished from frictional unemployment, institutional unemployment is caused by government interference in the economy: minimum wage laws, legal privileges for labor unions, unemployment compensation, *etc.*

interest arbitrage The transacting of business in loan markets in order to profit from interest rate differences among different loan markets. See **arbitrage.**

International Monetary Fund Established by the Bretton Woods (1944) conference and designed to meet the requirements of international monetary cooperation. I.M.F. originally had 38 member countries. In 1978 it had 134 members. The total paid subscriptions of the member countries are denominated in Special Drawing Rights (SDR's). The United States quota for 1978 was $8.4 billion. These funds can be drawn upon by the members for the purpose of bolstering their own inflated currencies. Because of this function, the I.M.F. has been called the engine of world inflation.

Terms

interventionism The unstable politico-economic system in which government regulations hamper the free market. Interventionism is the system that characterizes all free world countries today. It is unstable because the political interference has undesirable effects that force government to repeal or increase its regulation of the market. In most cases it leads to socialism.

Keynesianism The school of economic thought following John Maynard Keynes (1883-1946). The school disagrees with classical economics and Say's Law that supply creates its own demand. It believes that general overproduction leads to chronic unemployment, and therefore advocates governmental intervention in one form or another.

legal tender Any kind of money which by law must be accepted when offered in payment of a debt. Legal tender laws were enacted when contract law was rejected. They are designed to tell citizens what medium of exchange to use, rather than to allow the citizens mutually to agree upon medium of exchange in a contract. Governments made their *fiat* money legal tender and denied the status to gold and silver coin in order to force the people to use *fiat* money, which could be created at will.

long A term used by dealers in commodity and money markets to describe the action of holding goods or currencies in anticipation of a rise in prices.

macroeconomics From *macro*, large. Contemporary economic analysis is divided into macroeconomics and microeconomics. The former is the study of aggregates of prices, wages, and incomes, as opposed to that of the economic actions of individuals.

marginal productivity The market value imputed to the last (that is, marginal) unit of labor, land, or capital used in production.

marginal utility The least important (valuable) use to which a unit of a supply of identical goods can be put.

medium of exchange Any object that is used primarily for exchange rather than for production or consumption. Historically, gold, silver, iron, cattle, and beads, among other things, have functioned as media of exchange.

microeconomics From *micro*, small. As opposed to macroeconomics, which is statistical and mathematical in nature, microeconomics is the study of individual valuation and action.

185

monetizing debt The process by which government debt is used to issue more money. The central bank may purchase Treasury obligations, thus releasing newly created money.

money supply Money supply can be defined narrowly or broadly. The United States government uses at least five different definitions, ranging from actual currency to currency plus demand deposits, plus time deposits, plus certificates of deposits, plus deposits with institutions other than commercial banks. Some economists have even suggested the inclusion of food stamps, for they are accepted as media of exchange for food.

multiplier A Keynesian term used to describe the alleged effect government spending has on economic activity. When government spends one new dollar, it in turn is spent again and again, which is said to stimulate economic activity. In Keynesian usage, the multiplier is the ratio of the change in national income to a change in investment.

New Economics The name given to Keynesianism by proponents of the economic doctrines of Lord Keynes.

nominal wages Wages expressed in monetary units rather than purchasing power.

ontology That branch of philosophy that is concerned with the objects, physical and mental, that exist, and with their nature and interrelationships.

Phillips Curve Developed by Professor A.W. Phillips of the London School of Economics, the curve allegedly describes the relationship between inflation and unemployment. More inflation means less unemployment; less inflation means more unemployment. Because it ignores the factors that cause unemployment, the curve is an exercise in futility, and in recent years has fallen into disrepute with most economists.

praxeology The general theory of human action, whose most developed part is catallactics, the theory of the market economy.

price level A macroeconomic term which implies that all prices rise and fall uniformly. Actually, there are only prices, not price levels. Attempts to measure or determine a price level through such devices as the Consumer Price Index or the Wholesale Price Index are futile, for the very concept of a price level is chimerical.

producers' goods Goods that satisfy human wants indirectly, not being wanted for consumption but for the sake of creating goods that will satisfy wants directly. They include raw materials, machinery, and factories.

purchasing power Refers to the value of money in buying economic goods. The exchange value of a unit of currency is its purchasing power.

real goods Land, capital goods, gold, silver, precious stones, consumers' goods, all are real goods. They are distinguished from cash holdings of *fiat* money.

real wages Wages expressed in terms of real goods rather than monetary units. See **nominal wages.**

recession A mild economic readjustment made necessary by a prior inflation or credit expansion.

rediscount To discount again.

regression theorem Developed by the late Ludwig von Mises, the regression theorem traces the value of present *fiat* money back through its predecessors to the point where the medium of exchange served only non-monetary purposes. The theorem explains the value presently attached to *fiat* money on the basis that its predecessors had commodity value.

reserve requirements The legal requirements imposed on banks in order to force them to keep a certain fraction of their actual deposits on hand to meet cash withdrawals. In order to conduct inflationary policies the Federal Reserve has greatly reduced the reserve requirements. In a sound monetary system it would be in the interest of all banks to maintain a one hundred percent reserve.

scarcity The fundamental economic phenomenon is scarcity. If a good is not scarce (air, for example) it is not an economic good.

seigniorage The "profit" a government makes by coining money. The difference between the monetary value and the bullion value of coins.

short A term used by traders in commodity and currency markets to describe a commitment to deliver at a future date a security or commodity which the seller does not own, but which he hopes to buy later at a lower price.

shortage To be distinguished from scarcity, which is a natural phenomenon. A shortage is induced by political interference in the market economy, either through hampering production and distribution or through controlling prices.

space arbitrage The sale and purchase of goods on two or more markets separated by geographical location. Its effect is to equalize prices in both markets, except for the costs of transportation See **arbitrage.**

Special Drawing Rights The monetary unit created and used by the International Monetary Fund. Its value is based upon a "market basket" of leading currencies and may vary depending upon the value of the currencies in the basket. Also called "paper gold." It is designed to substitute for gold.

specie Coins or bars of precious metal, usually gold or silver.

statism The political doctrine that the state is the supreme institution in society and that all other individuals should be subjected to and controlled by it. It includes communism, socialism, fascism, Nazism, and interventionism.

subjective theory of value The theory that the value of economic goods is in the minds of individuals and is not quantifiable or objective. Its most consistent exponents are the members of the Austrian School of economic thought.

time deposit A bank deposit which is subject to at least thirty days' notice before withdrawal.

time arbitrage The simultaneous or nearly simultaneous purchase and sale of goods to profit from differences between present and future prices. See **arbitrage.**

trade deficit A mercantilistic term describing an excess of national imports over exports.

trade surplus A mercantilistic term describing an excess of exports over imports.

utility Usefulness. The ability of a material good or a service to satisfy human wants.

velocity of circulation The average number of times in a year which a given dollar serves as income (the income velocity) or as an expenditure (the transaction velocity).

Persons

Benjamin McAlester Anderson, Jr. 1886-1949. Eminent American economist and critic of Keynes; economist with the Chase National Bank, New York, 1920-1939; professor of economics, University of California at Los Angeles, 1939-1949; author of *The Value of Money* (1917) and *Economics and the Public Welfare (1949)*.

Ludwig Erhard 1897-1977. German statesman; West German minister of economics, 1949-1963; Vice Chancellor, 1959-1963; Chancellor, 1963-1966; architect of the German "economic miracle"; author of *Germany's Comeback in the World Market* (1954) and *Prosperity Through Competition* (1958).

John William Fellner 1905-   . American economist, born in Hungary; educated in Hungary and Germany; lecturer and professor of economics at the University of California at Berkeley and Yale University; Sterling Professor of Economics at Yale, 1959-1973. Presently associated with the American Enterprise Institute in Washington, D.C.; former member of the President's Council of Economic Advisors, 1973-1975, past president (1969) of the American Economic Association; author of *A Treatise on War Inflation* (1942); *Monetary Policies and Full Employment* (1949); *Competition Among the Few* (1949); *Trends and Cycles in Economic Activity* (1955); *Emergence and Content of Modern Economic Analysis* (1960); *Probability and Profit* (1965), and others.

Irving Fisher 1867-1947. Renowned American economist and professor of political economy at Yale University; author of *Mathematical Investigations in the Theory of Value and Prices* (1892); *Appreciation and Interest* (1896); *The Nature of Capital and Income* (1906); *The Rate of Interest* (1907); *The Purchasing Power of Money* (1911); *The Money Illusion* (1928); *The Theory of Interest* (1930); *Booms and Depressions* (1932); *Stable Money* (1934); *100 Percent Money* (1935), and others.

Milton Friedman 1912- . American economist; eminent member of the Chicago School of economic thought; past president of the American Economic Association; Nobel Laureate, 1976; author of *Essays in Positive Economics* (1953); *A Program for Monetary Stability* (1960); *Capitalism and Freedom* (1962); *Price Theory* (1962); *Inflation: Causes and Consequences* (1963); *A Monetary History of the United States* (1963); *Dollars and Deficits* (1968); *The Optimum Quantity of Money and Other Essays* (1969); *A Theoretical Framework for Monetary Analysis* (1970); *Monetary Statistics of the United States* (1970), and many others.

John Kenneth Galbraith 1908- . American economist and novelist; born in Canada; educated in Canada, the United States, and England; professor at Harvard and Princeton; employee of the Office of Price Administration, 1941-1943; past chairman of the Americans for Democratic Action; past president of American Economic Association; author of *American Capitalism* (1952); *A Theory of Price Control* (1952); *The Great Crash* (1955); *The Affluent Society* (1958); *The Liberal Hour* (1960); *Economic Development* (1963); *The Scotch* (1964); *The New Industrial State* (1967); *Indian Painting* (1968); *The Triumph* (1968); *Money* (1975), and others.

Elgin Groseclose 1899- . American economist and novelist; author of *Money — The Human Conflict* (1934); *The Persian Journey of the Rev. Ashley Wishard and His Servant Fathi* (1937); *Ararat* (1939); *The Firedrake* (1942); *Introduction to Iran* (1947); *The Carmelite* (1955); *The Scimitar of Saladin* (1956); *Money and Man* (1961); *Fifty Years of Managed Money, The Story of the Federal Reserve* (1966); and *Kiowa* (1978).

Alvin Harvey Hansen 1887-1975. American economist; disciple of John Maynard Keynes; professor at Harvard University; author of *Economic Policy and Full Employment* (1947); with Paul Samuelson, *Eco-*

nomic Analysis of Guaranteed Wages (1947); Monetary Theory and Fiscal Policy (1948); Business Cycle and National Income (1951); A Guide to Keynes (1953); The American Economy (1957); Economic Issues of the 1960's (1960); The Dollar and the International Monetary System (1965), and many others.

Sir Ralph G. Hawtrey 1879-   . English economist, educated at Eton and Trinity College, Cambridge; employee of the British Treasury 1904-1945; author of Good and Bad Trade (1913); Currency and Credit (1919); Art of Central Banking (1932); Capital and Employment (1937), and others.

Friedrich August von Hayek 1899-   . British economist; born in Austria, eminent member of the Austrian School of economic thought; professor at the Universities of London, Chicago, and Freiburg; Nobel Laureate, 1974; author of Monetary Theory and the Trade Cycle (1933); Prices and Production (1935); The Pure Theory of Capital (1941); The Road to Serfdom (1944); John Stuart Mill and Harriet Taylor (1951); Individualism and Economic Order (1952); The Counter-Revolution of Science (1952); Capitalism and the Historians, editor (1954); The Political Ideal of the Rule of Law (1955); The Constitution of Liberty (1960); Studies in Philosophy, Politics, and Economics (1967); Law, Legislation, and Liberty, Volume 1 (1973), Volume 2 (1977); New Studies in Philosophy, Politics, Economics, and History of Ideas (1977), and many others.

Karl Helfferich 1872-1924. German economist, banker, and politician; minister of finance, 1915-1916; minister of the interior, 1916-1918; author of Geld und Banken (1910) [English edition titled Money (1927)]; Deutschlands Volkswohlstand (1913); Der Weltkrieg (1919), and others.

William Stanley Jevons 1835-1882. English economist; lecturer and professor at Owens College and University College, London; author of Pure Logic (1864); Elementary Lessons in Logic (1870); Theory of Political Economy (1871); Studies in Deductive Logic (1880); The State in Relation to Labour (1882), and others.

Edwin Walter Kemmerer 1875-1945. American economist; professor at Princeton University, 1912-1945; advisor to the governments of Mexico, Guatemala, Colombia, Chile, Poland, Ecuador, Bolivia, China, and Peru; author of Money and Credit Instruments in Their Relation to General Prices (1907); Modern Currency Reforms (1916); The ABC of the Federal Reserve System (1918); High Prices and Deflation (1920); Kemmerer on Money (1934), and others.

John Maynard Keynes 1883-1946. Most influential economist of the century; professor of economics at Cambridge University; editor; government official; author of *Economic Consequences of the Peace* (1919); *A Revision of the Treaty* (1922); *A Tract on Monetary Reform* (1923); *The End of Laissez-Faire* (1926); *A Treatise on Money* (1930); *The General Theory of Employment, Interest and Money* (1936), and many others.

Frank Hyneman Knight 1885-1972. American economist; professor of economics at Cornell University, University of Chicago, University of Iowa; past president of the American Economic Association; author of *Risk, Uncertainty and Profit* (1921); *The Ethics of Competition and Other Essays* (1935); *Freedom and Reform* (1947); *The Economic Organization* (1951); *Essays on History and Method of Economics* (1956); *Intelligence and Democratic Action* (1960), and others.

James Laurence Laughlin 1850-1933. American economist; professor at Cornell University and Chicago University; author of *Study of Political Economy* (1885); *Facts About Money* (1885); *Gold and Prices Since 1873* (1887); *Reciprocity* (1903); *Money, Credit, and Prices* (1931), and others.

John Law 1671-1729. Scottish financier and speculator; induced Louis XV to establish a central bank in France which inflated the currency and met financial ruin in 1720; he fled to and died in Venice; author of *Money and Trade Considered, with a Proposal for supplying the Nation with Money* (1705).

Abba Ptachya Lerner 1903-   . American economist, born in Russia, educated in England; taught at the London School of Economics, University of Kansas City, New School for Social Research, New York, Michigan State University, University of California at Berkeley, Queens College, New York, and Florida State University; author of *Economics of Control* (1944); *Economics of Employment* (1951); *Essays in Economic Analysis* (1953); *Everybody's Business* (1962); *Flation* (1973).

Alfred Marshall 1842-1924. One of the most famous British economists since Ricardo; he predominated in England from 1890 until after his death, and exerted more influence on American economic thought than any other economist prior to Keynes; professor at Cambridge University, 1885-1908; author of *Economics of Industry* (1879); *Principles of Economics* (1890); *Industry and Trade* (1919); *Money, Credit and Commerce* (1923), and others.

Carl Menger 1840-1921. Austrian economist; founder of the Austrian School of economic thought; professor at the University of Vienna, 1873-1903; author of *Grundsätze der Volkswirtschaftslehre* (1871)

[English edition titled *Principles of Economics* (1950)]; *Untersuchungen über die Methode der Sozialwissenschaft* (1883) [English edition *Problems of Economics and Sociology* (1963)]; *Die Irrtümer des Historismus* (1884), and others.

Lloyd Wynn Mints 1888-   . American economist; professor of economics, University of Chicago; editor with F.A. Lutz, *Readings in Monetary Theory* (1951); author of *A History of Banking Theory in Great Britain and the United States* (1945); *Monetary Policy for a Competitive Society* (1950).

Ludwig von Mises 1881-1973. To many the greatest economist of the century; economic adviser to the Austrian Chamber of Commerce, 1909-1934; professor of economics, University of Vienna, 1913-1938; professor of international economic relations at the Graduate Institute of International Studies in Geneva, 1934-1940; professor of economics, New York University, 1946-1973; author of *Theorie des Geldes und der Umlaufsmittel* (1912) [English edition titled *The Theory of Money and Credit* (1934, 1953)]; *Die Gemeinwirtschaft* (1922) [English edition titled *Socialism* (1936, 1951, 1969)]; *Nationalökonomie* (1940); *Human Action* (1949, 1963, 1966); *Theory and History* (1957, 1969), and many others.

Sir Robert Peel 1788-1850. Outstanding British statesman and administrator; Prime Minister, 1834-1835, 1841-1846; leader of the Conservative Party, reformer of money and banking, 1844; repealer of the Corn Laws, 1846.

Arthur Cecil Pigou 1877-1959. British economist; Marshall's pupil and successor at Cambridge University; author of *Wealth and Welfare* (1912); *The Economics of Welfare* (1920); *Essays in Applied Economics* (1923); *The Theory of Unemployment* (1933); *Essays in Economics* (1952), and many others.

David Ricardo 1772-1823. To many the greatest English economist of the nineteenth century; Member of Parliment, 1819-1823; author of *The High Price of Bullion a Proof of the Depreciation of Bank Notes* (1809); *Principles of Political Economy and Taxation* (1817); *Plan for the Establishment of a National Bank* (1823, published posthumously).

Murray Rothbard 1926-   . American economist; professor of economics at Polytechnical Institute of New York, Brooklyn; author of *The Panic of 1819* (1952); *Man, Economy, and State* (1962), *America's Great Depression* (1963); *What Has Government Done to Our Money?* (1964); *Conceived in Liberty*, 3 volumes (1975-1976), and many others.

Age of Inflation

Jacques Rueff 1896-1978. French economist, government offical and adviser, vice governor of the Bank of France, 1939-1941; architect of the French financial reform of 1958; author of *Des Sciences Physiques aux Sciences Morales* (1922); *Theory of Monetary Phenomena* (1927); *The Social Order* (1945); *Letter to Policy Makers* (1949); *The Age of Inflation* (1963); *Balance of Payments* (1965); *Les Dieux et les Rois* (1967), and others.

Paul Anthony Samuelson 1915-   . American economist; consultant to the National Resources Planning Board, 1941-1943, to the United States Treasury, 1945-1952, to the Federal Reserve Board, since 1967; past president of the International Economic Association, the American Economic Association, and the Econometric Society; author of *Foundations of Economic Analysis* (1947); *Economics, An Introductory Analysis* (1948); *Readings in Economics* (1955); *Linear Programming and Economic Analysis* (1958); *Collected Scientific Papers* (1966), and others. His book, *Economics*, has gone through ten revisions and reprints and probably is the most influential college textbook at the present.

Hjalmar Schacht 1877-1970. German financier who occupied high official positions successively under the monarchy, the Weimar republic, and Nazism; president of the Reichsbank, 1923-1930, 1933-1939; economics minister, 1934-1937. He was acquitted of war crimes by the Nürenberg tribunal, 1946. Economic adviser to governments of Syria, Indonesia, Iran, and Egypt.

Henry Calvert Simons 1899-1946. American economist; professor of economics, University of Iowa and University of Chicago; editor of the *Journal of Political Economy;* consultant to Treasury Department, and to Committee for Economic Development. He was considered one of the foremost economists of his time, but unfortunately left no work in book form. *Economic Policy for a Free Society,* published posthumously, contains his most important writings.

O. M. W. Sprague 1873-1953. American economist; taught at Harvard University, Imperial University of Tokyo, and again at Harvard; economic adviser to the Bank of England, assistant to Secretary of the United States Treasury; author of *History of Crises Under the National Banking System* (1910); *Banking Reform in the United States* (1911); *Theory and History of Banking* (1929); *Recovery and Common Sense* (1934), and others.

Jacob Viner 1892-1970. American economist, born in Canada; educated at McGill and Harvard Universities; professor of economics at the University of Chicago and Princeton University; consultant to the United States Treasury and the State Department; past president of the American Economic Association; author of *Dumping: A Problem in International Trade* (1923); *Canada's Balance of International Indebtedness* (1924); *Studies in the Theory of International Trade* (1937); *Trade Relations Between Freemarket and Controlled Economics* (1943); *The Customs Union Issue* (1950); *International Economics* (1951); *International Trade and Economic Development* (1952); *The Long View and the Short* (1958), and others.

Sources

Articles

Brown, Sidney. "Final Balloon?" *The Commercial and Financial Chronicle,* June 7, 1971, p. 2.

Friedman, Milton. "A Monetary and Fiscal Framework for Monetary Stability." *American Economic Review,* Vol. 38 (June 1948), pp. 245-264.

_____. "The Monetary Theory and Policy of Henry Simons." *Journal of Law and Economics,* X (October 1967), pp. 1-13.

_____, and Meiselman, David. "The Relative Stability of Monetary Velocity and the Investment Multiplier in the United States, 1897-1958." *Stabilization Policies.* The Commission on Money and Credit: Prentice Hall, 1963.

Grünig, F. "Die Wirtschaftstätigkeit nach dem Zusammenbruch im Vergleich zur Vorkriegszeit." *Die deutsche Wirtschaft zwei Jahre nach dem Zusammenbruch.* Berlin: Deutsches Institut für Wirtschaftsordnung, 1947.

Halm, George N. "The 'Band' Proposal: The Limit of Permissible Exchange Rate Variations." *Princeton Special Papers in International Economics, No. 6.* Princeton, New Jersey: Princeton University Press, 1965.

Kemmerer, E. W. "Banking Reform in the United States." *American Economic Review Supplement,* III (March 1913), pp. 52-63.

Lerner, Abba Ptachya. "A Program for Monetary Stability." *Proceedings of the Conference on Savings and Residential Financing*. Chicago, 1962.

Pigou, Arthur Cecil. "The Value of Money." *Quarterly Journal of Economics*, XXXII (November 1917), pp. 38-65.

Ricardo, David. "The High Price of Bullion." *Works*, Volume III. Edited by Piero Sraffa. Cambridge: Cambridge University Press, 1951, pp. 47-127.

Schmölders, Günter. "Die Zigarettenwährung." *Kölner Universitätszeitung*, 5 (1947), p. 70.

Simons, Henry. "Keynes' Comments on Money." *Christian Century*, LIII (July 22, 1936), pp. 1016-1017.

Sumner, William Graham. "History of Banking in the U. S." *The Journal of Commerce and Commercial Bulletin* (1896), p. 472.

Viner, Jacob. Review of Keynes' *General Theory*. *Quarterly Journal of Economics*, LI (1936-1937), p. 149.

Williams, John Henry. "German Foreign Trade and the Reparations Payments." *Quarterly Journal of Economics*, Vol. 36 (May 1922), pp. 482-503.

Williamson, John H. "The Crawling Peg." *Princeton Essays in International Finance*, No. 50. Princeton, New Jersey: Princeton University Press, 1965.

Books

Anderson, Benjamin M. *The Value of Money*. New York: Richard R. Smith, 1936.

Angell, James W. *The Theory of International Prices*. Cambridge, Massachusetts: Harvard University Press, 1926.

Bresciani-Turroni, Costantino. *The Economics of Inflation*. Third impression. New York: Augustus M. Kelley, 1968 [1931].

Brown, A.J. *The Great Inflation 1939-1951*. London: Oxford University Press, 1955.

Burns, Arthur R. *Money and Monetary Policy in Early Times*. London: Routledge and Kegan Paul, 1927.

Cannan, Edwin. *Money*. Eighth edition. London: Staples Press, 1935.

Deutsche Bundesbank. *Währung und Wirtschaft, 1876-1975*. Frankfurt am Main: Fritz Knapp Verlag, 1976.

Einzig, Paul. *Primitive Money*. London: Eyre and Spottiswoode, 1948.

_____. *The Case Against Floating Exchanges*. London: St. Martin's Press, 1970.

Elster, Karl. *Von der Mark zur Reichsmark*. Jena: G. Fischer, 1928.

Federal Reserve Board. *Federal Reserve Bulletin*, July 1974; March 1977. Washington, D. C.: Government Printing Office.

_____. *The Federal Reserve System, Purposes and Functions*. Washington, D. C.: Government Printing Office, 1954.

Fellner, John William. *Maintaining and Restoring Balance in International Payments*. Princeton, New Jersey: Princeton University Press, 1966.

Fisher, Irving. *Inflation*. London: George Allen and Unwin, 1934 [first edition, New York: Adelphi Company, 1933].

Sources

_____.Mastering the Crises._ London: George Allen and Unwin, 1934 [first edition, _After Reflation, What?_ New York: Adelphi Company, 1933].

_____.100% Money._ New York: Adelphi Company, 1935.

_____.Purchasing Power of Money._ New York: Macmillan, 1926.

_____.Stabilized Money._ London: George Allen and Unwin, 1935.

Fisher, Irving N. _My Father, Irving Fisher._ New York: Commet Press, 1956.

Friedman, Milton. _Dollars and Deficits._ Englewood Cliffs, New Jersey: Prentice-Hall, 1968.

_____.Essays in Positive Economics._ Chicago: University of Chicago Press, 1953.

_____.Monetary vs. Fiscal Policy._ New York: W. W. Norton and Com- pany, 1969.

_____,editor. _Studies in the Quantity Theory of Money._ Chicago: University of Chicago Press, 1956.

_____. _The Optimum Quantity of Money and Other Essays._ Chicago: Aldine Publishing Company, 1969.

_____,and Schwartz, Anna Jacobson. _A Monetary History of the United States, 1867-1960._ National Bureau of Economic Research: Princeton University Press, 1963.

Galbraith, John Kenneth. _American Capitalism._ Boston: Houghton Mifflin Company, 1952.

_____. _Economic Development._ Cambridge, Massachusetts: Harvard University Press, 1962.

_____. _The Affluent Society._ Boston: Houghton Mifflin Company, 1958.

_____. _The New Industrial State._ Boston: Houghton Mifflin Company, 1967.

Grierson, Philip. _Coins and Medals: A Select Bibliography._ London: Published for the Historical Association, 1954.

Groseclose, Elgin. _Money and Man._ New York: Frederick Ungar Publishing Company, 1961.

Guillebaud, Claude. _The Economic Recovery of Germany._ London: Macmillan and Company, 1939.

Hansen, Alvin H. _A Guide to Keynes._ New York: McGraw-Hill, 1953.

_____. _Business Cycles and National Income._ New York: W. W. Norton and Company, 1951.

_____.Monetary Theory and Fiscal Policy._ New York: McGraw-Hill, 1949.

Hawtrey, Sir Ralph George. _A Century of Bank Rate._ Second edition. New York: Augustus M. Kelley, 1962 [1938].

_____. _Currency and Credit._ Third edition. London: Longmans, Green and Company, 1927.

_____. _Monetary Reconstruction._ Second edition. London: Longmans, Green and Company, 1926.

_____. _The Art of Central Banking._ London: Longmans, Green and Company, 1932.

_____.The Gold Standard in Theory and Practice._ Fourth edition. London: Longmans, Green and Company, 1939.

_____. _Trade and Credit._ London: Longmans, Green and Company, 1928.

Hayek, Friedrich August von. _Monetary Theory and the Trade Cycle._ New York: Augustus M. Kelley, 1966 [1933 title: _Geldtheorie und Konjunkturtheorie_].

_____.Profits, Interest and Investment._ London: G. Routledge and Sons, 1939.

Age of Inflation

_____.*The Counter-Revolution of Science*. Glencoe, Illinois: The Free Press, 1952.

Hazlitt, Henry. *Man vs. the Welfare State*. New Rochelle, New York: Arlington House, 1969.

_____.*The Failure of the "New Economics."* Princeton, New Jersey: D. van Nostrand, 1959.

Helfferich, Karl. *Das Geld*. Leipzig: C. L. Hirschfeld, 1923 [1910].

Jevons, William Stanley. *Investigations in Currency and Finance*. London: Macmillan and Company, 1884.

Keynes, John Maynard. *A Treatise on Money*. New York: Harcourt, Brace and Company, 1930.

_____.*The General Theory of Employment, Interest and Money*. New York: Harcourt, Brace and Company, 1936.

Länderrat of the American Occupation Zone. *Statistisches Handbuch von Deutschland*. Munich, 1949.

Laughlin, James Laurence. *Banking Reform*. Chicago: The National Citizens League, 1912.

Lerner, Abba Ptachya. *Essays in Economic Analysis*. London: Macmillan and Company, 1953.

MacDonald, George. *Evolution of Coinage*. New York: G.P. Putnam's Sons, 1916.

Marshall, Alfred. *Money, Credit and Commerce*. New York: Augustus M. Kelley, 1960 [London: Macmillan and Company, 1923].

Menger, Carl. *Principles of Economics*. Glencoe, Illinois: The Free Press, 1950.

Mises, Ludwig von. *Epistemological Problems of Economics*. Princeton, New Jersey: D. van Nostrand, 1960.

_____.*Human Action*. New Haven, Connecticut: Yale University Press, 1949.

_____.*Human Action*. Third edition. Chicago: Henry Regnery Company, 1966 [1949].

_____.*Theory and History*. New Haven, Connecticut: Yale University Press, 1957.

_____.*The Theory of Money and Credit*. Irvington-on-Hudson, New York: Foundation for Economic Education, 1971 [1912].

_____.*The Ultimate Foundation of Economic Science*. Princeton, New Jersey: D. Van Nostrand, 1962.

Monroe, Arthur Eli. *Monetary Theory Before Adam Smith*. New York: Augustus M. Kelley, 1966 [1923].

Muhleman, M.L. *Monetary and Banking Systems*. New York: Monetary Publishing Company, 1908.

Muthesius, Volkmar. *Augenzeuge von drei Inflationen*. Frankfurt am Main: Fritz Knapp Verlag, 1973.

National Monetary Commission. *Publications*. Washington, D.C.: Government Printing Office, 1909-1912.

Nurkse, Ragnar. *International Currency Experience: Lessons of the Interwar Period*. Geneva: League of Nations Secretariat, 1944.

Petrov, Vladimir. *Money and Conquest*. Baltimore: The Johns Hopkins University Press, 1967.

Pick, Franz. *Currency Yearbook*. New York: Pick Publishing Corporation, 1970.

Sources

Enterprise Association, 1957.

Powell, J. Enoch. *Exchange Rates and Liquidity.* London: Institute of Economic Affairs, 1967.

_____.*Freedom and Reality.* London: B.T. Batsford, 1969.

Quiggin, A. Hingston. *A Survey of Primitive Money.* London: Pall Mall Press Ltd., 1957.

Röpke, Wilhelm. *Welfare, Freedom and Inflation* London: Pall Mall Press Ltd., 1957.

Rothbard, Murray. *Man, Economy, and State.* Princeton, New Jersey: D. Van Nostrand, 1962.

_____.*What Has Government Done to Our Money?* Colorado Springs, Colorado: Pine Tree Press, 1963.

Rueff, Jacques. *The Age of Inflation.* Chicago: Henry Regnery Company, 1964.

Samuelson, Paul A. *Economics.* Tenth edition. New York: McGraw-Hill, 1976 [1948].

_____.*The Collected Scientific Papers of Paul A. Samuelson.* Edited by Joseph Stiglitz. Cambridge, Massachusetts: M.I.T. Press, 1966.

Schmölders, Günter. *Geldpolitik.* Tubingen, Mohr, and Zurich: Polygraphischer Verlag, 1968.

Schacht, Hjalmar. *Abrechnung mit Hitler.* Hamburg: Rowahlt Verlag, 1948.

Schultz, Bruno. *Kleine deutsche Geldgeschichte des 19. und 20. Jahrhunderts.* Berlin: Duncker und Humblot, 1976.

Sennholz, Hans, editor. *Gold Is Money.* Westport, Connecticut: Greenwood Press, 1975.

_____.*Inflation or Gold Standard?* Lansing, Michigan: Constitutional Alliance, 1970.

Simons, Henry. *Economic Policy for a Free Society.* Chicago: University of Chicago Press, 1948.

Sprague, O.M.W. *History of Crises under the National Banking System.* Washington, D.C.: Government Printing Office, 1910.

Statistisches Reichsamt. *Deutschlands Wirtschaftslage.* Berlin, March 1923, p. 24.

_____. *Wirtschaft und Statistik, No. 1.* Berlin, 1923.

Triffin, Robert. *Our International Monetary System: Yesterday, Today, and Tomorrow.* New York: Random House, 1968.

United States Government. *Budget of the United States Government, Fiscal Years 1965, 1978.* Washington, D.C.: Government Printing Office.

United States Senate. *Report of the Special Committee on the Termination of the National Emergency.* Washington, D.C.: Government Printing Office, September 1973, pp. 98-406.

Wolf, Julius. *Reparationen und russisches Geschäft.* Stuttgart: F. Enke Verlag, 1922.

Yeager, Leland B. *International Monetary Relations.* New York: Harper and Row, 1966.

Persons Index

Angell, James W., 85

Bischoff, F., 89
Burns, Arthur F., 58

Carter, Jimmy, 28, 33-34, 61, 166
Clay, Gen. Lucius D., 103

Dräger, H., 89

Eisenhower, Dwight D., 63, 103, 106
Elster, Karl, 81
Erhard, Ludwig, 103, 106
Erzberger (Secretary of Treasury), 83

Fick, H., 89
Fisher, Irving, 12, 40, 43, 43n, 44, 51
Friedländer - Prechtl, R., 89
Friedman, Milton, 40, 44-51, 54, 133-136

Galbraith, John Kenneth, 31
Gesell, Silvio, 132
Grofkopp, W., 89

Hansen, Alvin H., 30, 40, 44
Havenstein (President of Reichsbank), 80, 86
Hawtrey, Ralph George, 40-42
Hazlitt, Henry, 132
Helfferich, Karl, 80, 83, 85
Hitler, Adolf, 89, 92-94, 101
Hobson, John A., 132

Hoover, Herbert, 53, 63

Jevons, William Stanley, 40-41

Kennedy, John F., 30, 121
Keynes, John Maynard, 12, 18, 28, 29-30, 32, 40, 44-46, 64, 89, 129-133
Knight, Frank H., 44

Lautenbach, W., 89
Law, John, 18, 132
Lerner, Abba P., 31, 40
Lincoln, Abraham,33
Longfellow, Henry W., 178

Malthus, Thomas, 132
Mandeville, Bernard De, 132
Marshall, Alfred, 40-41, 44, 50
Menger, Carl, 9, 157
Mints, Lloyd, 44
Monroe, Arthur E., 12

Nixon, Richard, 25, 57-59, 61, 121, 145
North, Gary, 62

Peel, Sir Robert, 114
Pound, Roscoe, 154

Reinhardt, F., 91
Ricardo, David, 19
Roosevelt, Franklin, 28, 33-34, 43,53
Röpke, Wilhelm, 175

203

Subject Index

Subject Index

tariffs, 52, 128
taxes, 15-16, 63, 153
   business, 167
trade cycle theory (Mises), 50
Trading With the Enemy Act (1917),
    121
transfer agency, government a, 168
transfer society, 1

unemployment, 33-39
   cyclical, 35-38
   disintegration, 39
   hedge, 37
   inflation, 38
   institutional, 33-34
unemployment compensation, 155

Versailles Treaty, 83-85

Wall Street Journal, quoted, 26
war economy and inflation, German
    (1939-1945), 94-99
wealth, transfer of, 4